MALFEASANCE

PHIL RIBERA

This work is a memoir, a collection of memories covering a specific period of the author's life. Great care has been taken to verify and authenticate what has been written—facts have been crosschecked with personal notes, media accounts and official documents. Still, timelines have been compressed, and names, characters, locations and businesses names have been changed—to the extent that some characters are composites of more than one person. Any resemblance to actual persons, living or dead, events, or locales is entirely unintentional.

ISBN-13: 978-0-9962103-2-4
ISBN-10: 0-9962103-2-6

Published by Phil Ribera
[V: 2-8]

Learn more about the author by visiting: www.philribera.com

ACKNOWLEDGEMENTS

I have a wonderful wife and two very supportive daughters, all three of whom lived through my career right along with me. I could not have survived those years, much less written this book, without the love, trust and encouragement of my family.

I also want to thank my brother, Tyler, for all his help and encouragement; my nephew, Jacob Spillner, cover model; and my nephew, Zach Ribera, for his Kindle formatting and coding expertise. The task of editing is also one I dislike, and I'm so grateful to Norma Santos for all of her time and effort assisting me in that regard.

With great pride I became a police officer in the city where I grew up, lived, attended public school, and ultimately chose to raise my family. For thirty-one years I served a wonderful community full of good and decent people. Working alongside me were many honorable men and women—the ones who risked their lives and did their jobs well and with integrity. I dedicate this book to them. They are the strong and the brave, who, when things got tough, sucked it up and struggled through controversy and the difficult times. My eternal thanks to the ethical role models who showed me how to be good at what I did; men like Charles Plummer, Rick Parker, Charlie Heitz, Mark Collins, Dennis Rowe, Harry Bruno and the Muniz's— Walt, Eddie and Ted. And to the six most upstanding and principled people I know, Dennis Houghtelling, Cindy Waters, Raul Valdivia, Bob Palermini and Gerry Dinneen, you continue to have my unwavering respect.

To my Uncle Tony (retired San Francisco police chief) who was always in my corner, I have valued your wise advice throughout my years on the force. And finally, my deepest gratitude to Gil Ribera—a father whose lessons were taught mostly by example, and always with honesty and with my best interests at heart.

PROLOGUE

My father was a teacher.

For a curious, always-in-trouble, underperforming student like me, Dad's career choice made life a living hell. Aside from the constant scholastic challenges, my smallish eleven-year-old body fell somewhere around the 20th percentile for my age group, making me a poor fit for athletics—the second most important thing to my father. Add to that, a massive chip on my shoulder, a propensity for getting into fights, and a bent toward creative arts—which he never actually verbalized but always hinted were less than masculine—the differences between my dad and me felt like an ever worsening snag in the fabric of my young life.

Other than academics and sports though, my dad wasn't that big on offering up unsolicited advice. As if he expected me to somehow know, intuitively, how to deal with those prickly pre-teen issues, his facial expressions usually spoke louder than his words, and even then, only when he was annoyed with me. Occasionally, when I'd stray too far in the wrong direction, he'd surprise me—coming out of nowhere with a well-crafted lesson that I'd never forget.

He laid a few good ones on me over the years, but one of his more creative and memorable lessons came in October of 1967, a few months into my sixth grade year. And though I had absolutely no appreciation for it at the time, I now look back at the incident through completely different eyes—seeing clearly the manner in which he taught me one of the more important, yet subtle rules in life: *Be careful what you wish for.*

I had just brought home my grades—the first of the new school year. The report card was another real loser, and I was only mildly surprised that my dad had called for a parent-teacher conference on the heels of it. I was invited to attend the event, yet was sequestered to the hallway outside while the main participants met privately to compare notes.

Through the narrow window in the door, I was able to catch furtive glimpses of my dad and Mr. Moore as they greeted one another with stilted handshakes and stern faces.

I had hoped my teacher would say something about me that would piss off my dad, and that a flurry of wild punches would follow. The result, of course, would be a badly injured Mr. Moore, followed by a hushed absence for the rest of the school year as he convalesced. Instead, however, I soon witnessed the two of them laughing and chatting it up as if they were best buddies—roasting me, no doubt, with their comparative notes on my bad behavior. And why not? They were cut from the same cloth. It had become perfectly clear to me then, that my dad's allegiance to the United Brotherhood of Teachers far outweighed that of his own son.

Figures!

The tense silence of the ride home was finally broken by my father's words, half question and half deriding statement: "And music time! You even got a *needs to improve* in music time?"

I suppose he had long since given up on me academically, and that my failing grade in mathematics was, by that stage of the game, almost expected. But for some strange reason the music thing really ticked him off. My answer—though not very well stated—probably confirmed his suspicions: that the poor grade in music was more about poor attitude than my ability to carry a tune.

"Singing is stupid," I said. But as soon as the words left my mouth I knew I had done myself no favors. Quickly, but ineffectually I tried to repair the damage. "I mean, the songs Mr. Moore makes us sing are stupid."

My father shook his head, roughly palming the steering wheel of our green, two-tone Chevy Bellaire around the corner. I glanced at him as we turned onto our street, recognizing his tightly pressed lips and narrowing eyes as my clue to shut up—which I did. And when we rolled into our driveway, having had no further conversation about it, I was sure that the worst of it was behind me.

But then I caught sight of him following me down the hallway, and I quickstepped to my bedroom like a Chihuahua trying to get away from a Mastiff. He came into the room behind me, closing the door with a certain finality that conveyed that I was not free to leave.

"So you don't like the songs Mr. Moore has you sing in class?" He took a seat on my little brother's bed across from me.

Well, I guess I finally got Dad's attention. If I present this the right way, it may be a golden opportunity to sway him over to my side.

"Nah Dad, you know I like music. Music is great. In fact, I love to sing." (*Okay, I had better not overdo it*). "It's just that I feel really dumb singing *Inchworm, inchworm, measuring the marigolds.*"

When I detected a slight nod I was sure I had turned him around on the issue. "You get it, Dad. There's no way a guy my age should be expected to sing those tunes. It's just not *cool.*"

It was my closing statement to the jury, my final words that would undoubtedly seal the deal. After all, Dad was a guy once. He must have liked girls back before he got married and had us kids. Even *he* would have to know that the Inchworm song, even though the whole class was singing it too, wasn't going to make me popular with my buddies or win the attention of Gina Stefani. My buckteeth and early onset acne notwithstanding, I was more certain now than ever, that the source of all my troubles in life could be traced back to that damn Inchworm song. And I could tell by my dad's face that he was starting to see it the same way. He finally got it.

"What songs *do* you like?" He asked.

"Huh?"

"Your music." My dad seemed genuinely interested, but I thought I detected a grin concealed behind his curiosity. "The 'cool tunes,' as you say; the type of music that Mr. Moore *should* have the class sing . . . instead of that *dumb* Inchworm song."

He was up to something, but I wasn't sure what. Why couldn't we just leave it at that? I had said my piece and we had come to an understanding. But now his eyes wouldn't look away. I had to come up with a response.

I'd never been too good at thinking quickly on my feet. "I don't know," I said. "Just the groovy songs on the radio, I guess. Like, songs from this century."

The last sentence wasn't intended to be a dig on Dad, though it seemed like his lips grew a little tighter. It then occurred to me that he and Mr. Moore were probably around the same age. Maybe Dad loves the Inchworm song, too. *How could I have known?*

"Groovy songs." He repeated back, staring at me until I found myself fidgeting across my bed.

I only owned two records—both 78's (small vinyl disks with only one song recorded on either side). They were right there, on top of my record player, and my dad had gotten up and was now making his way over toward them. Suddenly this wasn't going well.

"What about this one?" My dad picked up the first 78, turning it to see the song title. "Build me up, Buttercup." He snapped his fingers rhythmically. "Looks like a groovy little song."

"Oh now, that isn't . . . I mean it's just --"

Before I could finish, he snatched the second record from the turntable. "Here's another one; from this century, too!" His eyes squinted to read orange and black label. "The Pata Pata Song?"

"Dad, those records . . . they're just my own type of music."

"Oh yeah, I know." He tossed the disks onto the bed next to me. "Not like those *dumb* songs that Mr. Moore makes you sing."

I looked down at the records, fearing the worst but still hopeful I could put a stop to this madness. "Okay, fine. I'll sing better in class. I'll really try. I promise."

My dad was already shaking his head—the insidious smile no longer concealed. At that moment, his cruel plan was clear to me.

"Too late for that," he said. "I want you to write down all the words to these two songs and I'll ditto them off for your class."

My head dropped to my chest and I closed my eyes, hoping to open them in another lifetime. And then my last ditch effort: "Mr. Moore won't like these songs . . ." (as if I suddenly cared about what Mr. Moore would or wouldn't like).

"He and I have already discussed it," Dad said. "And he's looking forward to you teaching the class some new music." By now my dad's smile had spread across his whole face, and I realized that I had been set up–ambushed by the both of them.

"Go ahead. Start writing the lyrics," my dad said. I started to protest, but he shook his head as if to say, *don't even try*.

As he left my room my little brother stuck his head through the doorway. I wanted to pound the little shit. He must have sensed it, because he took off down the hall and I could hear him asking my dad what was wrong with me.

I sat there staring down at the yellow notepad my dad had left. The touché he had just inflicted upon me was beyond his comprehension—*He knows not what he does*. This will destroy me. Build me up, Buttercup? Are you serious? And even worse, the Pata Pata Song? It's from South Africa, for Christ sakes! The words aren't even in English! I'll be the laughing stock of the entire school. The most hated guy in the sixth grade. There is no way Gina Stefani will ever like me now, even if I could somehow straighten my teeth and clear up my acne. My life is over, and just when I was hitting my peak.

I'm sure that to this day everyone in my sixth grade class remembers singing those ridiculous songs, hand written by me and dittoed by my dad. I can still recall the utter humiliation of standing in front of the class, leading them in lyrics that nobody even understood. African words that meant nothing to anybody.

And then there was the satisfied grin plastered on Mr. Moore's face—very similar to the one my dad had on his.

Although I ended the school year with satisfactory marks in music, I still spent a lot of time in the principal's office for fighting, and the rest of my grades continued to suffer. They improved marginally as I struggled through junior high and into high school, but nobody was ever going to see my name on the Dean's List. And despite the fact that I never drank liquor or did drugs, didn't steal, didn't cut school or lie to my folks, I grew through my teen years still feeling like a huge disappointment to my dad.

It wouldn't be until years later, when I was raising my own family and dealing with my own career, that we would develop a whole new relationship. The distance between us would close and we would understand one another with great compassion and great love. He would come to have a tremendous respect for me, for my decisions and for the man I had grown into. And I would see him not as an adversary, but as a father who only wanted the best for his son. I would realize that he always loved me, and only believed I could do better. He did the best he could, and as with many of life's events and obstacles, he had no roadmap to follow.

In the ensuing years of adulthood, I would face dozens of my own challenging situations, for which there would be no blueprint or plan to follow. As my father did, I would cobble together bits of experience and instinct, pieces from my successes and my failures, weaving them into new lessons from which to operate. I would eventually go back to school at night while working fulltime, and graduate from college—almost unbelievably with straight A's. Yet most of my education would still take place outside the classroom. These lessons would be shaped out of ugly crime scenes, or through the tears of a battered child, or while fighting for my life in a dark alleyway. But the worst of them would be learned in the halls of the police building, during staff meetings, and inside the council chambers at city hall. Unfortunately or fortunately, just as I did as a sixth-grader, I would have to live through the experiences in order to appreciate their value.

Though my father's role would become less of a teacher, and most of the lessons in my life would be self-taught, my dad would emerge as a close confidant and my most trusted advisor. We would find between us more similarities than differences, and the man from whom I once felt so disconnected would eventually appear as a reflection of myself. He would stand by me through the most difficult period in my 31-year career. We would finally come to be friends on equal terms.

Lessons.

LESSON 1

"Nearly all men can stand adversity, but if you want to test a man's character, give him power."
~ Abraham Lincoln

"We need a watch commander on the night shift," he says. "So I'm promoting you to lieutenant."

I glance around at the circa 1960's wall paneling—that dreary mahogany that I will forevermore associate with the police chief's office. He slides a finger across the organization chart on his desk then looks back at me. "You understand this is only a temporary promotion; you still have to do well in the testing process."

I nod. His eyes look odd and bulgy through his reading glasses, which somehow makes the statement seem more like a warning. I'm thinking about his word choice, noting that *earned* or *deserved* were conspicuously missing, at least to my ear. And though the delivery seems as ominous as my surroundings, I am definitely grateful for the overall gist of his message.

"As long as you don't make any waves between now and the next test, you'll probably do fine." He pauses again, as if dithering over just how much of a lead to give me. "The permanent position will go to a watch commander who can run his shift without any problems. You've heard the saying, '*It's better to be seen and not heard?*'"

I nod again.

"In your case it's better *not* to be seen *or* heard. Get my drift?"

I drive home, going over the conversation in my head. There was a time when I worked undercover narcotics, that Carl Bradford would have just as soon fire me. And there was a time when I wanted to strangle him with my bare hands. And now he's the chief of police and I'm his choice for the acting lieutenant spot. *Wow, what a difference seven years and a little judicious avoidance can make.*

I am eager to tell Gale the news. She'll be happy for me about the promotion, even if it's only temporary. I'll be assigned to a swing shift, working from 5 p.m. to 3 o'clock in the morning—the same shift I worked for years as a patrolman. But going back to nights always disrupts the house a bit. And since the girls are eleven and thirteen years old now, there is a lot more going on these days and a lot more to disrupt.

After all my antics as an undercover narc, and then bouncing through different assignments as a sergeant, I'm sure Gale would prefer that I just ride a desk on day shift. It's not like she hasn't paid her dues right along with me.

But just as I thought, she takes the news with optimistic enthusiasm. "I knew you would get it," Gale says. "We'll have to go out to dinner and celebrate."

I remind her that I still have to pass the written test and score well in the oral interviews. That is when her expression changes.

"Didn't you already take the lieutenant test?" Her frown tells me it's a rhetorical question—one she already knows the answer to. "In fact you're already ranked number one on the promotion list."

"I'm actually number two." I hang my jacket in the hall closet and follow her into the kitchen. "I don't think they want to promote the guy who's sitting on the number one spot, so they're letting the list die. I have to take the test again in a few months."

Gale shakes her head in disgust. "Because the chief doesn't have the guts to tell Walters that he isn't going to be promoted, you have to go through the whole testing process again?"

"Basically, yeah." I smile to let her know I'm not bothered by it. "It'll be fine. All I have to do is keep things quiet on my shift until they make it permanent."

Gale smirks. "Did the chief tell you that, too?"

By Friday I'm all ready to get started at my new rank. I drive to work plenty early, enjoying the warm July afternoon. Knowing the hot weather is a precursor for a violent mix of alcohol, family beefs and gang fights, I brace myself for what is sure to be a busy night. One in which I will be the highest-ranking officer on duty, where my decisions will be the final word and where the proverbial buck will actually stop. At least until Monday morning, when, over a latte and a croissant, each member of the command staff will read the weekend's logs and weigh in with the chief—giving either a thumbs-up or a thumbs-down to each of my decisions.

My first briefing as a lieutenant is a painful one. The street cops don't care too much one way or the other. To them I was already their boss as a sergeant, and one level or the next doesn't really make a difference in their world. But the sergeants working for me tonight—both of them a good ten years my senior—will have a difficult time taking direction from someone with less seniority.

"Good evening, *Lieu-tenant*." The sergeant stops the briefing to acknowledge me as I walk into the room, drawing out the word lieutenant as if the taste of it might make him puke.

I have considered neither of them a friend before tonight, but we haven't been enemies either. They are old-school street supervisors; secure in their stagnant careers and in the passive-aggressiveness it affords them. They wear long sleeve uniform shirts with a tie despite the summer heat, as some misguided statement that nobody understands. Their 70's haircuts are a little longer than regulation, but not quite enough that anybody ever makes the effort to write them up. Grumpy malcontents, the two could do their jobs with their eyes closed but choose instead to spend their shifts drinking coffee and smoking cigarettes together behind the 7-11 store.

I nod and take a seat by the door—the gold bars on my lapel suddenly feeling like they weigh ten pounds. But rather than get goaded into a pissing match with the duo, I figure showing up at their calls and asking them to explain their decisions will be penance enough. Besides, the worst thing I could do as a new boss is come on too hard. I've seen it before: guy gets full of himself after a promotion and quickly alienates his squad. It's always much easier to earn the asshole jacket than it is to lose it.

When the bookends are finished giving the briefing I step up to the podium at the front of the room. I tell the cops that the police chief has asked me to run their squad for a few months. I speak casually, turning to smile at the two grouses behind me as if we were all the best of buddies. It will make it harder for them to badmouth me once I leave the room. Either way, I am determined to keep the peace and make sure my shift runs smoothly and quietly.

After briefing I poke my head into the communications center, checking in with their supervisor and greeting each of the dispatchers before I head back to my office.

With large windows lining two walls, the watch commander's office is often referred to as the *fishbowl*. In it are file cabinets, desk drawers full of forms, a credenza stuffed with emergency operations binders, a computer terminal monitoring all the calls in dispatch, and a closed circuit TV with several views of the jail's interior. On top of my desk is a scanner programmed to our six radio channels, and also those of neighboring cities, the sheriff's department, and the highway patrol. Operationally, it is the *Situation Room* of the police department.

Around 10 p.m. the next oncoming shift arrives for work. Two other sergeants—supervisors for the midnight shift—stop by the office to welcome me. They are both around my age and are genuinely happy to have me there. I'll be their watch commander until 3 a.m., at which time I go off duty and they'll share the responsibilities for the next four hours until the day shift lieutenant comes on.

I stop into the jail, spending a few minutes to check on things and meet with the jail supervisor, and then head back down the hallway to my office. Suddenly the relative calm of my night is hijacked by a call over the radio: "All units . . . possible assault with a deadly weapon in progress on Olive Drive."

It isn't the severity of the crime that grabs my attention, assaults being more or less routine on a summer night; it is the location of the call. Olive Drive is less than a block from my house, running parallel to my street. In fact, our backyards butt up against the homes on Olive. I quickly sit down at the monitor and pull up the details—wanting to make certain I heard it correctly. Sure enough, a caller from an address close to my house has reported hearing someone yelling that they are about to either kill themselves or someone else. I frantically dial Gale at home.

"Hello?" She sounds worried, and I wonder if she's heard it, too.

"Are you alright?" I stare at the monitor, anxious for an update on the location of the suspect. "Lock all the doors and windows, and keep the girls with you!"

Gale is quiet for several seconds. "Why?"

"There's a crazy person somewhere in the neighborhood," I say. "It sounds like they may have a gun. We're on our way right now, but keep the girls away from the windows, just in case."

There is silence again and I wonder if I've woken her up. I look at the clock and it's too early for her to have been asleep. "Gale?"

"Phil?" She sounds even more scared now.

"What?"

"It's us," Gale whispers into the phone.

I blink my eyes, trying to understand the words. "What?"

"I think it's us that the person called about."

My heart begins to pound and my throat constricts to the size of a stir stick. "What the?" I quickly lower my voice. "What the hell do you mean, 'It's us'?"

Gale begins talking so fast I can barely understand her—like some obscure religion where they speak in tongues nobody else understands: "I was cleaning the house and the windows are all open, and you know, the girls were arguing and fighting, and I just mopped the floor and was letting it dry, and Megan was upset, and she was yelling to get my attention . . ."

"Stop!" I can't listen anymore. It feels like someone has thrown a sack over my head and is beating the shit out of me. I think I'm going to pass out. A dozen expletives fill my head, such that I can't be sure which, if any, are actually coming out of my mouth. At least a few, I think. "I haven't even had this promotion for five minutes!" I dig my palm into my temple. "My first night in charge of the goddamn police department and we get called to a crazed killer at my own fucking house?" Now it's me who is talking in tongues.

She takes a slow breath. "The girls have stopped fighting now."

I grit my teeth. "Well now, isn't that a load off."

As my vision starts to clear, I look up to find Sergeants Frick and Frack standing at the threshold to my office—like two kids who have rehearsed a song but are afraid to sing it without the other.

"Give me a minute, will you?" I say to them as I push the office door closed between us. I momentarily wonder how much they had overheard, but then figure it wasn't enough for them to put anything together.

I sit back down and try to appear unfazed. The two sergeants, apparently not getting the hint, stand at the window with their Brylcreemed hair and patronizing expressions. *God, I hate those two.*

"Phil?" Gale is about to cry. "I'm really sorry about this. What do you want me to do now?"

I look at the monitor. "The units we sent just hit off in the area. If they come to our door, just say that you had the TV too loud and the neighbor must have heard the show you were watching." I'm struggling to steady myself. "And for Christ's sake, keep the girls quiet!"

I exhale slowly after hanging up the phone then motion for the two supervisors to come in.

"There is a crazy woman with a gun up on Olive Drive," one of them says. "Did you happen to hear the call go out?"

I narrow my eyes. *If there were a crazy woman with a gun, then why aren't you two idiots there to supervise?* I casually look at the monitor and nod. "Yeah, I heard the call."

"It's only a few blocks from the county sheriff's house. Do you think you might want to give him a call at home and warn him?"

I wouldn't have believed I could get more irritated than I already was, but now I am. First, these two don't even know that I also live nearby and that the sheriff is my neighbor. Second, if I wanted to call the sheriff at home I would do so—without their unsolicited counsel. And lastly, there is no woman with a gun! It's my daughter!

The responding officers have been on-scene for a few minutes already, and I expect an update over the air soon. "No . . . but thanks." I try my best to be sincere. Actually, I am trying to subtly convey that I'm irritated, yet making an effort to *sound* sincere.

The scanner squawks the identifier of the officer on Olive. "Unable to locate any suspect. The call appears to be unfounded." It is a perfectly timed punctuation to my decision not to phone the sheriff. We all look at each other in silence for a second or two then I glance at my watch. They finally get the hint and head out to their cars to go in-service.

I catch the phone on the first ring. "Watch Commander."

It's Gale, telling me that two patrolmen had come to our door. She had stuck with the story about the loud TV, and though she thought they were doubtful, they left without checking any further.

"I don't think they believed me," she says. "Do you think they knew I was lying?"

I let out a sigh of relief. "I doubt it. Cops always act like they think you're lying."

She doesn't ask why, probably because she knows why. As I hang up the phone I realize that now I, like everyone else, lie to the cops.

The night is busy with a steady inflow of calls for service—all of which I monitor; yet none of which are terribly critical. No murders, no gang wars, and no cops injured. In other words, nothing has occurred on my first night in charge that would cause a political headache for the police chief.

Coming up on 3 a.m., I begin putting away the mound of operations folders and general order binders that I've been studying. The police chief has called for a mandatory training in the morning, for all supervisors and managers in the department. If I can get out of here on time, I may actually catch a few hours of sleep before I have to be up again.

The jail monitor shows everything calm there, and the radio is relatively quiet. Several of the swing shifters have already logged off the street and are writing reports down the hall from my office. I check my watch and am relieved to see that I have officially made it through the night unscathed. I have resisted the temptation to over-assert myself to the two older sergeants who work for me, and I've avoided drawing any negative attention to my shift or myself. And as far as my dysfunctional family goes, nobody is the wiser. All in all, it seems like a victorious first night.

Or so I think.

"Lieutenant?"

I look up to see a young street cop standing doe-eyed in front of my desk.

"Can I speak with you privately, sir?" he asks, easing my office door closed behind him.

I have him take a seat on the other side of my desk while I guardedly ease back into my chair. I have a fleeting hope that he's come to welcome me, or perhaps ask me a procedural question. After all, I've been a cop for sixteen years and there is little that can catch me off guard. I have worked undercover, done several years as a street sergeant and have even run tactical teams. My lieutenant exam study materials are all fresh in my head and I've just spent the entire shift pouring over the departmental rules and regulations. "Go ahead. What is it I can help you with?"

He glances around as if the CIA might be listening in, and I know then I can pretty much rule out the welcome wagon. "Sir, I just transported a guy into the jail on a traffic warrant arrest."

I nod. *So far, so good. This is going to be a piece of cake.*

"Well, sir," he continues. "On the way in, he asked what I was going to do to him. I explained the booking process and told him he could make a couple of calls to arrange bail."

I stifle the urge to yawn. "Sure . . . yeah, uh-huh."

"He said that wasn't what he was asking about." The cop clears his throat before continuing. "He asked me if I was going to sexually molest him."

An awkward stillness fills the room as my brain tries to jump ahead to the point he's trying to make. "Why would the guy ask that?" I say slowly, almost afraid to hear the answer.

"He claimed that the last time he was arrested, the cop forced him to strip and then . . . well, grabbed his . . . his genitals."

I pause for a second. "I suppose it's too much to hope that this all occurred in another city."

"I wish." The cop shakes his head. "He says it happened here."

I'm sure this arrestee, whoever he is, probably has a million reasons to make up an accusation like that. It happens all the time, though not usually claiming a sexual assault. *It's absurd, right?* Knowing just about every cop in the department, I wouldn't believe it about . . . well, about almost anyone. *Almost* anyone. In fact, out of nearly 400 employees, I can only imagine one guy weird enough to do something like that. "What's the cop's name? I ask"

The patrolman looks like he needs a drink. "Fred Bosworth."

And that would be the one guy.

I pull a notepad and pen from the top drawer.

So much for not drawing attention to my squad.

LESSON 2

"The time is always right to do what is right."
~Martin Luther King, Jr.

I head down the hallway to the jail and punch in a four-digit code. The heavy iron door opens with a loud clunk, alerting the jailers that someone is coming in. Two women dressed in utility uniforms, both community service officers, glance up from the booking area to see who it is.

"You want Wallace?" one of them asks, and then before I can answer she points across the open area to a cell we call *the cage*.

A young guy sits alone on a bench behind the wall of chain-linked fencing. He's a slight young man, maybe 120 pounds soaking wet, and he's wearing cotton pants tied at the waist with a drawstring, and a tight tee shirt. He looks more like a kid whose mother would be waiting for him outside of a karate class, than the hardened ex-con that I expected to see. He wouldn't be held here in the adult jail unless he was at least eighteen, but he sure doesn't look much older than that.

For a couple of reasons, I would have been happier to find a grizzled convict: First off, hoping to get the case against him dropped, he'd likely have a stronger motive to make up a story like that. And second, it's less likely a tough guy would allow himself to be the victim of a sexual assault by another male. It's stereotypes, I know, but with each new bit of information, I'm analyzing, cataloging, weighing, and putting it on one side of the scale or the other: legitimate complaint or total horseshit.

"Are you Darnell Wallace?" I ask.

"Who are you?" Darnell's manner is calm. His voice is curious but respectful as he gets up and moves to a small confessional-like opening in the screen. Normally I might have gone inside and sat next to him to build rapport, but considering the type of accusation he's made, I decide to remain outside.

I introduce myself as the boss of the guy he had complained to, making sure to let him know that the other cop, the one he complained about, does *not* work on my shift. I shake hands with him through the pass-through. He looks familiar to me and after a couple of minutes of small talk we realize that I had responded to an argument between him and his girlfriend about a year ago. As we talk, details of the call return to me. They seemed an odd match at the time—Darnell, a skinny, light-skinned black kid, and the girlfriend, a sloppy-looking white woman who weighed twice what he did. She was also older, as I recall.

"Are you two still together?"

Darnell smiles. "On and off. We still fight a lot."

The topic is a good icebreaker, and one that lets me know that Darnell is leading what appears to be a straight lifestyle. While it certainly doesn't rule out that he might play on both teams and may have come on to Bosworth, it's one more tiny piece of the puzzle.

We finally get around to the reason I am there talking with him, and I guess there's really no delicate way to transition. "So," I say with a bit of a pause, "I understand we might have a problem cop on our hands."

Darnell looks at me through the tiny opening, without so much as a blink. "If his hands on my dick is a problem cop, then you definitely got one."

I hadn't come back to the jail to conduct a formal interview or take an official statement; I just wanted to get a sense of the guy. I need to gauge how adamant he is, and to determine if he has a grudge against the cop. But he claims that he never saw or spoke with Bosworth before or since that night.

I have several questions for the guy, but decide to keep it short and only get what I need to convince myself whether or not he's telling the truth. The most pressing is how this could have happened in a crowded city jail, so I ask him about that.

"It didn't happen in the jail," Darnell says. "He walked me into the building, but took me past the jail into a dark area with blue carpet. I never been to that part of the police station before. After that, he brung me in the jail some kinda back way."

"One last question," I say. "Did you ever tell anybody else that it happened?"

"Only my girlfriend. I called her from the jail cell that night and told her." His head drops along with his voice. "I didn't think you guys would do anything about it. You know . . . my word against his."

10

I tell Darnell that a sergeant will be back shortly to take a written statement. I give him my business card and ask that he not discuss this case with anybody else.

Martin Nye has a knack for sexual abuse investigations. He happens to be one of the swing shift sergeants working for me tonight, and, thankfully, he's not part of the problem pair. Nye and me go back a long way and I trust him. Even before we worked together at the department, I remember competing against him at high school cross-country meets.

I call Nye into my office and lay it out for him: he's to take a full and complete written statement from Darnell Wallace about the alleged assault, place the statement in an envelope, and deliver it to me at the training class, first thing in the morning. "For my eyes only," I stress.

Nye is quick to read between the lines. He senses that this is an internal investigation, probably against another cop. He asks me who the suspect is and I provide the cop's name. Nye shakes his head, and I can tell he has the same discomfort with Bosworth as I do. "Nobody but me," I remind Nye.

I get about an hour of sleep then I'm up with the rest of the house. Gale asks me about my first night, then listens as best she can between fixing breakfast, getting the girls ready for school, and preparing for her own workday. We all leave together; she's driving the neighborhood carpool group in one direction, and I'm heading in the other to drop *the bomb* on the police chief.

The training class is held at a hotel near the airport—an odd venue, but it's a relaxed affair with tables and chairs loosely arranged around a group of flipcharts. At the front of the room is a long, cloth covered table set with a bounty of pastries, bagels and fresh fruit. Uncharacteristically, I pass by the spread altogether and scan the room for Martin Nye.

"Phil," a serious voice calls over my shoulder. "I'd like a minute."

I turn to see Lieutenant Frank Howard, an older guy who is one of the day shift watch commanders. I spot Nye on the other side of the room, and even though my sole purpose this morning is to retrieve Darnell's statement and then brief the police chief, I decide to give "a minute" to my co-worker.

"Sure, Frank." I smile politely, but the gesture is not returned.

"I'd like to know why we are making such a huge deal about this complaint." Howard leans into my space, an intimidating gesture that seems as if he forgot he no longer outranks me.

"What complaint is that?" I ask slowly, praying that he's talking about something completely different.

"This *supposed* assault that Bosworth is accused of."

I feel the volcano deep inside me, boiling its way to my head. I glance across the room at Martin Nye, narrowing my eyes when his meet mine—a silent message that I'm going to take that poppy seed bagel he's eating and shove it up his ass.

Howard continues, "Would we be bending over backwards to investigate something like this if it weren't a male-on-male contact?"

I get the inference he's trying to make, and I'm even more pissed off now. "You know what, Frank?" I take a second to slow my breathing and remind myself that he's barely worth the anger. "This complaint just fell into my lap last night. I wouldn't say at this point that anybody is 'bending over backwards,' however I have taken the complainant's statement as required by law." I smile again, hoping that it softens my next line. "Whatever happens from this point forward is up to the chief of police. And none of it really involves you."

"Well, I've already spoken with the chief about it."

Howard might as well have added, "So there!" The guy is a born-again gay advocate, but only when it serves him. He's a straight, married guy, but loves the trendy, progressive image of telling everyone that he and his wife went out to dinner and the theatre with a lesbian couple. Now he's managed to insert himself into this investigation, and worse, he's spun it to the chief as some sort of *gay* thing.

I see the chief and make my way toward him, stopping along the way to snatch the manila folder from the hands of a stammering Martin Nye. I pause only long enough to ask Nye, "What part of 'nobody but me' was unclear to you?"

I don't wait for Nye's answer, and continue through the crowd. When I reach Chief Bradford, he's standing with a cup of coffee and a freakish grin. He holds up a hand, ushering me to the quiet side of the room before beginning the conversation.

I hand him the envelope. "This is the kid's statement."

"I don't want it." The chief says through raised hands, as if I've just tried to hand him a Petri dish full of botulism.

I retract the envelope. "It's a pretty serious allegation. I just thought you'd want to - -"

"I know. Frank already told me all about it."

I bite furiously on the inside of my lip. "Okay. Well then, I guess I should just go ahead and forward this up to Internal Affairs?"

The chief gives me an appraising glance. "Why don't you just go ahead and run with it. It'll be good for you."

"Run with it," I repeat back. "As in, investigate the complaint while I'm managing the swing and midnight shifts?"

"Sure, why not? It'll be good experience for you going into the lieutenant promotional."

I'm dumbfounded. Internal investigations are tricky as hell. There are special rules, police officers' bill of rights, and procedural nuances that all need to be adhered to and complied with. Though I don't want to complain, especially now, I do feel that my hands are full just learning the watch commander ropes.

Bradford sees the reservation in my expression. "This one shouldn't be complicated, in fact I wouldn't put too much into it."

I realize that Chief Bradford has plenty on his plate—certainly more than my insecurities about investigating a major misconduct complaint. And having had my promotion for all of one night, I realize that I need to tread lightly.

"No problem, sir." I know it's the only response I can give. But I'm also wondering why he's minimizing the case's importance. *Wouldn't he want me to put together the best investigation I can?*

Something clicks in my mind and I decide to ask. "Has Bosworth had other complaints like this?"

The chief lets out a short, breathy laugh. "Sure, we've all heard things about that weirdo, but each complaint ends up being some crook's word against Bosworth's, and the tie always goes to the cop. We'll never be able to actually *prove* anything."

I glance at the envelope in my hand then back at the chief. "Maybe it's about time we try."

Bradford smiles. "Just cover the bases of the investigation and then kick it upstairs."

I'm working on little sleep and a lot of coffee, and I bail out of the training right after the catered lunch. I return to the station about an hour before Bosworth is scheduled to arrive for his shift. Protocol dictates that the officer being investigated has the right to be notified about any investigation or complaint they are named in. There are a number of forms that I need to gather together, most of which I've read about in my study materials, but have seldom used. Never having been assigned to IA, this is mostly new ground for me.

I pull Bosworth aside right after his squad's briefing, telling him that I need to speak with him about an urgent matter. I decide to walk him back to the department's youth services section. It's the most secluded area in the building, and based on Darnell's description of having blue carpeting, the most likely location that the assault would have taken place. In the event that Bosworth did it, this will be a subtle way to screw with his head.

His hands are trembling a bit as we walk into an empty office and I close the door behind us. "What's this all about, Phil?"

Normally a line-level cop in his situation would address a boss by rank, but his choice of the familiar tells me he's trying really hard to appear relaxed.

"Well, Fred . . ." *Two can play at this.* "I have to let you know that an internal investigation has been started against you because of a misconduct complaint."

"Misconduct?" He's flabbergasted.

I have Bosworth sign a form that shows he was officially notified, and hand him a copy of Darnell's statement.

"C'mon, Phil. You're freaking me out here." Bosworth forces a laugh and sets the statement aside without looking at it. "What's this all about?"

I tell him that it's all spelled out in the statement I just handed him, and that he should really take the time to read it over. I plan to give Bosworth an opportunity to provide his own statement in response to the allegations, and I advise him that he'll need to contact his PBA representative to arrange for an attorney before we talk again.

"I don't need a lawyer," Bosworth says. "I'll give a statement anytime you want."

"I don't think you want to do that," I tell him. "This is a serious complaint and you'll need representation." It's not that I'm trying to help the imbecile out, but I need to be able to document my repeated attempts to talk some sense into the guy. Otherwise it looks like I railroaded him and it jeopardizes the case. I'd lose credibility with the PBA, especially if they think I somehow bamboozled the sap into giving a statement he wasn't prepared to give. But after three tries, I acquiesce and pull out the tape recorder.

Bosworth denies everything except having arrested Darnell Wallace. I ask him to go over the details, and he says simply that he brought Darnell into the jail and had him booked for the domestic violence charge.

I walk him though it again, step-by-step, from the initial contact with the girlfriend to taking her written statement at the scene, then arresting and handcuffing Darnell and leaving him in the custody of the jailers.

"Which jail door did you use to bring him in?" I ask, suddenly remembering Darnell's description of entering through a back way.

Bosworth stutters a bit. "Through the m-m-main jail door."

Rather than ask anything else, I just stare at him. It works.

He shifts uncomfortably in his seat. "Where else would I have supposedly done this to him, anyway?"

I raise my eyebrows. "Don't know, Fred." I look around casually. "Maybe back here."

Bosworth tosses his head back, a sincere attempt at a convincing laugh. "Back here in youth s-s-services?"

I make a mental note that I had never told him it didn't happen in the jail. In fact, Bosworth hadn't even read enough of Darnell's statement to see what was alleged to have occurred. As a result, he just implicated himself with his stupid question.

I wrap up the interview and thank him for meeting with me. As we walk out, I stop to take in the long corridor of busy offices. Counselors and school cops everywhere, finishing for the day.

"It's amazing how busy this place is," I say.

Bosworth agrees.

"I imagine it's pretty quiet on Sunday nights." I look back at him. "Dark, too."

I wait until Bosworth is gone, and then use the empty counseling office to phone a friend at the Department of Justice. He gives me the name and number of a reputable polygraph examiner, and I'm able to speak directly to her. Without going into much detail, I ask if she would be willing to drive down from Sacramento to interview a complainant in a police misconduct investigation. She agrees, and I suppose she'll bill the department for her time.

I stop in to see Evan Casey, the lieutenant in charge of the department's investigation bureau. He's a slick operator who puts more effort into buying a suit for work than actually doing the work, but we get along pretty well. You never really know with a guy like that. Anyway, I need him to approve the polygraph payment out of his budget.

I explain the basics of the investigation, which somehow he also seems to know about. Casey agrees to cover the cost of the examiner, as if the money's coming out of his own wallet, but apparently the approval also comes with his unsolicited commentary.

"You think busting that freak Bosworth is going to make your promotion permanent?" Casey smirks as he checks his pager.

I stand in his office, barely managing to retain my friendly face.

"I'm just screwing with you," Casey says, now laughing like we're chums. "The chief likes you, he does. Just don't try too hard, and you'll do okay."

Another country heard from. I leave Casey's office having gotten what I wanted, though somehow I feel worse than when I went in. I suppose it's natural for a guy like Casey to suspect my motives as self-serving. His always seem to be. But then a voice inside me asks, exactly how much of what you're doing is motivated by wanting to look good in the new position?

I think about that as I drive out to Liberty Street where Darnell Wallace stays off-and-on with his girlfriend. By the time I get to the pink, flat-roofed cottage, I have figured it out. I'd be lying to myself if I didn't think that catching a rat like Bosworth, if he is guilty, would probably benefit me. But the whole investigation is already littered with landmines, and it would be a hell of a lot easier to hand this thing off to IA and simply keep my head down for the next few months. The last thing I need is to piss off other lieutenants, make waves for the chief, and upset the police benevolent association—who will ultimately have to come to Bosworth's defense. But the overriding motivation for me, that nobody else seems to get, is what if this allegation is true? How can I just throw up my hands and act as if there's nothing anybody can do about it?

I finally come away content that, although I want to prove myself as a competent lieutenant, I am thoroughly disgusted by bad cops. And my fervor to rid the department of Bosworth—if he is guilty—is only fueled by the latter. Had I been a sergeant or even a newly hired officer, I would have felt and behaved in the same way.

I'm parked in front of the house, thumbing through the case file. I read Bosworth's original report again. He had responded here after Darnell's girlfriend called 9-1-1 about a domestic violence complaint. Bosworth ended up arresting Darnell and taking a statement from the girlfriend, Maryann Fletcher. Seems pretty basic—until I get to the last page of the report. It's the written statement Maryann gave about Darnell smacking her in the mouth that doesn't set right. I read it again and something at the very end of the statement suddenly stands out like a giant pointing finger.

I smile to myself as I gather the file and head up the walk.

Maryann answers the front door, looking about the same as I remember. I don't bother reminding her that I've been to the house before, figuring she's probably seen more cops than she cares to remember. I tell her that I'm there about a misconduct complaint against a cop, and not about Darnell's most recent arrest. She's a friendly lady, and doesn't seem to mind talking to me either way.

I ask if she remembers the evening last October when she had Darnell arrested for hitting her. She recalls the incident, and describes Bosworth as the cop who responded and arrested Darnell. She also remembers Darnell phoning her from jail to tell her that the arresting officer had sexually assaulted him.

At my request, Maryann reads the statement she gave that night.

"Is that the same statement you gave the officer?" I ask.

"Pretty much, yeah." She's studying the last sentence.

"Pretty much?" I make like I'm surprised. "Is there anything that isn't completely accurate?"

"Well, yeah, sort of." Maryann points to the last line. "I didn't say this."

It's the same line I spotted in the car before coming in. An oddly placed sentence that looks like it was squeezed in after the fact. Not even written with the same pen. I read the line back to her: "Darnell was very drunk."

"I never told the officer that," Maryann says. "Darnell had been asleep on my couch. He hadn't had anything to drink."

I leave Maryann's house feeling pretty good about my case. The new turn of events seems fairly compelling. The misfit sentence definitely looks like an unauthorized addition—which, under normal circumstances, would have had to be initialed by the person giving the statement. This one wasn't. It was also a pretty obvious attempt by Bosworth to cover his tracks. In the event Darnell complained, here it was on paper that he was drunk and therefore not credible.

I'm exhausted by the time I get back to the station, but I still have to interview the jailers working the night Darnell was brought in. The three who were on duty that night just happen to be working the same shift tonight. I poll each of them separately, showing them Darnell's photograph. Since it's been several months, the chances of recalling a single, unremarkable arrest is improbable.

The first two have no recollection whatsoever. The third, a guy named Voss, studies the photo and seems uncertain. He looks at the photo again. "Something about this guy rings a bell," Voss says.

I tell him to take his time, and then I show him the sheet with all his booking information.

"Would it be okay if I look through the old logs while I'm working tonight?" he asks. "Maybe seeing what else was going on that night will jog my memory."

It's a great idea—one that I probably should have thought of. "Take as much time as you need, Voss." I leave the paperwork with him. "And call or leave me a message if you remember anything."

I secure the entire case file in my uniform locker and head home.

Gale sits at the table with me while I heat the Saran-wrapped dinner I missed. The girls finish their homework and we all turn in early. My mind isn't quite as tired as my body, and I keep going over the investigative steps I still need to take. I finally drift off around nine-thirty.

9:40 p.m.

"Phil." The voice is familiar and seems to fit perfectly into my dream. I hear my name again and it draws me out, the soothing images slowly vanishing from my mind. I open my eyes to total darkness. "Phil, wake up."

I sit up and Gale hands me the phone. "Hello?"

"Lieutenant?" I hear the title and it doesn't sound right. Then there's the unmistakable beep of the department's tape-recorded emergency line, and my mind starts to focus. "This is Jan in dispatch."

I clear my throat. "Yes?"

"Sorry to wake you, sir. We have a situation . . ."

LESSON 3

"It is a man's own mind, not his enemy or foe, that lures him to evil ways."
~Buddha

I'm driving to the station with my window open, the cold air blowing life back into me. The SWAT team callout has come on a bad night; one in which I could really use some sleep. It crosses my mind that I'm so tired I could literally fall asleep in the middle of the operation, which I actually did once. But that was years ago, and I was a different guy when I worked undercover narcotics. In my present role as team commander, I need not only to be here, but to be awake and on top of every single decision. A lot of lives depend on it.

The gate slides open and I pull into the back lot. As I do, I see the equipment van and armored car parked at the curb amidst a haze of warming exhaust. Their rear doors are propped open as guys in black jumpsuits load tools, test electronics, and stock the van with weapons, ammo and provisions.

I see one of the team's sergeants and I lean out the window. "Whadda we got, Bobby?"

"It started as an FBI case," he says. "Their San Jose office has been working a hostage for ransom investigation all day, and they've apparently tracked the victim to a house up here. They're going to brief our guys on the specifics in ten minutes."

Bobby Roselli has dark eyes, a heavy brow, and he sports a five o'clock shadow even after he's just shaved. He's also a good friend and he's as solid as they come. I've decided that if and when my lieutenant promotion becomes permanent and I'm officially given command of the SWAT team, Bobby will be my second. What I really like about the guy is that he's not a 'yes man.' In fact there are times he'll tell me what he thinks, even if I don't think I want to hear it. But it always turns out that I'm glad I listened.

Infused with a good dose of adrenaline now, it takes me only a few heartbeats to change into my tactical uniform and gear-up. Instead of wool patrol uniforms and shiny shoes, we wear black jumpsuits and boots; lapel microphones are threaded through a heavier bullet resistant vest and clipped in place, and in addition to my sidearm, I carry a small sub-machine gun with a folding stock.

Though we're in our own police building, the FBI bigwigs have moved a group of chairs onto the dais for their people. It tells me that they have made themselves at home here, and in my mind it sets the tone for a long night of us playing the little dog in our own house. Their briefing is charged with a palpable urgency, since they believe their victim may be killed if his ransom is not paid. The special agent in charge, or SAC, as they like to be called, spits those details out with federal agency parlance that seems to swell the magnitude of the whole thing—especially for the younger cops.

It turns out that their "victim" is a drug trafficker who transports tar heroin across the border from Mexico, up the I-5 corridor into the San Francisco Bay Area. Someone familiar with his routine had abducted him from his San Jose home earlier in the day. His family had contacted the FBI, who brought in their high-tech equipment and somehow managed to track phone calls from the kidnappers. Apparently the suspects were stupid enough to make the ransom requests using the victim's own cell phone.

Most of the information disseminated to us has to do with the victim, but little is known about the suspects. That bothers me. In cases like this, what we *don't* know can cause us serious problems. At the very least, it makes it more difficult to know what to plan for.

The briefing room is a Sunday potluck of titles, agencies, and uniforms. With their bureaucratic protocols—approvals from headquarters and the like—the sheer number of personnel involved and the incompatibility of our radio equipment conjures up a few more concerns; less about the outcome of their case and more about the safety of my team. I glance over at Bobby who is already making his way toward me.

"What do you think?" he whispers, twisting his head and neck uncomfortably as his eyes drill into me.

"I think it's a well planned operation." I keep a straight face. "I'm going to have your team hit the door as soon as we get on-scene."

His eyebrows morph into one solid line. "They don't know shit about the suspects--"

I crack a smile before I lose my team leader to a cardiac arrest. "Easy, my man." I get up and he follows me out to the hallway. "I'm kidding. I can see that this thing is already a clusterfuck."

Bobby looks somewhat relieved. "Did you hear those guys?" he asks. "They want us to rush an entry into the place."

I nod. "It may be an FBI case, but the tactical part belongs to us. So don't worry; we're not going to bum rush our way in and get somebody hurt. We'll take some time and get the Intel we need. The negotiations team just got here. Let's have them do a workup on the address."

We finally gather everyone and drive to the other side of the city, across the Western Pacific tracks and onto a potholed road with no sidewalks or streetlights. The neighborhood is older, and sits in a rural section of the city on the fringes of an industrial track. It used to be an unincorporated part of the county, but we annexed it into the city several years back and then simply left the whole area to rot out here on its own.

By now it's nearly midnight. We set up a command post a couple of blocks away from the house and establish a sort of hybrid joint command—the FBI's upper ranks together with our boss, Patrol Captain Danny Jenner.

"Phil," Jenner calls out in a low voice. He rolls his eyes to let me know that the command post is as big a mess as the briefing was. "What do you think?"

I step out of the way as two guys in dark business suits stride past. "We're going to slow this thing down a bit," I tell Jenner. "We couldn't come up with much info about the house or any suspects, other than they're Mexican and probably undocumented."

"Any idea how many are inside?"

"Not for sure, sir." I motion toward a white van parked about fifty yards further down the street. "That's the FBI's surveillance van, and the target house is down a dirt driveway just off to the right of it. The agents in the van reported hearing several male voices coming from the house, and they've estimated five or six suspects. Nobody's been in or out since the van arrived, and that's been almost three hours now."

The captain smiles. He used to be SWAT before he moved up the ranks. He knows that this is the kind of callout I like to manage, because it's the kind of callout he would have liked—not the garden-variety domestic brawl with an armed, drunk husband.

Captain Jenner is one of the good guys. He was my patrol sergeant years ago, and I remember when I accidentally broke a guy's nose one night in front of a liquor store. The guy was a big biker and he had just burglarized an apartment. I was going to take his boots for evidence of mud—the same mud he left shoe prints in outside the apartment. So, the guy tried to get rid of the evidence by smacking the mud off the tread. As I made a grab for the boots, I ended up smacking him. Jenner was standing right there, saw the whole thing. But instead of making a big deal out of it, like other sergeants would have, Jenner laughed. He knew I was going for the boots and that my palm-strike was an unintentional reaction, more or less. And he also knew the guy had it coming.

"The suspects just made contact with the hostage's wife again," says the FBI's case agent, leaning out of the command trailer. "They're still using the victim's cell phone."

I follow Captain Jenner inside and listen as the higher-ups are briefed. Apparently the feds have been able to pinpoint the origin of the phone calls to within a hundred feet by using local cell towers to triangulate the source signal. The technology is new and less than exact, and it still doesn't give any clue to the location of the hostage—just his phone. The agents aren't saying it, but Jenner and I both realize that the guy could be dead by now and dumped in the bay, or buried a hundred miles from here.

"We just monitored another call to the wife," says the agent. "They want a hundred thousand dollars before they will release the victim." It occurs to me that our team could easily be drawn into a shootout, and at the end have nothing to show for it but a stolen cell phone.

"So, is your team ready to go in?" asks the FBI SAC.

Go in? Yea, sure thing! There's a pressed suit if I ever saw one. I flash the okay sign. "Got to go over a few things with my guys first," I say. "Should be ready to roll out in about ten."

The volume rises to a fervent buzz as the briefing breaks up. The captain wishes me good luck, but doesn't tell me how it should be handled. Like I say, Jenner is one of the good guys.

I move down the street a half-block to the SWAT van. The team is already huddled into three groups of six, inclusive of a supervisor for each group. I address the snipers first. "I want somebody on the roof behind the target house, with a clear view of the number three side. Two other sniper teams at the front—the one/two and the one/four corners. One team high and the other at ground level."

The sergeant and his snipers dissolve into the darkness without a word.

"Arrest team! You guys are going to stage at the rear of the detached garage. As we make contact with the suspects, you'll be responsible for securing them and getting them out to a patrol car. We'll need you back in place quickly, though. There may be a lot of them in there to deal with."

Their sergeant, a quiet, serious guy named Nakamura, leans slightly into the radio mic on his lapel. "Nakamura to Command. Have somebody move three patrol cars from the command post to our location. Make sure the cars are lined up and ready to go, just behind the white FBI van. And keep them out of sight."

He and his arrest team silently move off into position.

Less than a minute passes when a uniformed officer pulls up, lights out, behind the van. I recognize her as a street cop named Patricia Irons. She's got a reputation as a solid, kickass type, who takes care of her beat and handles herself well.

Bobby Roselli stands with his entry team, waiting for their orders. One guy steadies a heavy battering ram against his hip, while another carries a pneumatic wedge—a compressed air-powered pry tool. His guys are itching to hit the door.

I motion for Bobby to come with me. We move further down the street to the mouth of the target driveway. It's little more than a spit of dirt sandwiched between a dilapidated clapboard garage and an overgrown honeysuckle bush. The house itself is set back another 50 yards off the street. Other than a couple of outbuildings, which look like chicken coups, there are no other houses in the immediate area.

"How do you think we should handle it?" I ask him.

"They've threatened to shoot the victim," Bobby says. "So we've got to assume they're armed." He hesitates a second. "And it sounds like there are quite a few suspects inside there."

I nod as we both lean around the hedge to glance down the dark driveway.

"We could hit it fast with a flash-bang grenade, and hope we can get to the hostage before they shoot him."

"But what if the hostage isn't even in there?" I peer down the driveway again, as if the answer to my question will somehow show itself. I come to the conclusion that the number of suspects inside presents too many variables. We may not be able to gain control in time, and all it would take is for one of them to get to the hostage and take him out.

Bobby and I are still brainstorming ideas at the foot of the driveway when the front door of the house opens. A pale yellow wedge of light falls across the porch and onto the dirt. We duck back into the shadows as Bobby alerts the team over the radio that someone may be coming out.

Nakamura and his arrest team are already hunkered down behind the garage, but only one of the sniper units is in place—the guy in the back of the house. The other two are still working their way over fences so the suspects won't see them. Those two acknowledge over the air, and hold in place.

The silhouetted figure of a man emerges onto the porch, pausing there to look around. His head slowly turns one way and then the other. I'm worried that he may have heard one of us and now they are on heightened alert.

The guy holds a beer bottle to his lips and takes a long swing, then stumbles down the couple of steps to the driveway. My relief lasts only a second before he turns and starts slowly toward us. Bobby and I suck back as far as possible into the bush.

"Everybody on the inner-perimeter hold tight. Suspect is out and walking toward the street."

The air is still. The figure in the driveway is almost lost in the heavy shadows of the lot, and then suddenly I can't see him.

"Where did he go?" I whisper to Bobby.

We lean out, ever so slightly, straining into the darkness. "There he is," Bobby says. "He's taking a piss."

My eyes finally adjust enough to see the forward hunching shadow, one arm propped against the fence for support. I grab my mic. "Nakamura, take him now!"

Within only a couple of seconds, two black-clad figures shuffle silently across my field of view—inches from one another, like a railcar behind a locomotive. The suspect holds the beer gingerly in one hand as he mercilessly shakes himself dry with the other. The two commandos arrive just as the guy finishes stuffing himself back into his pants. Before he can even secure the zipper, he's snared around the neck and jerked backwards like a rodeo steer. Not a sound emits, as he's drug on his heels to the back of the garage. Then, finally, only a tiny '*tink*' as his bottle of Modelo Especial drops to the dirt.

"One down," Bobby whispers with a grin.

"They're going to be looking for him soon," I say over the air. "Make sure we're ready to move if they come back out."

24

From the corner of my eye, I see two more members of the arrest team inching up the side of the garage. They stop when they're about even with us, and then condense themselves down to a formless black mound.

Meanwhile, I know that the negotiators are interrogating the arrested suspect only a stone's throw away.

We wait in silence for several minutes. I'm about to reach for my radio and ask for an update when the door opens again.

"Front door on number one side just opened," a voice reports into my earpiece. "And all snipers are now in place."

Another man steps onto the porch, repeating the survey of the environs. He pauses there, and I see the tiny orange glow of his cigarette. The guy leans casually against the railing for a second then calls into the darkness for his buddy. "Javier!"

He steps onto the dirt and stares in our direction. Slowly, the orange glow makes its way toward us. As he gets close, I see he's taller than the first guy. And he's wearing a cowboy hat.

We're perfectly still now, waiting until he moves just a few steps closer.

"Javier!" he says again.

I grunt back from the bushes, and the guy stops. Leaning slightly forward, he glares into the shadows. "Javier?"

He takes another halting step toward us, and then suddenly he's on his back. The two arrest team members had crept up behind him, and have muzzled him with their padded forearms. Another few seconds to cuff him and he's whisked away.

The odds are looking better for an entry now, but I'm still hoping we can pick off one more suspect. Another silhouette steps out and we scrunch back. Snipers advise that he's on the porch, and we wait. This guy stands casually for a minute and then goes back inside. I can't tell if they're suddenly hinked up or just completely oblivious.

Finally word comes over the air from the negotiators. They've been questioning the two suspects that we bagged. "We found the victim's cell phone and wallet on the second guy," they report. "But he won't talk. The first guy says there are three more suspects inside. Neither one admits to knowing where the hostage is."

Dammit!

Bobby's entry team joins us and we shrink the inner-perimeter down to just the house. We decide to try snagging one more suspect before making entry. I have Nakamura and the arrest team ready for another takedown, and Bobby's guys are staged to hit the door as soon as that happens. Only problem is, nobody's coming out.

A sudden crashing sound sends us all scrambling for cover. Glass and debris shower me as I dive toward some construction equipment laying in the yard. An overturned wheelbarrow is the only protection I can find. All firearms are pointed toward the house, and I'm expecting to hear gunfire at any second. There's nothing.

"What the hell was that?" Bobby barks into my ear. I turn to find him spooning me from behind.

I brush some dirt from my hair and find tiny bits of yellow ceramic. A gouge on the side of the house and more ceramic pieces on the ground beneath it confirms my suspicion. "That didn't come from the house, it came from behind the team."

We look back to see that one of the negotiators has joined us. Apparently he had decided to help expedite the process.

"Somebody threw a goddamn ceramic vase at the house." Bobby is ready for the cardiac unit again.

Thankfully, the vase toss against the wall—though not one of the tactics we train for—seemed to work quite well. The front door opens and two of the suspected hostage-takers walk out. They're looking around curiously, presumably as confused by the crash as we had been. The arrest team slams them into the dirt as the entry team whizzes past and through the front door.

"The house is clear!" a voice blares over the radio.

"Check it again," says Bobby.

A second, and then a third check are made. Still no hostage.

The team calls for the ladder and they hoist a man into the attic. "All clear," he reports.

We post two guys inside while the rest of them move out to the porch. I join them as they make a circle around the house, checking each shed and outbuilding. Nothing.

Two of the leaner members of the entry team shimmy over a cement lip and down into a crawlspace beneath the house.

"Down here, Sarge!" The muffled voice permeates up to us.

I follow Bobby over and we drop onto our bellies. Peering through the opening into the basement, I focus on the converging beams of their flashlights. There, strung up like a drying mackerel, our kidnap victim hangs handcuffed from a drainpipe. He's unshaven and dirty, and his tousled hair is knitted with cobwebs. The poor guy seems half out of it as he tries to focus his eyes.

The two cops crawl over and use their own keys to release the cuffs. They drag the guy out to the street, where the team medic does a quick triage, and then we hand him over to the paramedics.

By this time the whole area is swarming with FBI agents. Since kidnap for ransom is a federal crime, they regain operational control of the case. A couple of them escort the victim in the ambulance, and their crime scene folks take custody of the house.

Suddenly, it's over.

The weight of the operation starts to flow out of me—a sensation similar to watching dirty shower water swirling down the drain. Except what's washing off of me is the stress I never knew was there. It's close to an emotional release, and I take my time walking back down the road to our equipment van. As I reflect on the night's events, a seesaw of pride and relief surges back and forth inside me. I'm intensely happy that the callout ended well—my team is in one piece and we're all alive. In truth, it was Javier's decision to step outside and pee that allowed us to pick them off, one-by-one. I chuckle as I replay how it happened. And though I know I'll get credited with running a successful operation, it's really the guys on the team who did their jobs so well. I trust them, and respect them, and care for them very much.

"Nice job, guys." It's about as much as I say when I get back to the van. Anything more would make them uncomfortable. It doesn't matter anyway, because they know how I feel.

It's nearly daylight by the time we stow all our gear, collect our people and get back to the station. We hold a quick debrief to go over any tactical or procedural hiccups that occurred, but I can see that the potency of the rush has waned. Once in the comfortable seats of the warm classroom, none of us can keep our eyes open. The guy who threw the vase is a good friend, and I'm not going to embarrass him here. We'll deal with that privately at another time.

I thank everybody for their dedication, and call it a night.

Before leaving, I head upstairs to check in with the captain. He seems pleased with the results and has already called the police chief to let him know that it ended peacefully.

The overcast morning is only a few shades lighter than the night that just passed. I'm parked in the back of the secured lot, listening to the radio, waiting for the heater to warm the cold air blowing on my legs, and anticipating how nice my bed is going to feel. Suddenly, I see something that jolts me upright. I peer through the foggy windshield as Fred Bosworth drives in and parks his car. Since we just met about his misconduct complaint, I'm acutely familiar with his assigned hours and workdays. And today is Bosworth's day off.

Interesting.

27

I slink down in my seat and watch. Bosworth stands with his hands in his pockets, glancing back and forth in the lot. A few of the day shift officers arrive for work, park their cars, and head inside to the locker room, but Bosworth says nothing to any of them.

A few more minutes pass and I see a tiny gray Toyota pull in and park. Bosworth spots it and hurries purposefully over. I use my shirt to wipe a small peephole on my side window, through which I watch as the driver gets out of the car and is immediately be set upon by Bosworth. The guy in the Toyota is a new kid, a community service officer assigned to the jail. Other than the fact that he works day shift and his last name is Chambers, I know nothing else about him.

Bosworth is standing so close that the kid has to lean away. I can almost imagine the morning breath that poor Chambers is enduring. Bosworth's animated gestures and non-stop monologue are interspersed with what appears to be nervous glances around the lot. Chambers doesn't seem to be saying much, and definitely looks as if he's been caught off guard by the encounter.

The onslaught lasts only a few minutes, and then Bosworth jumps back in his car and drives out of the lot. Chambers takes his dry-cleaned uniform from the Toyota and ambles into the building. I'm wondering if I should approach the kid to find out what was said. But my car has warmed now, and the chances that their conversation has anything to do with my investigation is about one in a hundred. Besides, I have to be back this afternoon for Darnell Wallace's polygraph exam.

Sleep comes quickly, but my wake-up alarm seems to come quicker. I enjoy a cup of tea with Gale before starting back to work. She's made me two ham sandwiches, one for the drive to work and one for my dinner break later in the evening. The first sandwich is devoured before I reach the main boulevard.

I stow my gear and hustle upstairs, where I find Darnell sitting in a small waiting area outside the second floor elevator. He nods to me as I walk past and I thank him for coming in. I continue to the far end of the bureau to find one of the interview rooms already set up for the examination.

Shirley Daneke is a middle-aged woman with the same frosted hair that my fifth grade teacher had. She's painfully thin and smells of cigarettes and coffee. Not quite what I imagined a DOJ examiner would look like.

We make introductions, and I notice Evan Casey hovering in close proximity. I know that his investigations budget is paying for Daneke's services, but I'd rather not include him in this. I escort the woman into the detectives' lunchroom and close the door. For the next few minutes I explain the specific details of the misconduct investigation against Bosworth.

First thing out of her mouth: "There are a number of reasons a prisoner would make complaints such as these against a policeman. I find it highly unlikely that this Officer Bosworth assaulted him."

What in the hell? She hasn't even turned on her damn machine and she already finds the complaint, "highly unlikely?" I clear my throat and stretch my neck from side to side. I immediately wonder if Evan Casey got to her. Or worse yet, that nosy day shift lieutenant, Frank Howard.

"You don't even know Bosworth," I tell her. "I'm sure he's not like other cops you may have worked with. Just try to keep it objective, will you?"

Daneke flashes an indignant glare. "The polygraph is a scientific instrument. My role is only to interpret the readings, not to pass judgment."

I try my best to verbally dust the woman off, after having clumsily insulted her. The message behind my words was genuine, but probably ill timed. I want to tell her that Bosworth has had other complaints of this nature, and that he is one weird son-of-a-bitch. But my window for personal commentary has closed, and it wouldn't be right to try to poison her in the opposite direction.

"By the way," she says. "You've got a blob of mustard on your cheek."

So, as she and Darnell go into the small interview room, I sit outside wiping the dried remnants of a sandwich off of my face.

The examination goes on for 90 minutes, and finally Daneke emerges with a beleaguered Darnell Wallace. She sends him on his way and waits until the elevator doors close to fill me in.

"Deceptive," she says.

I take a breath to steady my climbing blood pressure "I beg your pardon?"

"He seemed pretty straight forward with most of the questions," she says as she disconnects wires and rolls them into neat bundles. "But when we got to the *alleged* sexual assault, I detected some deception."

I stare at her, hoping for more. Finally I ask, "So that's it? He failed the polygraph?"

"Basically, yes. Mr. Wallace indicated deception."

From the corner of my eye I see Evan Casey, lingering close enough to hear our conversation. He quickly heads off toward the chief's office. I offer Daneke a lackluster thank you, and walk down to the locker room to dress for my shift. I relieve the day shift watch commander and organize my things on the desk.

"So, the kid failed the poly." The police chief plops himself into the chair across from me.

I nod my head. "According to Mrs. Daneke."

A look of relief crosses his face, as if a doctor had just told him the giant tumor they found is benign. "Well, I guess that's the end of your investigation. If the complaining victim isn't telling the truth, you've got no case."

He didn't say it like a question, but more like a period at the end of a sentence. I try to force another nod. "Guess so."

I feel the need to tell him that the woman had her mind made up before she even interviewed Darnell Wallace. I want to describe the strange encounter I witnessed between Bosworth and the jailer in the back lot, and about the written statement Bosworth forged. And I'm aching to tell him that Frank Howard and Evan Casey are a couple of idiots, and that he shouldn't listen to a thing they say.

"Have a good night, Chief." It's the only thing that comes out of my mouth. He checks his watch, picks up his briefcase and walks out of my office, content that the Bosworth investigation is all but a distant memory.

I need some air. The back lot is quiet, and I stand just outside the door watching the last of the orange sun duck behind the coastal range across the bay. I take a deep breath and let it out slowly.

"Good night, LT," says a voice in the parking lot.

I glance over to see Chambers, the jailer who Bosworth bushwhacked this morning. He gives me a friendly wave as he heads across the lot to his little Toyota.

"Chambers," I call to him in desperation. "Can I have a minute?" Poor kid has the same look on his face that he had earlier when Bosworth approached him.

I walk with him toward his car, but out of respect for my rank he keeps trying to stop and show his attentiveness. I'm doing my best to put the kid at ease, soften it with my words, as if this is just a casual conversation between two regular guys. But he's not fooled. So I dispense with the façade.

"I need to ask you about the conversation you had with Fred Bosworth this morning." I refrain from telling him how I even know about it. "If it was of a personal nature, and it had nothing to do with work, I completely understand. You're under no obligation to discuss that with me."

The kid stares at me with a wide-eyed stupor. I feel a little creepy doing this, almost like I'm abusing my power, but I know the payoff could make it worthwhile. "However," I continue. "If the conversation had anything to do with his internal investigation, then I need you to tell me about it."

Chambers takes in a gulp. "Sir, I didn't know anything about an internal investigation. Officer Bosworth just asked me about an arrest he brought into the jail a couple of weeks ago."

"A couple of weeks ago?"

"Yes, sir. A guy arrested for being under the influence of drugs."

I'm at a loss. Darnell Wallace was arrested months ago, and not on drug charges. "Do you know why Bosworth was interested in that particular arrest?"

"Something about when he collected the urine sample," says Chambers. "Officer Bosworth wanted to know if I saw the prisoner pee on him."

"Pee on him." I stare off, trying to make sense of it. I turn back to Chambers. "So, do you recall that?"

"Not really," Chambers says apologetically. "I mean, I remember the prisoner, and I remember Officer Bosworth collecting the urine specimen, but I never saw anyone pee on him."

"Interesting that you would remember that arrest, out of all the prisoners you've booked."

"Sir?" He's looking at me like he doesn't want to go *there*. "The reason I remember it is because, well, Officer Bosworth collected the urine sample himself. The cops usually have us jailers do it, and we always wear gloves. I came around the corner after putting on my gloves, and Officer Bosworth was already up against him."

"What do you mean, 'up against him'?"

"He was smack-dab against the guy, holding the cup up to the guy's dick, uh, I mean penis."

I roll my eyes. "Go on, Chambers."

"Well, sir . . . Officer Bosworth wasn't even wearing gloves."

I ask Chambers if he remembers anything else about the incident, and he swears he doesn't. I feel badly jamming him out of the blue like this, but it might be well worth the discomfort.

This isn't making any sense to me. It can't be Darnell Wallace; the timing doesn't work at all. *Is it possible there could there be a second victim?*

"Why would Bosworth want to make sure you saw the guy pee on him?" Although I ask, I'm really thinking it through aloud. I don't expect an answer, but I'm happily surprised when I get it.

"Because he wanted to make sure I knew that's why he pushed the prisoner's dick away."

"Run that one by me again?"

"Officer Bosworth told me that the only reason he had his hands on the guy's dick was to keep him from peeing on him."

This just keeps getting weirder. "So, you saw Bosworth grab him?"

"That's just it," says Chambers. "I never saw anything like that. Officer Bosworth just took the urine sample and left."

"Do me a favor," I ask the kid. "Go back through the booking sheets when you get in to work tonight, and try to find the prisoner's name for me. Don't mention it to anyone, and just send me an email with the information."

Chambers promises he will. I see him driving out of the lot and I know he won't be able to sleep today. But the tinge of guilt I feel about that is quickly dwarfed by Bosworth's vile smell. I've investigated enough people to know when someone is dirty. And though it's too early to be 100% certain, there's just something about these accusations that ring true in my gut.

I know that freak is up to something, and I'm going to find out what it is. Even if the police chief and his *trusted advisors* don't want to deal with it.

LESSON 4

*"Transcend political correctness and
strive for human righteousness."*
~Anthony J. D'Angelo

I met Jimerson Thomas in 1989, when my street drug team raided
his mother's apartment. He was only thirteen years old then, and his
mother, Uniqua Thomas, was a crack whore. Now, after the
forgettable boy had receded into the abyss of my memory, I sit
staring at his face again.

"I've been trying to find you for a couple of weeks." I study the
nineteen-year-old in the dim light of the courthouse basement.
"How's your mom doing?"

Jimerson flashes a half-smile that tells me he doesn't know,
doesn't care, or doesn't believe that I care. "You spent two weeks
looking for me so you could ask, how's my mother?"

He was arrested last night on a traffic warrant for unpaid tickets,
and it was a stroke of luck that I happened to check the logs this
morning. Until then I wasn't having any luck locating him. Even if I
had found him, I'm sure he would have told me nothing and walked
out, had he not been in custody.

I decide to use another angle. "I'm trying to bust a dirty cop."

"Why?" he asks. "Thought all y'all stick together."

"Sometimes. But only to a point."

I tell Jimerson that the jailer who had booked him six weeks ago
had given me his name. Jimerson's face remains expressionless as I
explain that the cop who had arrested him is the one I'm after. I
remind Jimerson that he was charged that night with a drug offense,
and that the cop's name was Bosworth. I'm watching for the, 'ah-ha'
reaction, but there's none. "So, did you have any problem with the
cop?"

"No," he says flatly.

"Did the officer grab you . . . touch you in any way?"

Jimerson shakes his head. Now he's frowning in confusion, and
so am I.

I deicide I'm just going to ask the question, flat-out. "Is there any possibility that the cop grabbed your dick?"

"Hell no!" Jimerson pushes back from the table. "If that mutha fucka done something like that, it would have been on."

He leaves no ambiguity for me to work with. "You were arrested for being under the influence," I remind him again. "Maybe you were so high that - -"

Jimerson interrupts before I can finish. "Look, I was high, but I ain't never been that high. I'm telling you, it never happened."

I thank him for taking the time to talk to me, and we shake hands. I tap on the door, signaling to the bailiff that the interview is over. He steps in to handcuff Jimerson and return him to court.

The guy was my last hope, and he swears it didn't happen. That's even more definitive than a deceptive polygraph. Now, I've got zip. With nothing to lose, I decide to take one final shot. "You know, if you're worried about how talking to me will affect the drug case, you don't have to. I can put in a good word with the judge."

"Nah, I ain't worried none 'bout that shit." Jimerson shrugs. "Them charges already got dropped."

Jimerson and the bailiff disappear down the hall as I stand alone in the basement, thinking. *His charges were dismissed.*

Interesting.

As I walk across the lot from the courthouse to the police building, I have to ask myself if this is all worth it. Since I'm assigned to night shift as the watch commander and I'm responsible for both the swing and the midnight shifts, the bulk of this investigation is being done on my own time. *Who even does that?*

Then again, every time the flame sputters to nothing, a small gust of new information blows it back to life. Or does it? Maybe this thing really is dead, and I've lost my objectivity. *Do I want to be right so badly that I'm willing to nail Bosworth at any cost?*

I think about these questions while changing into my uniform to start my shift. Sitting through the squad briefing, I'm only half listening to the sergeant as he rattles on about stolen cars and runaway teens. Later, in the relative solitude of my 'fishbowl' office, I close the door and pull out Bosworth's file.

The desk phone rings and it's the communications center. "The chief wants to know if you can meet him at City Hall," the dispatcher asks. "He's there for the city council meeting tonight."

I check my watch and see that the council meeting doesn't start for an hour. "Tell him I'll meet him there in fifteen."

The police chief is waiting in the rotunda when I walk in. He's a physically fit guy, but he's lost a lot of weight lately. His rumpled gray suit is a couple of inches too loose now and looks like he's been mountain biking in it. I should see a leader when I look at him, but I can't help but flash back to the guy who took over the narcotics unit when I was halfway through my undercover assignment. He was disorganized then, and he's still a mess. On the plus side, at least we no longer hate each other.

"Dispatch said you wanted to see me, Chief." I glance around the empty hall, wondering why the intrigue.

"Have you wrapped up the Bosworth IA yet?"

I'm unsure if he wants to know if it's closed, cleared off my plate, or if I'm done typing it all up—none of which I can respond to in the affirmative. And I definitely get the feeling he's got something riding on my answer. I measure my response against his expression, and try to say it as sedately as a bowl of lime jell-o.

"Pretty much," I lift my eyebrows like a guy who can't wait to get rid of the case. "Just need to tie up a few loose ends and I'll be done."

Chief Bradford tilts awkwardly, pitching forward as if someone just pushed him from behind.

I take a small step backwards. "I'm probably going to have to interview Bosworth one more time, just to put a couple of questions to rest, once and for all."

He grimaces. "You know, I'm getting some heat from the gays about this."

"The gays." I drop my shoulders. "Would that be Frank Howard and company?"

"Doesn't matter," the chief says. "I just want to make sure we're not bending over backwards to hang Bosworth just because this is a male-on-male contact."

Interesting choice of words. They might as well have come right out of Howard's mouth.

"You know . . . Fred Bosworth is married to a woman and has kids," I tell him. "In any case, I'm not sure why *'the gays'* would be upset by a misconduct investigation." As if gays in the department, or any other group for that matter, ever speak with a single voice or can agree on anything.

He nods, almost apologetically. "I know, I know." He pulls out his cell phone and glances at a text message. "Just wrap up the case as soon as you can and turn it over to Internal Affairs. It's all about a negative image, and I really don't need that."

I leave City Hall pissed off. Too many weird things have come up to just walk away from this investigation. I'm more determined now to ignore the political overtones and dig deeper into it, regardless of what it might mean for my career. *I liked being a sergeant much better than a lieutenant anyway.*

As I drive back to the station, I'm trying to figure out where this investigation could possibly go from here. I feel like I'm out of tricks. I've really got no more cards to play, other than to interview Bosworth and flat-out ask him if he did it. By now he'll have an attorney, and no matter how stupid the guy is, my chances of getting a confession from him are zero.

A motorcycle zips across the intersection in front of me, and I glance up from my daze to see that my light is green. It's been a while since I wrote a ticket, but I still remember that if my light is green, his light must be red. I step on the accelerator and make the turn to go after him.

"L-56, I'm going to be stopping a Harley at G and Davis." I set the microphone back in its holder and flip on my emergency lights.

The biker is hunched over his wide handlebars, and the broad back of his Levi vest blazes the name of his club. A ponytail swings wildly from the back of his helmet as he turns to throw me a look. Then, in an instant, he's a quarter mile down the road. I stomp on the gas, and the watch commander's heavy Ford lurches like an old man in line at the Early Bird Special. *Damn these cars!*

The cruiser swings spastically onto a narrow street and I see the guy's exhaust cloud half a block ahead. It's a hot summer night and the avenue is lined with apartment houses. I don't want to run over anybody, much less a kid, but I would definitely like to catch this son-of-a-bitch. "L-56, I'm in pursuit of a black motorcycle, heading westbound on Sacramento from Wilcox."

The dispatcher repeats my location, and I assume other cops are starting to head in my direction. Farther up the road ahead of me, people are running to cross the street in advance of my siren. Blurred figures flash in my periphery, and I try to make myself aware of how fast I'm driving and how long it would take to stop this boat. It feels as if the car's seat has been spit-shined with Armor All, because I'm sliding halfway across the car every time I round a corner.

To my surprise, I've gained on the biker. We head down Burnett Street, which I know ends just after the continuation high school. From the motorcycle's speed, I don't think he's aware of that.

I back off the gas as we near the end, and I see the guy suddenly stand on the footbrake. His bike fishtails and he lays it down, sliding across the roadway and up onto a private drive. I'm out of the car running, my nightstick in one hand and my radio mic in the other.

The biker has abandoned his rattling motorcycle, trying his best to run. I notice a pronounced waddle, which I figure is either a result of the fall or a consequence of his heavy leather boots. Perhaps he's just out of shape.

I catch up to the guy and use my nightstick as a calling card to the back of the thighs, just to let him know I'm there. He crumples to the pavement, and I dive onto his back. He tries to raise his arms in defense or submission, but I snap a cuff on his hand before I can figure out which way he's going. I yank him up and start back for my screaming patrol car just as a Sheriff's unit skids to a stop. Behind them are two more of our guys, lights and sirens blaring.

The street cops hustle to take the arrest off my hands, and I'm reminded that I have more important things to do. It's not a bad image for the patrol officers to see—a lieutenant who still goes out once in a while and makes arrests. But if I'm being honest, it wasn't anything I was trying to do. It was just a red light violation that happened right in front of me when I was in a lousy mood.

As I exchange my handcuffs with the transporting officer's, I ask the biker why he ran. The cop pulls a small baggie of marijuana from the guy's pocket and sets it on the hood of the car.

"'Cause 'o that," he says. "Didn't want to get busted with weed."

I shake my head and start back to my car. Something suddenly occurs to me, and it feels as if all the colors of my Rubik's Cube have suddenly come together at once. The biker didn't know that minor possession of marijuana is hardly even a crime anymore—about the equivalent of a jaywalking ticket. But he was willing to risk a felony evading charge to avoid being caught with the dope.

Bosworth! Just like the biker, he panicked and did something that made matters worse; he dumped his own case in order to cover up something else. *But why Jimerson's case? He wasn't the victim.*

I go to the Jimerson Thomas arrest file and find a supplement in the jacket. It hadn't been there when I originally copied the report, and the date shows that it was added the day *after* I notified Bosworth of the investigation against him. Besides the suspicious timing, the supplement, written by Bosworth, actually requests that the charges against Jimerson be dropped—the same charges that Bosworth brought against Jimerson in the original report.

With the new supplement in hand, I draw back into my office and start reading. In it, Bosworth claims to have changed his mind about which drug Jimerson was under the influence of. Originally thought to be methamphetamine, after mulling it over (for 28 days), Bosworth suddenly decided that it was PCP—a hallucinogen with physical characteristics that are nothing even close to Meth. As if that isn't enough, Bosworth claims to have mistakenly mixed up the urine sample with one taken from another suspect. That too, apparently, only dawned on Bosworth nearly a month later. And, coincidentally, all of this realization occurred the very day after I confronted him about the sexual assault allegation.

My only problem remains that Jimerson insists Bosworth never victimized him. *So what the hell is Bosworth hiding?*

I come in early the following day to meet with Evan Casey. Not that I have any desire to talk to the puffy narcissist, but I have no choice. He oversees the District Attorney Liaison officer—the cop who brings all our criminal cases to court. I'm particularly interested in the Jimerson Thomas arrest, and how Bosworth managed to get it dumped. I mean, the supplement Bosworth wrote makes it clear enough, but I'm wondering how it is that nobody noticed. *What cop writes an addition to an arrest report a month later, saying they changed their mind?*

I show Casey the supplement report and ask what he knows about it. Casey's eyebrows dip as he reads Bosworth's remarks and then sees the date it was written. "What the hell is this?"

"That's what I want to know."

"But this isn't even the guy who complained," Casey says. "What is Bosworth up to?" Casey's sudden interest whiffs of cooperation toward a common goal, while at the same time glossing over the fact that he never spotted any red flags. Bosworth's supplement went through his unit, and I know for a fact that the DA liaison officer alerted him to the oddness of it.

Casey pulls out a folder containing test results for all of the criminal cases where physical evidence has been sent to the crime lab. "The urine sample came back positive for meth," he says. "So why would Bosworth try to say it was PCP?"

"He claims to have accidentally mixed it up with another prisoner's piss," I say, wondering how much to even tell this shyster. "But I checked the records and there were no other urine specimens even collected in the jail that night."

Casey picks up the supplement. "So this whole thing is bullshit?"

I nod, knowing it will probably take less than 30 seconds for him to report this new information back to the chief.

As I'm leaving Casey's office, I spot Nora Morales at the copy machine. She's a detective who worked for me when I ran TNT—a high-energy street drug unit. She was also one of the first lesbians in the department to 'come out,' years ago when the culture was much less welcoming.

We greet one another and I ask if we can talk privately. We duck into a conference room and without mentioning a name, I give her a rough idea of what my investigation involves. Though she doesn't say, it seems she may have already heard about the case. Either that or she's quick to figure out that only Bosworth could be the culprit. In any event, I mention that there are concerns at the top about how this may be perceived by the gays in the department.

Nora coughs out a laugh. "First off, Bosworth is a straight-up bizarro. If he's trying to claim gay, he's delusional. There's not one of us who would back his play. Besides that," Nora says. "What does it matter if he is or isn't gay? Sexual battery is gross misconduct, and no decent cop of any ilk would want to see him get away with that. It gives everybody in the department a black eye."

I smile and thank her. *Finally, a voice of reason.*

Chief Bradford is sitting in my office when I get back downstairs. He's got that ants-in-his-pants look again, and I can only guess that Evan Casey has alerted him to the Jimerson Thomas direction the case has taken.

"Is it true? You have another victim?" He wipes his forehead like a politician trying to contain a scandal.

I explain that Bosworth seems concerned about the Jimerson arrest, but that so far I'm unable to find a connection to the original complainant, Darnell Wallace.

"Have you questioned this Jimerson kid yet?" he asks.

I tell the chief that I have. "Unfortunately, he's telling me that nothing happened."

The chief perks up. "You mean, he wasn't a victim?"

"Well, apparently not the victim of an assault." I pull out Bosworth's supplement report, the one requesting the case be dismissed. "But Bosworth wrote here that he . . ."

The chief bats my words out of the air with a swipe of the hand. "Never mind all that. One guy didn't pass the poly and the other says he wasn't molested. Time to drop this thing before we look like a bunch of homophobes."

I take a breath. "Speaking of that," I ease myself into my chair. "I'm not so sure that's how we would be seen." I then recount my conversation with Nora. I finish by telling the chief, "Nobody seems to have an issue with this thing, but Frank Howard."

Chief Bradford ignores the point and focuses on my decision to discuss a sensitive internal investigation with Nora Morales.

"She seemed to have already heard about it," I say. "Probably from some of the same people who've been telling . . ." I stop myself before implicating Howard or Casey. Before I say, the same people who have been telling *you!*

"I'm not sure how she knew." I leave it there.

The chief rubs his forehead and then purses his lips until I can no longer see them.

"I agree." I toss the file onto my desk. "It doesn't serve anyone's interest to draw this thing out any longer."

He leans back as if his load has suddenly been lifted.

"Bosworth probably has a PBA attorney by now," I say. "How about I call them in to give a statement, and that will be it. He can tell his side, refuse to talk, whatever, and I'll write it up after that.

Bradford's lips slowly emerge from his mouth. "Good, yeah. Let's do that. Give them a chance to clear his name, and that will be that."

I smile to myself, knowing that I'm going to grill Bosworth like a ballpark frank. "Yep. Then that will be that."

I've moved to day shift, and my new squad hits the street with two new sergeants. The switch was necessitated by the quarterly shift change, rotating the entire division. I'm glad to be rid of the two old-time sergeants, along with the smell of their Polo cologne.

My new shift sergeants stop into my office before briefing so I can go over a few things with them: progress of probationary officers, a couple of new policies, and the types of calls I want to be notified about. Pretty standard stuff, really.

We break lineup and I head back to my office. It's only 8 a.m., but I'm already hungry. I pull out my lunch bag, unwrap a BLT sandwich, and settle back into my seat. The sergeants haven't been on the street for more than ten minutes when I get a call from one of them. Sergeant Thurmond Morris. He sounds out of breath.

"Lieutenant, we got problems!"

I glance at the status screen on my desk to see what type of call he's on. It looks like a welfare check of a woman downtown. "What's going on, Thurmond?"

"Whoa boy," he wheezes into my ear. "We got a bad one down here. It's some kind of serial murder."

"Serial murder?" I press my thumb and forefinger into my closed eyes. "Isn't that, like, three or more victims?"

"Oh, well, maybe. But we've only come up with one so far. A city worker found her."

"Found who, Thurmond?"

"The murder victim. A dead whore." He lowers his voice as if the press may be listening in on our call. "She's been gutted and disemboweled, and then her body was dumped in the bushes!"

LESSON 5

"A judge who cannot punish, in the end associates themselves with the criminal."
~Johann Wolfgang Von Goethe

I've known Morris for years, and he's always been a little jumpy. In fact, he once fumbled a loaded shotgun at the scene of a SWAT standoff, accidentally firing a round just inches over my head.

"The press is going to be all over this," he says. "Do you want me to notify the chief?"

"No!" It comes out a little harsher than I intended, so I add a thank you. "Just cordon off the scene and I'll be right there."

I see the coroner's van parked near a clump of bushes and I pull up behind it. Morris hustles over to my car before I can even put it in park. His uniform pants are hiked high around his bowling pin body, the woolen fabric wedged securely into his ass.

He lifts his hands as if to calm *me*. "It's okay, it's okay," he says. "It's not as bad as we thought."

We? I get out of the car. "What's changed? The disemboweled whore is feeling better now?"

"Well, no. She's still dead." Morris totally misses the sarcasm. "But as it turns out, she's been living in the bushes over there where she was found. The chick's homeless."

"A homeless prostitute who lives in the bushes?"

"I guess she's not really a prostitute after all," says Morris. "And the coroner thinks she died of natural causes."

"Disemboweled?" I glance past him to the cluster of police and deputy coroners gathered behind the crime scene tape.

"Dogs," Morris says. "The dogs got to her after she died."

I close my eyes, trying to hold down the BLT. "So, let me see if I get this right; no whore, no serial killing, and no disembowelment. Just a dead homeless woman who was chewed on by some dogs after she died."

"Yup." Morris adjusts his pants. "Sorry about that, boss."

I opt not to view the gnawed remains, and head back to the station instead.

There is a message in my mailbox from the president of the police officer's benevolent association advising me that Daphne Mullan, an association attorney, is now representing Fred Bosworth. I assume that means that any communication with Bosworth now has to go through, or at least include, her.

I wait until the end of my shift, when I'm certain a real person won't answer the phone, and I call Daphne Mullan's number. I leave a message introducing myself as the lieutenant investigating the complaint against Fred Bosworth. I leave my contact information, and request she call me to set up a re-interview of her client.

After waiting two days, I leave another message for Mullan. My message is essentially the same as the first, but with perhaps a little less friendly tone.

Another day goes by without hearing back from her, and I come in for my last workday of the week. I'm in the locker room changing when the chief's secretary pages me over the intercom. I dial her office from the wall phone next to me.

"The chief wants to see you right away," she says, in her usual hurried manner.

After changing, I go up to his outer-office where I'm asked to wait while the chief finishes a phone call. A couple of minutes pass and then he ushers me in and closes the door.

"Daphne Mullan called." He studies me for a reaction, but I give none. "She represents Bosworth."

I recognize a shade of irritation in his tone. It's probably because he's got better things to do than field calls about an investigation that his subordinate is conducting. I can't say that I blame him, either. "I've left several messages for her," I tell the chief, adjusting the annoying velcro strap on my ballistic vest. "But she hasn't returned any of them."

"I don't think Daphne likes you," he says.

"We've never even met."

The chief shrugs. "She says you don't know what you're doing."

I'm not sure why the attorney would tell the chief that, other than the fact that I'm not an Internal Affairs investigator, and in truth, this is all new territory for me. On the other hand, it could be typical lawyerly maneuvering: Call up the head guy, tell him his investigator screwed up the case, and try to get the whole thing dropped.

"Is she pressuring you to intervene?" I ask, intentionally using the word 'pressuring' to my benefit. *What man likes to admit he's being pressured to do something?*

"No, nothing like that." The chief crumples the message and tosses it decisively into the trash.

"Oh, okay." I pause a second. "So, did you happen to mention to her that I'd like to re-interview Bosworth?"

"Uh, no." He stirs in his high back, faux-leather chair. "I told Daphne that I'd talk to you first."

Talk to me about what, I don't know. I'm guessing she did put the screws to the chief, and he's been feeling me out about dropping the whole damn thing. "Okay then." I check my watch. "I'd better get down to briefing."

Not really sure what the meeting was all about, I quickly leave the office before he actually finds enough pluck to order me to dump the investigation.

After our squad's briefing, they all hit the street. I watch with longing from the back door as the patrol cars file out the gate, before finally succumbing to my desk. I'd so much rather be taking calls out on the street.

I leave the attorney another message asking for a re-interview, mentioning that she can feel free to respond directly to me instead of the police chief. It's my way of letting her know that I know what she did. It also insinuates that the chief told me about her call, yet did not order me to drop the case. I'm trying to make it appear as if he is backing my play—which, of course, he is doing in only the most frail sense of the word. I note the date and time of the call in my case file.

I check the clock and see that the shift is past its halfway mark. I make myself a cup of tea, and then ease back into my chair just as the jail line rings on my desk.

"Lieutenant? It's Tremon Voss."

It takes me a second to remember the context, and then I realize he's one of the jailers who were working the night Bosworth brought in the complainant, Darnell Wallace. "Yeah, yeah, how's everything going back there tonight, Tremon?"

"Fine, sir. I just wanted to get back to you about that *thing* you had asked me about."

I'm searching my memory. "Oh, yeah. You were going to let me know if you remembered anything about Bosworth's arrest."

"Yes," he says, sounding as if he's shielding the phone. "I've been thinking about it, and I do recall something. That night was busy, and several female prisoners were brought in. I hadn't really remembered that until I looked over the logs."

So far it doesn't sound like a nugget in this recollection that I'll be able to use. But I give an encouraging, "Uh huh," just the same.

"So we had to convert cell number six to an all female cell."

It's been seventeen years since I worked in the jail as a police assistant, and they've remodeled it twice. I have no idea which cell is number six or why any of this is important to me, but I go ahead and keep listening.

"So that's how I remembered it," he says.

"Remembered what?"

"I was over on that side of the jail, checking on the cell full of females when they came in. Officer Bosworth and Darnell Wallace."

"I see." I clear my throat, not really understanding. "Did you see something out of the ordinary when they came in?"

"Well, sir. Nothing too out of the ordinary. Just that they came in from the youth services side of the jail, instead of using the main entrance like everyone else."

I walk back to the jail and make a copy of the log that Jailer Voss had used to jog his memory. Interestingly, it also lists the times each prisoner was brought in—including Bosworth's prisoner, Darnell Wallace.

Voss finishes fingerprinting an arrestee and then comes over to me. "I don't know if that helps at all, but it's the only thing I can remember about it."

I thank Voss and tell him that it did help.

"I should have called you sooner," he adds. "But I was confused about which arrest we were talking about."

My attention is focused on the log, and I'm only half-listening to Voss.

"There's some other guy Officer Bosworth brought in recently who looks exactly like Darnell Wallace, so that's what confused me."

Voss goes back to what he was doing, and I stand there staring into space.

"Wait a minute, Voss!" I step around the counter. "What other prisoner are you talking about. The guy who looks just like Wallace, what's his name?"

Voss looks at me like I've gone mad. "Uh, his name is Jimerson Thomas, sir. He's in here all the time."

"That's it!" I slap my hand against the counter.

"Sir?"

"Oh, nothing Voss. Thanks for all your help."

I go back to the fishbowl and close the door. Pulling the two booking photographs out, I set them side-by-side. I look at Darnell Wallace and then at Jimerson Thomas. *Holy shit—these two guys could almost be twins!*

Another four days go by before I hear back from Daphne Mullan, and even then it's through the chief's office again. She set the date of the re-interview for the following week. The slight delay gives me time to pull the case together and document it right up to the final interview.

I also put together a visual timeline based on radio logs, jail logs, police reports and evidence collection times—primarily the urine specimen collected from Jimerson Thomas. It shows inconsistencies in the time Jimerson's urine specimen was collected; at the time noted on the evidence tag, Bosworth, who supposedly obtained the specimen, was across the city taking a petty theft report. The sloppy documentation alone could be job threatening.

Another important point the timeline illustrates is a ten-minute gap between the time Bosworth logged off at the station with his other prisoner (the victim, Darnell Wallace), and the time he actually brought that prisoner into the jail.

A week later I'm well prepared for the Bosworth re-interview. Before going upstairs to the interview room I run into Captain Danny Jenner. He knows about the investigation, which I suppose has been a topic of discussion in their command staff meetings. I only wish I were a fly on the wall to hear the potpourri of haughty opinions. Thankfully, Jenner is not like that.

"Good luck," he says. "Do you think you'll be able to nail him?"

I nod optimistically. "I'm pretty sure that idiot, Bosworth, got two guys mixed up. In a pathetic effort to cover his tracks, Bosworth screwed up the evidence on the wrong case and then wrote a supplement to get it dismissed. Wasn't even the guy he molested."

I approach Ms. Mullan as if she had returned all my calls, not gone over my head to the police chief, and hadn't badmouthed me to my boss. In other words, I kiss her ass. It's only a temporary condition however, because as soon as I finish kissing it, I plan to ram the Bosworth case directly therein.

The attorney's role in this type of interview is to act as an advisor to the client, nothing more. She can't interrupt, answer for him, or interfere in any way. Mullan does all of them. I have to remind her several times to stop talking and let Bosworth answer the questions himself. She is livid, and I can barely contain myself.

Part of my strategy is to let Bosworth continue thinking that the Jimerson Thomas arrest is the one in question. It works.

"At any time during the booking or evidence collection process did you come in physical contact with the prisoner's genitals?" I ask.

Bosworth claims he did not.

I remind him that I interviewed the jailer, Community Service Officer Chambers, who witnessed the urine specimen collection—though I don't let him know that Chambers never saw any contact.

"At one point he was spattering his urine against the wall and also on me. So I tried to push him away and his baggy pants kind of slid toward his penis where my hand touched his penis."

After further questioning on this point, Bosworth admits he had "some of [the prisoner's] flesh" between his fingers, but couldn't tell if it was his penis or a testicle.

I ask Bosworth to hold his hand in the air to demonstrate, and he does a pinch-like movement with his forefinger and thumb.

"Well, I had him like this, okay?" Bosworth pinches the air. "And I did squeeze on them, because all I wanted to do was to prevent him from peeing on me."

I finally tell him that the prisoner he collected the urine from, Jimerson Thomas, never complained, and denied that Bosworth even touched him. "Did you get Thomas and Wallace confused?"

The color drains from Bosworth's face and his attorney finally shuts up. Unfortunately, I am not able to sustain the sexual misconduct complaint because of the deceptive polygraph results. But with the mislabeling of evidence and the erroneous supplement report Bosworth wrote—he's as good as gone.

I write everything up and turn it in two days after the interview.

I'm sitting in my office, finally able to put some time into watch commanding. I have a new squad with fairly decent sergeants working for me, and now I actually have the luxury of going out on the street once in a while.

It's been a few weeks since the Bosworth IA was submitted, and I've got visions of a criminal case against him and possibly jail time. If not that, at least a termination of employment, such that he can never work in law enforcement again.

"Knock-knock," Evan Casey rounds the corner into my office. His cheesy grin tells me that he's excited to share some little bit of gossip. In my experience, Casey's exuberance usually precipitates my being pissed off.

"What is it?"

"Did you hear the outcome of the Bosworth disciplinary review board?"

I don't think I can stand this. "Go ahead."

"They're going to allow him to resign, in lieu of." Casey flips out his gold-trimmed pager, checks it, and then slips it back in its holder, just in case I hadn't noticed it the last time he flashed it around. "No charges against him, no termination of employment, nothing. He just gets to resign and walk out of here as if nothing ever happened."

I gaze away, through the glass partition, out to the busy front office. It's where I started my career—a 19-year-old police assistant working the night shift. I remember how strongly I believed then that this place, the police department, was where everything was finally fair and just.

"You don't understand the big picture yet," Casey says with a smirk. "You'll learn."

He wants so badly for me to ask, but I just lean my head back and close my eyes for a second. When I open them, Casey has plopped himself into the chair across from me.

"Okay," he continues. "If *we* fire Bosworth, Daphne Mullan files an appeal. Case gets kicked downtown, and now the city attorney's office and personnel department are involved. Press gets wind of it and . . ."

I don't respond, but my eyes inadvertently flash up toward the chief's office.

Casey grins. "Municipal Administrator gets heat from the mayor and city council because the pervert cop makes them all look bad, and then the MA blames Bradford for letting the police department run amuck. See how it works? It's all about image. Nobody really gives a shit that Bosworth grabbed some guy's prick."

I let out a sigh. "Thanks for the civics lesson."

Casey forces a phony laugh. "You new lieutenants crack me up."

As he walks out of my office, the hand resting on my lap is flipping him off. *New lieutenants. That ass bite was only promoted a year ago.*

* * *

48

I set my folder down in front of the only chair on this side of the table. My gaze falls on the panel members seated across from me, and I shake each of their hands—remembering to make eye contact. Unbuttoning my suit jacket like a guy who actually wears one every day, I calmly take my seat. In my folder is the meticulously prepared promotability packet. It's essentially the history of my career, a compulsory phase of the testing process. That, and this interview itself, combines for a whopping 70% of the final score—a fact of which I am acutely aware.

My opening statement is fairly brief, consisting of a quick rundown of my previous assignments and significant certifications. I want to leave them plenty of time for questions.

I watch as the five of them flip open their copies of my packet. They are the handpicked henchmen of the police chief—guardians of fairness, purveyors of proficiency, and assessors of my readiness for promotion. It's an unsettling thought that these jurists make up the same tribunal who judged it more appropriate to let Bosworth walk than hold him accountable for sexually molesting a prisoner.

They take turns questioning me about my accomplishments, pointing out documents in my packet and quoting lines from them. It's not quite contentious, but there's a definite pointedness that's hard not to take personally. I'm sure it's meant to gauge how well one reacts under stress.

The one panel member who seems to be getting the most pleasure out of the intense questioning is Bill Preston. He looks like he's about to ask me a zinger, but one of the other captains beats him to the punch with his own question.

"Here in the management section, page 10, it asks you to discuss a program or project that you initiated. One in which you took all the way to fruition."

"Yes, sir." I thumb through my copy, trying to locate my written response.

The captain continues, "You've listed the gunfire suppression initiative."

I nod, waiting for his question. When none comes, I answer with a stronger affirmation. "Yes. As it says in the packet, the initiative was my idea. I wrote the proposal, submitted it up the chain of command, and managed the program for a little over a year."

The room suddenly grows silent and the panel members glance nervously back and forth at one another. I'm beginning to wonder if I've got a piece of spinach stuck in my teeth.

The captain who's asking the question slowly removes his eyeglasses and leans forward in his seat. "Well now, we were all under the impression that Captain Preston came up with that idea, and that *he assigned* the project to *you*."

I set my folder down and stare at the page for a second, as if to double check that it is indeed my signature on the memo. The momentary second-guessing is quickly replaced with disbelief and finally outrage.

Preston! That son-of-a-bitch took credit for my project and now they all think I'm lying!

LESSON 6

"My grandfather once told me that there are two kinds of people: those who work and those who take credit. He told me to try to be in the first group; there is less competition there."
~Indira Gandhi

I'm tiptoeing around in the dark, gathering my clothes, wallet, keys, shoes and socks, when my phone goes off. Gale groans and I make my way out to the family room to talk.

"I wanted to catch you before you ate breakfast," says the night shift sergeant—a buddy named Gary Donahue. "We have a pretty bad one on train tracks this morning."

"Anything out of the ordinary?"

Gary pauses. "Not really, but it's probably a teenage kid."

"Any missing persons calls from the parents?"

"Not yet."

"Swell, I'm on my way." Now, normally I wouldn't even bother ruining my day with a scene like that, but I get a feeling from Gary—the fact that he called me, plus the troubled hesitation in his voice—that there may be more to this.

First off, it's still dark, and an eerie silence hangs over the gray and red bits of body parts scattered up and down the rails. There's a tennis shoe, which is usually the point of impact, and then a smeared trail of bloody clothing that extends about 50 yards in a northerly direction along the tracks. Among these is a busted headphone and a Sony Walkman with the cassette tape spun next to the rail—like a string connecting the chunks of flesh. Okay, so we deduce from that that this was a kid, listening to music and walking down the train tracks in the middle of the night. Didn't hear the train coming.

"Train didn't stop?" I ask Gary.

"Nope."

They usually do. They'll see the guy, hit the breaks, and slide over him going about 70 MPH, until the train finally stops about a mile later. "Conductor might have been asleep," I say.

"Or didn't see the kid." Gary motions toward a hump of black—a jacket. "It looks like his pants were dark, too."

"Hmm." We walk along the scene, both looking down. Gary's on one side of the tracks and I'm on the other. "Do we know what time the train hit him?"

The sergeant checks his notes. "The last train came through at 6:34 a.m. A southbound Amtrak."

"Southbound?" I look at Gary. He checks his notes and glances back at me. We both turn around at the same time and walk the other way, back past the original point of impact. Sure enough, there are traces of blood—not much, but a little—and then the bottom portion of a leg and the other shoe. It's sitting off to the side of the tracks about 15 yards in the opposite direction.

Gary and I look at each other and then walk through it again.

"Okay, here is where he was struck," I say, pointing out the first shoe. We walk north, slowly, following the winding strip of cassette tape and broken bits of Walkman. We stop at the jacket, a bloody torso oozing from the bottom of it. "And this is where he ended up."

Gary is already on the phone. We wait in the quiet dark of the Sunday morning. The patrol cop who initially responded to check the suspicious form laying on the train tracks is sitting in his patrol car working on the report.

Finally Gary ends the phone call and turns back toward me.

"5:50 a.m.," he says. "A Western Pacific freight came through, *northbound*."

"That's what hit him," I say. "Well, the first one that hit him."

"And what's worse than getting run over by a train?" says Gary.

I grimace. "Getting run over by two trains."

We figure out that the first one did the majority of the damage—carrying most of the body north along the tracks. When the second train came by 54 minutes later, heading the other way, it dragged a leg and shoe with it in the other direction—past the original impact location. *Wow!*

I glance down at the cassette tape snaking along, and as I walk back to my car I find myself wondering what the kid was listening to. His was a terrible way to die, I think to myself. But then again, it came so quickly that he never felt it. It's probably more painful for those who have to see its aftermath, and even worse for those who have to clean it all up.

By daylight a coroner's wagon will come out and two of their people will collect all the pieces into plastic bags. Once that's done the fire department will be called to hose off whatever's left. It's an imprecise process, full of all the gory realities that nobody wants to know. *And what of the boy's family? Will they come down to see where it happened? Will they examine the scene? Find a piece of a finger or a nose that was missed?* I wonder about those things.

"Congratulations on the promotion."

I glance up from the newspaper spread out on my desk. It's Danny Jenner, the captain of my division, and my boss. "I hear you came out number one on the list, that's really good."

I thank him, relieved to have the whole *acting* thing behind me. I'm also pleased that none of my missteps as a temporary watch commander seem to have compromised my ranking.

Jenner sets a mug of hot coffee on my desk and takes a seat across from me. "I also heard that one of my colleagues got busted trying to take credit for your project." He lets out a little chuckle. "Did they really say that Bill had claimed the project as his?"

I nod, pausing long enough to realize that Jenner is the only captain I trust enough to tell. "I was staring at my packet, wondering if they would automatically believe Preston over me. I thought about arguing that the project was my idea, and confronting Preston right there in the interview, but that was a *lose-lose* for me. I'd appear defensive and I'd look like a hothead."

"You must have been pissed." The captain takes a sip of coffee. "How did you handle it?"

"I didn't, really. When they said that Captain Preston had claimed the project as his brainchild . . . well, after a few seconds of panic, I just closed my file and sat back in my chair. I looked at all of them, Preston included, and said, 'Since I have no way of knowing what you've been told, I can't really comment on that. But perhaps you'll want to address that question to Captain Preston.'"

Jenner bursts out laughing, so much that he has to steady his splashing mug. "I heard Bill was back-peddling all over the place."

"Pretty much," I say. "I'm just thankful the panel didn't take the side of the rank."

I tell Jenner about the train case and then ask what he's doing here on a Saturday. With a shrug that says it's part of the job, he tells me he's going to a community thing that the chief asked him to attend—a business opening in a small strip mall on Mission Street.

It seems Jenner gets tapped for a lot of these events—probably because, like me, Jenner also lives in the city. The chief doesn't.

The captain invites me to stop by if I want, and though I can't tell whether or not he's kidding, I assure him that I'll try to be there. I actually don't mind these kinds of events.

Later in the morning I'm walking out to my car, ready to head out to the business opening, when a hot call goes out. Three alert tones over the radio followed by the details: "Any unit to break – multiple calls of shots fired in the Shop Smart lot, downtown."

I head that way, but not too fast mind you. As a street cop, and even as a sergeant, I remember lieutenants who would race, balls-to-the-wall, to all the big calls. They generally wouldn't do anything helpful once they got there, just nose around, get in the way, and basically tell everyone else what to do. To my way of thinking, it's like a show of confidence when the boss takes his time responding, trusting that his people will do their jobs.

As it turns out, I'm right to trust the cops. It's the firefighters who screw everything up.

Their downtown fire station is close to the Shop Smart lot, so they get there before we do. Within seconds of their arrival, the beat unit and the sergeant both pull up. [I'm listening to all of this on my radio as I approach the scene].

A white Ford Pinto is stopped, cockeyed, in the middle of the lot. Its engine is running and its front end is pressed up against a lamppost. Through the webbed shatter patterns of bullet holes in the windshield, I see a black man slumped in the driver's seat. His door is partially open.

One of my dayshift sergeants, Thurmond Morris, seems to be in a heated discussion with one of the firemen. I take it from all of this that the shooter is gone, and there is no need to try to save the poor guy who's lying bloody in the car.

Morris sees me and chugs over to my car. With his hands tossed upward like a kid who's given up all hope, he says, "The foundation recovery team did it again."

"Wait, what?" Then I suddenly get the joke. *The fire department is such an inept bunch that they can't save a burning house—just the foundation.* "Morris, what the hell is going on here?"

His hands go skyward again. "That hotdog, Diaz." Morris extends his chin in the direction of a pretty boy firefighter named Greg Diaz. "Before I could stop him he jumped up on the hood of the victim's car and ran across it. Some kind of heroics, I guess."

54

I glance at the dented hood, black boot prints across it. "What, like he was trying to save the guy? Couldn't just walk around it?"

Morris shrugs. "Knocked shell casings all over the place, even crushed a few of them. No use printing the car either, Diaz hand-fucked the door, window, the seat . . . and get this, he pulls a bag of cocaine off of the dead guy, holds it up for everyone to see and says, 'Look at what I found.'"

I squint over at Diaz, giving him my best *You're a dumbshit* look. "So I guess there's no use in fingerprinting the bag of drugs either." I say it loud enough for Diaz and the other firemen to hear.

By now the crime scene tech has arrived, and she and the beat cop are stringing crime scene tape around the car.

"Make Diaz write out a statement," I tell Morris. "And have him do it himself. That might cool his heels the next time he wants to be a big shot."

"Yeah, I'll make him write out a statement." Morris heads back to the huddle of firefighters with a shit-eating grin. The only thing the firefighters hate worse than a cop telling them what to do, is actually writing a report.

I make sure the homicide detectives have everything they need before swinging by the store opening, even though I'm an hour late. The strip mall is an old set of buildings—a restaurant, a couple of stores and a flower shop. All of them either Indian or Pakistani owned. Captain Jenner is gone, and so are the few customers who showed up. I find the owner and introduce myself, giving him my business card in case he ever needs anything. He offers me tea, which I don't really feel like, but I drink some with him, anyway.

On my way out, I hear tapping on a window to the side of me. A woman waves from inside the store next door—one that sells Indian saris. I wave back, trying to see through my reflection in the glass.

She comes out, and slowly I begin to connect the face with the memory. She's older now, but so am I. We met on a call years ago, somewhere off of Montara Avenue in an apartment house we used to call the Curry Palace. A guy had overdosed on heroin, and his friends left him in a bathtub full of ice. This woman lived in an apartment across the hall at the time.

Normally I might not have recalled a single incident such as that, but she was very kind to me. I remember it being a stiflingly hot day, and she offered me a cold coke. She also phoned me once after that, to ask if I could help her husband. Apparently he had a problem with his visa and was being deported. This woman thought I might have some pull with immigration. *What?*

"How are you?" She springs from the doorway with surprising delight on her face. I immediately wonder if she is showing off for someone inside—like, look how well I know a cop. Then she hugs me. *Yep, this must be a show.*

"Oh yeah, hi, how have you been?" I step back and my badge is momentarily tangled in her scarf.

"I am Shanti!" she says. "You remember me, yes?"

"Yes, of course." *Just barely.* She looked like a skinny little girl the last time I saw her. She's a little rounder now, not in a bad way, just more like an actual woman. "How's your husband? Did he ever get that immigration thing cleared up?"

"No, he was deported." She bobs her head and shrugs. "He lost the gas station and had to move back home. I have a son now; he's four. But he stays in India with relatives."

"Great, well . . . good to see you again."

"This is my store now," she says, motioning to the sari shop. "Remember? I used to sell the clothes out of my little apartment."

The vague memory of a tiny apartment stuffed with racks of Indian clothing comes back. "Oh yeah, that's right." I pause again. "Well, gotta get back out on the street. Nice talking to you, Shanti."

She invites me to stop by her store anytime I'm in the area. She also makes it a point to let me know she's living at some newer, more modern apartments near the city center.

The next five months pass without any real excitement. Well, nothing that I'd consider excitement. Others might call it a crazy life, but to me it's just the norm.

During one of our watch commander meetings with Bill Preston, the new captain of our division, he mentions—kind of in a bragging way—that he's already off probation. As I sit through his meeting, I'm trying to figure it out. He was promoted to captain at the same time that I was promoted to lieutenant—same day, in fact. Both positions have a one-year probationary period.

I later ask Jenner about it and he tells me that Preston wrote up a request to the chief; apparently there's a caveat in our contracts that allows for up to six months of "acting" time to be counted toward probation. The only requirements are that the acting assignment be contemporaneous to the actual promotion, and that the chief approve it. *Why wouldn't he? My situation is exactly the same as that windbag, Preston's—both of us did six months of acting time before our permanent promotions.*

56

But the chief never even sees my request. Preston denies it, flat-out. No explanation, just sends a note back saying that he's not going to sign off on it. Probably payback for the thinly veiled kick in the balls I gave him for taking credit for my project.

I suppose I could go over his head, go directly to the chief, but that would put Bradford in a tough spot: back the young lieutenant, or back his captain? I decide to suck it up for the next half-year.

Not really that big a deal, I guess.

One sunny afternoon, I'm compiling the shift's monthly stats when a call catches my attention. It's the code for a bomb threat—which is never broadcasted in words, only in code. *Ten-seventy*, or something like that. Everyone always has to look it up, because we don't get enough of them to commit the code to memory. Anyway, it's the location of the bomb that gets me—the catholic high school where both of my daughters go.

Needless to say, I get in the car and head that way—thinking to myself that it's probably some loser kid who needs to get out of a test. Why in the hell would anyone plant a bomb in a nice little school like that? Seriously, how many of these are real? *None.*

As I'm driving, I roll through the facts in my mind. Daughter number one is a sophomore—has a boyfriend who's conned her into doing his homework for him. To the point that she's fallen so far behind in her own work that she's nearly failing out of the school. Daughter number two is in a world all her own. She can't stand the rigid structure, has challenged the principal a number of times, she's already been suspended once for flat-palming some girl in the forehead, and she holds the school record for detentions—103. Nothing too serious, mostly gum chewing, dresses too short or wearing unapproved shoes. Once she even tried to run from the principal, but got caught when her backless sandal fell off.

The principal meets me in the horseshoe driveway in front of the school and asks me to have all the responding patrol cars pull around back. Apparently it's something to do with school image.

They've already evacuated all the students, moving them onto the soccer field at the rear of the campus. I'm imagining them, a total social hour with no teachers, no tests and no work. Just what the prank caller was hoping for. I can picture my oldest daughter, snuggled up next to her boyfriend while touching up her eye makeup. Then there's my younger daughter—eyes on the target, scanning the area, watching for anything that looks like a bomb.

57

The cops check the entire school, all the buildings, lockers and classrooms. It takes well over an hour, almost two. Afterwards, I approach the principal, a fastidious British woman named Hocking. "All clear," I tell her. "How have the students handled the disruption?"

"Pretty well, for the most part." She dabs at her shiny brow. "Out of 1,600 students 1,599 were fine with the evacuation drill."

It takes me a half-second to do the math, and I quickly come up with my youngest.

"Your daughter, Megan, had an issue with the handling of it."

I close my eyes and nod, imagining myself in Meg's position.

"She was the only student who demanded to know what the threat was, and if placing the students in the open field was the most prudent decision. She mentioned the Columbine school shooting, and said that a sniper hiding in the hills behind the school could take out hundreds of students. Megan said they were 'sitting ducks', actually accused us of playing right into the killers' hands."

"The killers." I let out a long breath. "Yeah, sorry about that." Actually, I'm not. I'm glad Megan thinks like me. And I'm also glad my older daughter, Cari, is indifferent to all of it. High school kids shouldn't have to concern themselves with things like this.

LESSON 7

"Murderers are not monsters, they're men. And that's the most frightening thing about them."
~Alice Sebold

Sunday morning is usually the quietest time of the entire week. As I arrive at the PD, I notice an inordinate number of personal cars scattered throughout the secured back lot. Inside the building, the energy is palpable and more comparable to a busy weekday.

"What's going on?" I ask one of the night shifters.

"Homicide this morning, around three o'clock, sir." The officer looks like he's right in the middle of something, so I don't ask any more questions.

I meet with the lead detective, K.C. Clifford, who gives me additional details. He tells me that the victim, a young man in his 20's, was found in the middle of West 12th Street with a shotgun blast to the chest. The victim had no identification, suspect was long gone, and no witnesses were located in the neighborhood.

"We're just coming on," I tell him. "Anything you need from us?"

"Not really, thanks. My partner and I are going to head up to the coroner's office. Not much more we can do until we come up with an identity on the victim."

I'm an hour into my shift, just past 8 a.m., when I get a phone call from the communications center.

"LT? We've got a report of a suspicious vehicle holding on the board, and I think you better take a look at it."

The status monitor on my desk shows only four calls that have yet to be dispatched, and I quickly spot the one she's talking about. "On Chambers Street?"

"Yeah, a neighbor just called it in. Silver Mazda parked there with its motor running, but nobody's around."

The distance from where the car is parked is less than a mile from where the body was found last night. I assume the dispatcher has already put together a possible connection between the two. "Have you run the license number yet?" I ask.

"It's not reported stolen." In the background I hear the battering of her keyboard. "It's registered to Allen Edward Yago, with a listed address on Hartford. He lives right there, two blocks from where the car is parked."

I thank her for letting me know, and then I add, "Check to see if we've got a mug on file, and get a hotprint of his license photo from DMV."

In the meantime, I drive out to the scene to take a look at the car. A sergeant and two cops have already arrived. With a dissipating stream of exhaust behind it, the Mazda sits sputtering in the morning dew. As the four of us stand around it, an ominous feeling settles on me. *I know this is the dead guy's car.*

"It's him." The night shift cop sets the faxed driver's license photo on my desk. The cop had arrived first on the scene of the 'man down' call, and positively identifies the car's registered owner as our homicide victim.

I watch the young cop walk, slumped-shouldered, back down the hall, knowing the sizable report that awaits him. It will keep him here for hours, and when he finally gets to bed, I know that the haunting image of the horrific scene will prevent him from getting any sleep. I slip the photo into a folder and dial Clifford's cell.

"Detective Clifford," he answers on the first ring. Done with the coroner, he's already on his way back to the city. I tell him about the abandoned Mazda found idling on Chambers Street, and give him the name of the registered owner.

"Holcombe from midnights identified Yago's photo," I tell him. "No criminal record, no history with us whatsoever."

Not knowing what precipitated Yago's murder, we decide not to make contact at his apartment, at least until Clifford gets back in here. For all we know, the suspect could be a roommate or domestic partner, still inside the residence. Instead, I have the sergeant pull a beat cop from the street and have him watch the apartment from an unmarked car.

Detective Clifford comes into the office and I brief him on our stakeout of the victim's residence. By now Clifford has done a more complete background workup on Allen Yago. The detective has a sick look on his face, beyond his obvious lack of sleep.

He props himself against the credenza and offers a weak smile. "Thanks for the help this morning with the car and the apartment."

"Sure, K.C., anything else you need?"

"This . . . this is really a tragic case." Clifford swallows a lump of emotion. He rubs his bloodshot eyes. "We found out that Yago attended a bachelor party last night, and he was seen leaving around 2 a.m. We think he arrived home by himself and was confronted after parking his car. He was most likely forced to drive his car around the corner, where he was abducted and robbed."

I'm picturing the chronology of events as Clifford describes them to me. I swear I felt the whole thing when I was at his car earlier.

"We checked the status of Yago's bankcard and there were two withdrawals last night—right before he was killed. We're trying to come up with a photo from the bank's ATM camera."

"Does his family know yet?"

Clifford shakes his head. "That's the most tragic part. The bachelor party Yago was at? It was for him. Today was supposed to be his wedding day."

"Oh, my God." I now realize why this is hitting Clifford so hard.

"His family and his fiancé are all at the church, getting ready for the wedding. They have no idea yet."

I glance at my watch. "What time was the wedding?"

"Eleven o'clock," Clifford says. "A half-hour from now."

The church where the victim's wedding was supposed to take place is across the bay in Redwood City. I offer to handle the family notification, via Redwood City police department. Clifford thanks me, and then he leaves the office.

A horrendous image gushes into my mind and curdles there, blocking out everything else. It's the picture of Yago's bride, waiting at the church, not knowing the whereabouts of her fiancé. The happiest day of her life, robbed from her, and turned into the day that will destroy her forever. I envision Yago, a guy I've only seen in his smiling driver's license photo, and I imagine the fear he must have felt. Not only facing certain death, but on the night before his wedding, alone on a dark, empty street.

I dial the phone and ask for Redwood City's watch commander. A heavy silence hangs over the line as I explain what we know and what we hypothesize about Allen Edward Yago's last moments alive. The lieutenant groans when I get to the part about the church, and I feel for him. He's now got to pull together a group of his most sensitive and emotionally strong police officers, and then send them into an encounter more heartbreaking than war.

"I'm sorry," is all I can offer him.

I hang up the phone, sitting weepy-eyed and drained of all my energy. I've always been told that hate and vengeance are unhealthy emotions, both without any upside. But no matter how hard I try to avoid it, this searing anger is metastasizing inside me—laying waste to any good that was ever there. Someone needs to pay for doing this. I can only imagine what Detective Clifford is going through.

By early afternoon the investigation is in full swing. Clifford's partner and two other detectives have joined in to ferret out clues to the identity of Yago's killer. I wander upstairs and find Clifford at his desk, staring at a series of grainy black & white photographs.

"This is Allen, trying to withdraw money from his ATM," he says. "Look at his face; he's terrified."

I study the top photo—a close-up view seen through a fisheye lens at head level. Yago's dark eyes are wide, panicked, as if he knows the fate that awaits him.

"Look at this frame," says Clifford. "In the background, three dark-skinned males. One looks heavy and the other two look thin."

Clifford leaves to brief his partners and his bosses, while I head back downstairs. I wish I hadn't seen the photographs. Now I have a real image that will cement itself, along with a few select others, into the darkest part of my memory. *Why couldn't the suspects have just taken his money and let him go?*

At 4:30 in the afternoon I get word that they've identified the suspects: two brothers and a cousin from a Tongan family residing on Grattan Road—only a half-mile from the murder scene. Whatever their source, the detectives seem to be pretty certain it's them.

Two detectives in an unmarked car have set up on the house, and they report back that there doesn't appear to be much activity.

I get a phone call from Captain Jenner 30 minutes before the end of my shift. He says that the detectives have secured a search warrant, and they want the SWAT team called in for a high-risk entry of the Tongans' residence.

I phone Gale to let her know I won't be home for dinner, and then I change into my tactical uniform. It takes the team about 45 minutes to get to the station, dress, and assemble for a briefing. You would never guess that they were all pulled away from a quiet Sunday with their families; each one of them bounds into the room, spirited and enthusiastic. The mood quickly sobers to a single-minded intensity as they listen to the facts of the case.

Looking at the faces around the room, I see the same outrage in them that I've felt all day. Although vengeance and justice have little in common, today the distance between the two has narrowed. These guys are good—the best of the best in the department—but I can't help but wonder if there is a limit to a man's restraint. We all want to avenge the groom's killing.

K.C. Clifford addresses the group, providing us with the latest intelligence about the suspect house. "At present, there are at least two men inside the house. The family van is gone, and we think at least one of the suspects is in it."

The detectives have no idea where the van is or when it might return. Based on that, we organize the team in three units with an additional two veteran uniformed cops assigned to assist us. One of them is Patricia Irons, a take-care-of-business patrol officer that I really like. The plan is for the marked car to follow us into the area and stage a couple of blocks away, just in case the van returns while we are at the house. We decide to keep one team mobile with them, and deploy a small sniper unit around the perimeter of the residence. I'll be with the main assault unit when we hit the house.

The team snakes across the city in a caravan led by the marked patrol car. We're about a mile from the target house when the uniform cop radios me from the front of the pack.

"We've spotted the suspect's van stopped at a red light two cars ahead of us," Irons advises. "Just came off the freeway, now heading southbound. Appears to be loaded with passengers."

My mind runs quickly over the possible scenarios. If we allow them to make it to the house, they could run inside before we get to them. That would definitely complicate our entry. Even if we can contain them in the van out front, those already inside the house could pose a threat. *Better to take the van down right here.*

I respond back over the air, "Command to the marked unit, we'll take them off before they get to the house—SWAT Unit One will be your support. Sniper Unit Two and Entry Unit Three, standby."

We've got to do this quickly, before a passerby or someone in the neighborhood has time to notify the people still at the house.

The patrol car's red and blue flashing lights come on, and after a few tense seconds of indecision, the van pulls to the curb. Behind the patrol car is the armored truck we use as a personnel carrier. Teams of black-clad officers are perched on fold-down running boards mounted on either side of it. As our truck lumbers to an elephantine stop, Unit One deploys from the sideboards onto the ground.

With a dozen weapons pointed at them, the Tongans are ordered from the van, one-by-one, and onto their stomachs in the middle of the street. These are big people, and I know we are going to have to secure them before we can move on to the house. I call for the assistance of two more patrol cars.

Irons and her partner already have the handcuffed occupants of the van lined up on the side of the street. I take my best guess at a family inventory; the papa bear, the mama bear, a couple of hefty baby bears, and one fat son-of-a-bitch that matches the guy in the ATM photograph. *One suspect down, two to go.*

I rotate my hand over my head. "Let's move out!"

As the newly promoted SWAT commander, I'm really trying to take a step back. But after years of running the entry team, I'm not quite ready for a headset and clipboard. Especially when it comes to this particular case and these particular suspects.

With all three SWAT teams back onboard, the armored truck complains its way another five blocks. We pull up just shy of a lime green, ranch-style house. It's dark and overgrown with shrubs. We're off the skids and moving into position across the front yard before the truck has even stopped.

The front door is covered with an outer metal security door, which takes the lead man only a few seconds to pry open. The rest of the entry unit is stacked off to the right side, with me in the middle of the group.

On the left is a large picture window. A picture of what, I don't know, since ivy has long since shrouded any view. Unfortunately, the ivy also blocks most of our light, creating only shadowy silhouettes of the suspects moving around inside.

As the battering ram is hefted back, ready for its obliterating forward swing, a figure moves across the room. It's only a shadow, but clearly that of a young man—tall and lean . . . and armed. In his hands a long, barrel-shaped object about the same size and diameter as a shotgun.

"Shotgun!" one of the entry guys calls out, just as the ram strikes the door. Splinters fly in all directions as the door succumbs to the weight of eight men bursting through it—each one hungry to face down the armed killer.

We fan into the room, weapons sweeping back and forth just below eye level. Over the shoulder of the guy in front of me, I see our prey—frozen in the center of the room, shotgun in hand.

Only it's not a shotgun, it's a broom.

I prepare myself for gunfire, especially given the emotionally charged case and the erroneous warning of a shotgun, but I'm not surprised when there's none. The first two cops through the door advance swiftly, closing the space between them and the suspect before he can even blink. The broom sails in one direction and the suspect is swept off his feet. He hits the floor with a thud and the rest of the team files past them, paying little notice. *Suspect number two, down and handcuffed.*

We breach the door of a dark bedroom at the back of the house. Muzzle lights illuminate a man in a sleeping bag, huddled on a mattress in the corner. Twice he's ordered to show his hands, but he only squints into the light beam—probably more confused than defiant. A booted foot swings from my periphery, catching the guy in the sternum. The impact sends him flopping backward in the bag. With a wheezing gasp, the man's empty hands creep into view and are immediately handcuffed. *Suspect number three, down.*

With all suspects in custody and the house secured, I turn the scene over to Detective Clifford and his partners. They and the crime scene technicians will begin a thorough search, inventory and processing of any evidence associated with the homicide. As it turns out, the evidence recovered includes the victim's wallet and the shotgun believed to be the murder weapon. Clifford phones me later to say that a girlfriend of one of the suspects was found wearing the wedding ring that Yago had planned to give his bride.

It's difficult to find an upside to any of this. I suppose for me it's the satisfaction of a job well done. In every respect, the outcome was successful—especially given the level of restraint shown by the team. None of our guys were hurt, and everyone held their fire when it could have easily gone the other direction. A boot to the chest of a noncompliant murder suspect, I'm not going to lose any sleep over.

My route home takes an unplanned detour, and I find myself driving down West 12th Street. The magnesium residue of burnt road flares litter one end of the block, revealing the spot on the empty street where Allen Edward Yago was found. Less than 24 hours has passed, yet the only marker to signify the man's life, on what would have been his wedding night, is a chalk outline of his body.

LESSON 8

*"A man should never neglect
his family for business."*
~*Walt Disney*

After a couple of years of having me assigned as watch commander, the chief decides to move me into Community Policing. I'll be one of two commanders working directly under the deputy chief—who by this time is that blowhard, Preston. *I can't seem to get away from the guy.*

I'm relieved of day-to-day street operations in the new role, to focus on building community, business, school, and government partnerships in the northern half of the city. I successfully negotiate to keep my command of the SWAT team—thank God, otherwise I'd be a total pencil pusher.

The new position, with all its political correctness, feels like a complete waste of taxpayer money. But it makes a lot of people in the community feel good, feel listened to, and feel valued. Those aren't bad things, but I'm not sure you need a deputy chief and two lieutenants in order to accomplish that. Regardless, the job also has its perks: I'm now working a day shift, mostly 9-to-5, and mostly weekends off. And because I'll now have a set schedule, I decide to enroll in a degree program at night in order to finish college.

It doesn't take long though, before Preston starts loading me up with jobs. Most of them, I suspect, were delegated to him, and he in turn, delegates them to me; things like middle school kids who jaywalk on Mission Street, bother patrons of the library, and intimidate people at the downtown transit station.

Some of the projects Preston gives me are so bizarre that I wonder if he's just thinking them up to justify his position—like the time he popped into my office and asked me to "look into" building a two-story parking garage in the back lot. And then he adds, "And since the chief has his pilot's license, see about putting a helipad on the top deck.

What? Sure, let me jump right on that. Like . . . would that project take precedence over the pet parade, and the food drive? What about the downtown skateboard ordinance? The Day Laborers and the federal immigration compliance policy? Don't forget the pushcart ice cream vendors licensing ordinance. Or the gasoline pumps and the freak'n carwash for the back lot you also ordered me to "look into". And by the way, what the hell does any of this have to do with community policing, much less police work?

Then Preston sends me, at the last minute, to speak at a community meeting on Highcliff Avenue. Chief Bradford was supposed to address the group, but I assume part of my role on the management team means stepping up when the police chief and deputy chief can't be there. Only thing is, the deputy chief can do it but chooses me to fill in instead. But the guy shows up halfway though my talk, watching me from the doorway as if he's going to hold up a scorecard when I'm done. Then Preston interrupts me, and in front of the whole group, corrects me by citing some obscure criminology study that he once read about.

At the conclusion of the meeting, the community members, hungry to talk turkey with the chief, start peppering me with dicey philosophical questions about marijuana legalization, gun control, and about the city council's position on property taxes. That's when Preston suddenly disappears.

The guy hasn't changed much. Years ago when I was an undercover narc, Preston found out during a departmental inspection that I wasn't wearing the proper uniform under my Class-A jacket. He thought it would be funny to give the order to remove jackets—which he did, roasting me in front of the entire department in the process. To pay him back I convinced a goofy snitch to come in and deliver his feces to Preston in a glass jar. I always felt a little guilty for doing that, and thankfully Preston never figured out who was behind it. But after the way the guy's been treating me, I no longer have any remorse about the turd.

I've been telling my dad about the workload. He feels for me, offers a few ideas, but he admits that his life as a college professor was nothing like the police environment. And now that he's retired, his day-to-day routine is even simpler. I'm glad for him; he worked hard to give us a good life.

When the two of us get together for breakfast I always ask what he's been doing with his time. He smiles, usually telling me that he and his retired teacher buddies are going to the Indian casinos. He says that this weekend, he and his pals are heading to Tahoe. "One guy owns a cabin," he says. "And this is our annual trip."

Most of his cronies are PE instructors—actually a more natural fit for Dad than some of his coworkers in the business division. Accordingly, they watch a lot of sports. They also gamble, drink, eat, and then gamble some more.

At my dad's urging I have lunch with my uncle in San Francisco the following week. I tell him about the dilemma of working for Preston, the difficulty of staying up on all the projects he's assigned me, and the fact that I'm also trying to go to school at night. Uncle Tony is a retired police chief, and if anyone gets it, he does.

After listening to all the things Preston has laid on me, Uncle Tony asks if there's a sergeant I can reassign from elsewhere in the department—someone I can pull in to help me. Unfortunately, we're not like San Francisco PD. He had a few thousand cops—probably 300 sergeants. My department has only 24 of them, and they're all committed to other assignments.

I mull over my hopeless situation during the drive back. Knowing that things can change quickly at the department, I resolve to keep my cool with Preston while I try to figure something out.

Every summer the community bands together for the National Night Out. It's a crime prevention thing, and an opportunity for neighborhood folks to meet the cops who patrol their areas. Police administrators generally spread their time at four or five of the block parties, chauffeuring members of the city council to them as well. We're supposed to behave like real people, talk to neighbors and eat their food, no matter how bad it looks—which for me is not a problem. I'll eat anything. But Chief Bradford can't do it.

That night, the chief looks like he's getting ill just thinking about someone's mucky bean dip or crusty potato salad. Then, no sooner does he glad hand around the table with all the city big wigs, than he disappears. I glimpse him jumping into his car and racing out the back gate before the event even begins. Deputy Chief Preston, never one to miss an opportunity to kiss some ass, takes the mayor in his car for the night. To me, he passes off a pickled old boozer who's serving his last term on the council. Not only does the councilman keep calling me officer, but his breath is enough to make me gag.

Meanwhile, back on the home front, Cari is getting real cozy with this kid she calls her *boyfriend*. I've sworn to myself that I'd never be one of those "cop dads" who hounds their kids and treats them like one of their suspects. On the other hand, this boyfriend situation is one that I need to pay attention to. Don't get me wrong, I trust my daughter. But I know girls her age can see things a little out of whack. And I actually don't mind the kid she's seeing. He's a quiet guy from Costa Rica—kind of a James Dean look, with a black leather jacket and black boots that he never laces up.

Other than the fact that his black boots scuff the hell out of her kitchen floor, Gale likes the kid too. She has really been staying on top of this thing, and tips me off to an upcoming request that'll find its way to me soon. The *boyfriend* wants to take Cari to a concert at the Shoreline Amphitheater across the bay. I have no issue with trusting them not to drink or do drugs, but the kid's car is a beat up little hand me down that would be lucky to make it over the bridge.

Gale and I talk about it and we decide on a negotiated position— Cari can go to the concert, as long as I can drive them to and from the Shoreline.

When I'm officially presented with the idea, Cari is fine with my counter offer. She just feels badly for me having to wait alone in the parking lot while the concert takes place. *Believe me, it's better than the other option—waiting up, worrying that they'll break down on the bridge.*

Back at work I find that Preston has other plans for me. Turns out the guy has had a federal grant application on his desk for over a month, and has been trying to palm it off on one of his subordinates. He's already approached my counterpart, the southern district commander, about writing the thing, but he doesn't want to do it. So Preston, lacking the balls to force the older and more seasoned lieutenant to write it, lays the grant application on me.

"The chief and I would like you to put together this grant application," he says, handing it to me as if it's a gift.

I notice that the damn thing is due next week. "You want me to write a federal grant in six days?"

Without the slightest bit of sheepishness, he lifts his arms out to the side like wings. "It'll help you to s-t-r-e-t-c-h yourself."

"Stretch myself." I repeat back. As if this jerk hasn't already stretched me like a Gumby toy.

Preston puts a finger to his lip. "And I was thinking *we* could structure it around the creation of a South End resource center."

"That's not even in my area," I say. "If it's a South End thing, why isn't Frank Howard writing it?"

"Too busy," he says.

I nod. Not in an eager way, but in more of a dumbfounded way. Then a thought crosses my mind—a counter offer tactic I recently used successfully at home. I turn back toward Preston.

"I'll do what I can in the time I've been given," I say. "But I'm not going to do Frank's work for him. If I write this thing up, it's going to be for something in my district."

Preston tilts his head, cautioning me with his sideways look. "I'm not sure the chief--"

I tilt my head back at him and he stops mid-sentence. I realize that the last thing Preston wants to do is go back to Bradford with this. He'd have to admit to the chief that he couldn't make Frank Howard do it and he couldn't make me do it.

I return to my office and stare at the grease board listing all my assignments—twenty-seven projects that Preston has dumped on me. I now have twenty-eight. I shake my head and toss the folder on my desk, feeling so stressed that I want to hit something. I walk to the workout room at the end of the hallway. Nobody is in there, so I unleash my anger on the heavy bag hanging in the corner. I punch the thing, bare knuckled, for five minutes straight, until I can no longer lift my arms. I run my raw hands under the cold water in the locker room before taking the grant file, getting in my car and driving home. It's the middle of the day, and I just leave. If that jackass wants me to do a decent job on this grant, I'll have to work at a place where he won't bother me.

The next day at the police department I run into one of the patrol sergeants, Bruce Roberts. He was my boss for a couple of years when I worked undercover narcotics—a good guy who has always watched out for me and given me sound advice. He must have noticed that I'm beat up pretty bad, because he follows me with a concerned look, down the hallway and into my tiny office. He's getting close to retirement but still cares a great deal about doing a solid job. And thankfully, he still cares about helping me.

"How've you been, Soto?" He chuckles at the use of my old undercover name.

I shake my head, nodding toward the grease board. "Preston is stretching my ass."

70

"Everybody sees it," says Roberts. "The guy's always been that way." He pauses. "I know how much of a family guy you are. It may be none of my business, but you're not going to do Gale or your daughters any good if you're dead from a heart attack."

Roberts and I have joked a lot over the years, had a lot of laughs and have never taken things too literally. But I can see that the sergeant is serious—really concerned. I realize that I need to listen.

"My dad has told me the same thing," I say. "But I have school tonight, and I've got this grant that's due."

Roberts rolls his eyes. "Just make sure you find some time for yourself. This place will still be here long after you and I are gone."

The lunch with my uncle, and the talks with my dad and with Bruce Roberts have got me thinking. The idea of self-preservation spawns an idea that never would have occurred to me on my own.

What if I wrote the grant to fund another sergeant position? One who would work under me, and who could help me with some of these *community* projects that Preston has dumped on me?

I read through each line of the grant goals, objectives, and criteria. It stresses that any personnel funding request should be for "line level/direct service providers." This means an officer or a civilian crime prevention person, not a sergeant—they'd be considered a supervisor. But the paperwork doesn't strictly prohibit it, only discourages it. And when I call back to Washington D.C., and speak to the division within the Department of Justice offering the grant, I get my answer. Any request for supervisory personnel would be highly scrutinized, and would have to be *very* compelling.

Compelling? I can do compelling.

I come up with a strategy that nobody in the federal government could possibly say no to. It's a downtown resource office, right in the city hall rotunda—directly across from the transit station. We would partner with a senior volunteer group, who would act as downtown ambassadors. The middle school would sign on, as would the city library staff, and the transit police department. It's an answer to half of the shitty little problems that Preston has heaped on me. And just for a little more icing on the cake, I contact the NAACP and get the endorsement of the most liberal element of the community. Lastly, I tap into the chamber of commerce and a few of the business honchos in the city, all of whom support the plan. Some also agree to subtly garner the support of the council members, which should be easy since the senior volunteers come from the mobile home parks—the largest single voting block in the city.

And to manage the senior ambassadors and run this community resource office? A police sergeant, assigned to yours truly—all paid for by Clinton's Community Oriented Policing Services. Now all I have to do is sit down and actually apply for this thing. I've got three more days. Really, only two days, considering that a family pool party at my sister's house will take up my entire Sunday.

I stay home, working on the grant all day Friday—sun up to sundown, and beyond. It's slow, technical work, and I have to run out a couple of times to get signed letters of commitment from some of the other community partners. By Saturday, I've still got a lot to write and I'm feeling the pinch—it's going to be tight.

"You remember about this afternoon," says Gale.

I look up from my papers, stacked in neat little piles around the dining room table. "What?"

"Cari's concert? With Alberto? At the Shoreline Amphitheater?" She smiles through her delivery, but knows that my head is about to blow off.

I have no idea how I'll be able to finish this grant as it is, much less play chauffeur and still attend the family party tomorrow.

It's a warm night in Mountain View, and I'm listening to the music of the concert through my open window. Inside the car, piled all around me, are stacks of folders. I've parked under a lamppost, which helps some with lighting, as I feverishly type into my laptop. Four hours later, I've got this thing damn near completed.

Cari and the *boyfriend* come out at the end of the concert, and huddle together in the back seat. I try not to look in the mirror, too much.

The next day is the family swim party. For the first time in a while, I'm able to relax and enjoy the day. My brother takes a seat next to me, hands me a beer, and leans back under the shade of the patio umbrella.

As I take a swig, he tilts his head down and looks over the tops of his sunglasses. "What did you do to your knuckles?"

I glance at the molten scabs as I take another sip. "Oh, those. I worked out on the heavy bag the other day at work."

He nods. "You didn't put on gloves?"

"Well," I pause, trying to think of a logical answer. "I was kind of in a hurry."

Tyler laughs and leans back into the lounger. *He knows me.*

On Monday I turn the finished grant over to Preston. He doesn't even bother reading it, just sprints off with it toward the chief's office. He'll probably tell Bradford that he wrote it.

Later in the day Preston stops by my office. He's got his coffee mug in hand, and two of the secretaries are with him—one on each side. "We're on our way to lunch," he says. "But I wanted to let you know that the chief doesn't think we'll get the grant. Needs to be for a *direct service provider*."

I nod, but resist the temptation to respond with a few sharp words. Anyway, it wasn't like he really asked me a question. Preston takes a gulp of his coffee and grins. Then he turns awkwardly on his lanky legs and walks off, followed closely by the two secretaries. Not a *thank you* for working so hard on the grant that sat on his desk for a month, just a wiseass crack to impress the ladies.

Preston's treatment of me is an embarrassment and it feels devaluing. The big laugh is that much like Frank Howard, Preston prides himself on being so damn considerate of protected classes—a cutting edge, all-inclusive progressive. Perhaps if I were black, or gay, or a woman, he'd treat me differently. At the very least, others would see his behavior as discriminatory and harassing—definitely outrageous and unfair. But I'm finding that nobody notices, and this kind of mistreatment seems easier for people to accept when the victim is a white male.

One night around this time I'm called at home by police dispatch. They advise that the watch commander has activated the SWAT team—including hostage negotiators. As I'm driving in, the watch commander calls to brief me further. Two SWAT team guys, working as part of a street crime suppression unit, rolled up on an armed robbery in progress at a neighborhood bar. Three or four suspects, described as young black males, tried to shoot their way out. The two cops returned fire, pinning the robbers inside the bar with over a dozen patrons as hostages.

None of our guys were hit, and we held our fire when the suspects used the hostages as human shields at the door. We don't believe anybody has been injured.

"Who called it in?" I ask.

"The bar manager" says the lieutenant. "Apparently he was counting cash in a back office when the suspects burst into the place. He watched what was going on via closed circuit monitor in the office and called 9-1-1. Our two cops were riding double, and just happened to be a block away."

73

My mind immediately goes into planning mode. These types of callouts—armed takeovers with hostages—are rare, and I'll need to be mentally prepared to make the right decisions.

Everybody is moving faster than normal, because when hostages are involved we don't have the luxury of time. The robbers could turn the guns on them at any moment, and I want to be ready to storm the place if things go that way. So we immediately stage an emergency entry team at the corner of the building. Protocol dictates that we do what we can to quickly relieve and replace an officer who's been involved in a shooting—but these two guys are solid, and we need them holding the corners, right where they are.

The second thing we do is stage the negotiators' command post—a motor home—closer than usual. I'm anticipating a lot of witnesses when this thing ends, and we're going to use both the negotiators and the detectives who are on-scene, to interview them.

What we don't know at the time is that a drunken customer sitting at the bar stabbed one of the suspects in the leg. The suspect was so keyed up that he thought the man had only pushed him; he had no idea that his femoral artery had been severed and he was bleeding to death. When the robber finally noticed the fountain of blood emanating from his crotch, who knows what he thought? Maybe that the cops had shot him, or maybe that he was pissing blood. In any case, he ultimately crumbles against the jukebox and dies there. The other two desperados panic, trade shirts with a couple of the bar patrons, and they herd everybody outside.

We're not exactly ready for that; it happens too fast—a whole bunch of drunks suddenly walking out the front door with their hands in the air. Luckily, it isn't too difficult to put the pieces together: fifteen middle-aged white people, and two young black men with eyes as big as saucers. We pounce on them, and then find the third guy dead inside. We also find the manager cowering in his office. The entire crime—from start to finish—has been recorded on his closed circuit monitor.

A month or two later Chief Bradford calls me to his office. He congratulates me on the successful grant application. We've been awarded funding for a sergeant, a community service officer, and a bunch of equipment—radios, jackets, and such for the volunteer ambassadors. The chief confides that he didn't think we'd get it, but he seems genuinely pleased. The municipal administrator and the council are also happy about it. But none of them can be as pleased as I am.

The selection process begins immediately, and within a few weeks I have an assistant to give me some breathing room. He's a great guy by the name of Paul Vega—perfect for the position. A hard worker who can think outside the box, he's friendly and engaging, and wears really nice suits. City Hall is going to love this guy.

Through my interactions within the community about the grant, one particularly unexpected partnership comes out of it. I meet Russ Emory, an influential business owner who is very close with one of the city councilmen. Every time we talk, Emory hints at the behind-the-scenes scuttlebutt within the city government. I'm not the least bit interested in it, so I never take the bait. But he always leaves it hanging there—like the shadowy stain of city hall politics is part of the bigger picture that I've yet to see.

Anyway, with Sergeant Vega now managing the downtown resource center, I'm able to avoid most of my dealings with the local bureaucrats. He also makes the remainder of my time working under Preston much easier. Besides, I think the writing on the wall for Preston is that he'll never be chief here, and there are rumors that he's looking elsewhere.

If this works out the way I hope it will, I'll actually have some time on my days off to relax a little. I've been toying with the idea of building a small art studio in the side yard of our house. Gale knows how much I enjoy my artwork, and she encourages me to move forward with the plan. The eight-by-ten foot shed turns out to be a lifesaver. I'm able to listen to my music and sit out there for hours, painting with oils and watercolors, and drawing with my pastels.

Between the solace of my art studio, Paul Vega's help, and much needed breakfast meetings with my dad, I'm able to survive the two years of hell working under Preston. I also graduate from college with a bachelor's degree, just about the same time as I'm finishing my three-year community policing commitment. The degree is a requirement for a promotion to captain—a position that I've recently tested for.

In any case, my transfer away from Preston, back to dayshift patrol as the watch commander, comes with a great sense of relief.

LESSON 9

"What is right is too often forgotten by what is convenient."

~Bodie Thoene

Between my watch commander duties, my responsibilities as the SWAT commander, and an occasional personnel investigation, I've also been delegated as the department's representative to the city's Emergency Operations Center. Nothing like the load that Preston had me saddled with, the EOC gig only calls for a meeting or two every few months—really no big deal. And occasionally, because of it, I find myself on some interesting federal email lists.

I'm in my office one day, reading through all of the law enforcement courses being offered, when a class catches my eye. I find it posted under the counterterrorism heading. It's a weeklong bioterrorism instructor's course put on by the U.S. Department of Justice at their center for domestic preparedness in Anniston, Alabama. I have an intense interest in such things, and it falls directly under my area of responsibility within the organization. Graduates of the training will be federally licensed to teach the course, which would benefit the rest of the police department, should we ever need to organize a first responder course for patrol officers. Best of all, the training is being offered free of charge. The police department pays nothing.

So, I go ahead and fill out the applications for myself and for one of my sergeants—the guy named Nye, who is now assigned under me in the emergency preparedness function. I mail off the forms and that's the last I think of it.

* * *

First order of business of the new workweek is the SWAT team. Seven officers have tested for two spots. Only four have passed all three phases; the physical agility, weapons proficiency and the oral interview. Now I have an important decision to make.

Formed in 1978, SWAT has since been comprised of only men. First, a handful of Vietnam veterans based solely on firearms experience, and then a second wave of team members a year later. Just off of my rookie probation, I was part of the third group, formed in 1981.

To say the SWAT team has been the 'Good Old Boys Club' wouldn't be *exactly* accurate, but pretty close. I was always told it had to do with simple physiology—women lack many of the skills required to be effective on the team. In truth, most females, and quite a few of the males, lack the upper body strength to pull themselves onto a roof, much less lift another team member up and support his body weight. But over the years that reality has been swallowed by a widely held perception: The white male officers who make up the team have been disproportionately promoted into command positions, and now comprise the power structure in the organization. In fact, the 'disenfranchised' around the department have even coined the term "SWAT or not"—a sardonic reference to team membership's sway over one's career opportunities.

Women in the department have either accepted the rhetoric or have simply been uninterested in breaking through that particular ceiling, because not one has ever actually tested to be a member.

But I've always wondered, *what if there was a woman who tested for the team? And what if she did possess the required skills?*

I glance down at my list of successful candidates—three men and one woman. The woman is Patricia Irons, an officer for whom I have a very high regard. Probably the only female officer I've known who possesses the skills to be a SWAT officer. And just to add a little more controversy into the decision I have to make, Patricia is also black and lesbian.

I stop by the captain's office later to advise him of my decision, but he's in a meeting. I return to the fishbowl, opting to send him an email rather than leave a note on his desk. There are far too many nosy co-workers around here.

I'm back in my office and I find a phone message taped to my chair. It's from one of the secretaries at city hall, "inviting" me to meet with the municipal administrator, Hector Lara. I agree to the already-selected date and time, and hang up the phone a bit puzzled. The MA is at the very top of the city's food chain. The mayor and council hire him to oversee every city department—including police. As a matter of fact, he's Chief Bradford's boss.

What could the municipal administrator possibly want with me?

77

I glance at the note again and a shadow buzzes my periphery, just outside the office window. It's gone by the time I look up. A few seconds later, it's there again, this time lingering near my door. The shadow disappears around the corner, but not before I glimpse the back of a uniform. With a cocked head, I stare at the open door, knowing he'll be back around.

Finally, Johnny Lang pokes his head in. He sees me, and then turns abruptly to leave.

"Hey, hey," I call out. "Not so fast, Johnny. Get over here."

"You're busy," says Lang, a young cop who used to be on my midnight squad. "I can come back later."

I need to stretch my legs anyway, so I stand and remove my reading glasses. "Come on in, Johnny. You know I'm never too busy for you. Besides, I've been watching you pace around my doorway for the past five minutes."

His shoulders pitch forward, as if what I just said made him feel worse. He's got terror in his eyes, and he looks like what he really wants to do is run in the other direction.

"Johnny?" I step around the desk. "You got off work over an hour ago; you ought to be home in bed by now. What's on your mind?"

"I think I need to sit down, sir." He wipes his forehead. "What I'm about to tell you . . . well, sir, it's probably going to cost me my job."

I ease myself into the chair near the door. "Better take my seat," I tell him. "You look like you could use one with more support." Though the gesture is genuine, Johnny's too distraught to see it was meant to lighten the exchange.

He drops onto it with a thump then straightens as if seated at attention. "I was checking on the police explorer scouts at Columbus Park last night. You know they're stationed there to keep an eye on all the booths set up for the big city festival. It's this weekend."

I smile.

"Yes, of course you know that. You're the watch commander." Johnny stretches his neck before continuing. "Well, sir, they've been provided a park district golf cart, the scouts have, in order to patrol the grounds more efficiently."

"Johnny," I lift my eyebrows. "Get to it. What happened?"

"Well, sir, I was . . . one of the female scouts . . . you see, she was driving me around to show me . . . sir, we struck a tree. Actually *we* didn't strike the tree, *she* did. I managed to jettison myself from the vehicle moments before impact."

"Was anybody hurt?"

"No, sir. No injuries were sustained by either occupant."

"So that's it?" I ask him. "Nothing else? You just jacked up one of the golf carts?"

"Yes, sir."

"Then you're not going to lose your job."

"I'm not?"

I let out a howl, unintentional but hardy. "Unless the reason she lost control was because your head was buried in her lap . . ."

"Oh no, sir. Nothing like that!"

"Then we're okay." I come around the desk and swat Johnny on the shoulder. "Just fill out a property damage report, and then go home and get some rest."

Captain Jenner appears at my office door and poor Johnny nearly collapses. The look on Johnny's face reads guiltier than any polygraph machine could.

"Morning, sir," Johnny says to the captain, saluting while at the same time squeezing past him in the doorway. "I was just leaving."

Jenner waits until he's gone before speaking to me. "So you're going to put Irons on SWAT?"

I nod. "It wasn't really a difficult decision. She's far and away the best candidate."

He smiles. "I agree."

"Did you tell the chief yet?"

Jenner lifts an eyebrow. "Yeah." His expression cautions me that there's more.

"What is it?"

The captain's smile changes to a grimace. "He agrees that Irons is probably a worthy candidate, but I think he's worried about what the guys on the team will say. You know how Bradford is, he doesn't like controversy."

"Controversy . . ."

He shrugs. "Easier for him to keep the status quo, I guess."

I roll my eyes. "He underestimates these guys. They'll be fine."

"How do you plan to handle it with them?"

"Same way I would if *she* were a *he*." I lean my head back and stare up at the ceiling for a second before looking back at Jenner. "I'll tell Irons that she made it onto SWAT, and then I'll simply introduce her to the rest of the team at our training on Friday. It doesn't need to be any more complicated than that."

* * *

I'm sitting on a padded yellow chair with my hands on my knees, and suddenly I feel like my feet can barely touch the floor—just like when I used to be "invited" to meet with my grammar school principal. Only now I'm a grown man wearing a police uniform. Yet, when I notice the secretary giving me the fisheye, the feeling comes back to me like it was yesterday.

"The MA will see you now," she says.

Hector Lara greets me with a warm smile and a weak, but friendly, handshake. "Congratulations," he says, as if I already have the new position. Then he corrects himself, "for doing well in the promotional testing process for police captain."

He's got a nice corner office, sleek lines, polished metal and glass. The desk has been cleared of work, leaving no hint of what he does with his day. No family photos, no flag, no mementos from that family trip to Disneyworld. Only a pen set mounted on a small piece of marble that bears the city seal.

Lara clasps his hands and leans into his desk. "So, the chief has recommended you to fill the captain vacancy. How do you feel about that?"

Uh . . . good? An odd start to the conversation. "Well-prepared," I say. "I think the positions I've held in the department have put me in a good place . . . make me uniquely qualified to run the patrol division." It had come out awkwardly, almost as lame as *his* icebreaker, and I consider going back to try to fix it.

"What are those assignments?" Lara asks, as if he's unfamiliar with my career, though I somehow doubt there's anything in my file he hasn't read.

I give him the rundown: this, that and the other. After going through the promotional interviews, I'm able to rattle them off without having to think too much. He nods as if bored by the answer to his own question, so I wrap it up.

"How do you feel about officers living outside the city?" he asks.

Now we get down to the meat and potatoes. Lara obviously knows that I live in the city—one of only a handful of police employees. Well over 90% live elsewhere. I'd bet that most don't even live in the same county. Clearly, Lara is already aware of this, too. I know it's a tricky subject, and he probably thinks I'm going to dance around it. I'm not.

"Since there's nothing to prohibit officers from living outside the city, I suppose it's their right to do so." I pause for a second to consider the entirety of my opinion. "I don't like it though."

Lara's eyes spring open.

"In my opinion, they don't have the same buy-in as someone who lives here. How could they?" It's a rhetorical question, and I answer it before he does. "It's natural to be more concerned about the safety of your own community; the streets where your wife drives, the schools your kids attend, the stores where you shop. Any off-duty contribution to the community, be it coaching, involvement in the arts, service clubs, whatever, is going to benefit their own cities. I think we miss out all the way around."

It suddenly occurs to me that Carl Bradford was allowed to continue living outside the city when he was promoted to chief—the first time in city history that the police chief hasn't been a resident of the city. I realize I sort of walked into his next question.

"What would you do about that?"

Start with making sure the chief lives in the city; the example has to start at the top.

I decide to temper my real answer with at least a little bit of restraint. "I would focus more of our recruitment efforts on city residents—people who have grown up here, have gone to school here, and have family here. Even if they relocate outside the city later, they still have ties here in town."

"Of course," he says. "I believe we actively recruit from . . ."

Lara's words fade from my hearing as I realize he's now more concerned about defending his human resources department, and letting me know that *the city* has it all covered already. *Whatever.*

Then he throws the haymaker. "What do you think about the chief living so far away? What message does that send?"

I look at Lara across the austere desk. He knows the answer as well as I do: *it sends a shitty message.* Obviously, his question is some kind of test. Do I back peddle off my initial position? Or do I torpedo the chief that he hired, and who he has allowed to continue living where he does?

"Well," I say with a slight laugh. "As you know, Chief Bradford spends so much time here that it almost seems as if he lives in his office."

It's the biggest crock of shit I have ever uttered, but what the hell? I'm here to show the municipal administrator what I've got. And yes, I can bring a convincing line of bullshit when I have to.

We talk casually about a few non-essential things, and then Lara glances at his watch—a sure signal that my time is up.

"One more question," he says. "What are your future plans?"

Future plans? It catches me off-guard, and I'm suddenly picturing myself as a fat old man, sitting on a lake in an aluminum boat, with a fishing rod in one hand and a cold beer in the other.

"With the department," he says. "Have you got any aspirations beyond captain? Given any thought to becoming police chief?"

I try to read his expression for a clue as to why he would ask me that. I haven't even secured the captain job yet. *Does he think I'd leave for a better offer or is he talking about grooming me for the position when my chief retires?* But I feel as if Lara and I made a bit of a connection, and his question does seem sincere.

"I've never really given it much thought," I tell him. "If the position were to come up *here* someday, and if I felt ready, and if I were a good fit, then sure, I would probably consider it. You know, I've been with the city and the department since I was nineteen years old. I certainly don't want to be a chief anywhere, just for the sake of being a chief. In other words, I can't see myself leaving to take a position somewhere else."

Lara doesn't really react, but smiles, stands up and shakes my hand. "It was a pleasure getting to hear your thoughts."

I thank him for his time and I leave.

A few days later I meet my dad for breakfast and I tell him all about the meeting with Lara. I can see by Dad's face that he doesn't think much of the guy. I'm not too sure why—The MA seems nice enough to me.

My dad asks me the names of the other commanders that I'll be working with, and I name them: "Besides Chief Bradford, there's Bill Preston, the deputy chief, and Captain Jenner, and then there's Captain Casey."

Dad's eyebrows arch upward. "Evan Casey?"

Now my eyebrows do the same. "Yeah, you know him?"

"I didn't know he was a captain," he says. "I ran into him up in Tahoe a couple of weeks ago. He was hanging around some of the PE teachers I went up with."

"Yeah, I think Casey and his wife have got a little vacation condo somewhere around there. Reno, I think."

My dad nods. "Well, Casey wasn't with his wife. He was hanging around with some little gal. The teachers I was with all knew her, said she was his secretary."

I describe Casey's secretary to my dad. "Her nickname around the department is Cheesecakes," I tell him.

"Yep, that's her," he says. "But once the two of them found out that you were my son, they both took off and we never saw them the rest of the weekend."

I laugh. *Doesn't surprise me.*

"Casey seems kind of weaselly," says Dad. "Do you get along with him?"

I shrug my ambivalence. "I don't give the guy much play," I tell him. "Evan Casey is sort of like . . . a case of jock itch. It's not going to ruin your life, but it's always creeping around where you don't want it. He's more of an annoyance than anything else."

A few days later I find out that I have officially been promoted. It comes in the form of a message from the chief of police, along with an invitation to his Christmas party.

I've barely had a chance to read the thing when Evan Casey swoops around the corner, into my office.

"Chief's Christmas party, eh?" He's holding his invitation in front of him with both hands—a hyena with a hunk of meat. I can almost imagine the chittering laugh as he protects it. "You know it's at his house," he says. "Half acre. 3,700 square feet right on the golf course. It's a nice place, don't get me wrong, but every time me and Shelly get invited there I'm worried my Vet will get dinged by a golf ball."

"Hmm." I nod.

Casey has managed to squeeze a lot of crowing into a short conversation, including mention of his prized Corvette—which I couldn't care any less about. And about his many visits to the chief's home. He seems to measure his self-worth by these things.

Casey loiters in the doorway for a minute and I'm wondering if he's feeling me out to see what, if anything, my dad told me. He's about to leave my office when he suddenly turns back. And with an earnest look on his face he says, "I don't think you're a piece of shit or anything—I don't."

I stare back with an unchanged expression. *Really? Where in the hell did that come from? It's like, out of the blue someone says, "Hey, I don't have a wine colored birthmark on my left ass cheek or anything—I don't."*

The night of the party arrives amidst a calendar full of family events and other obligations. But this, being my first dip into the pool of police bigwigs, isn't optional—we have to take the dive.

For some reason, women seem to find these events more intimidating than men do. Between the good or bad hair, finding just the right outfit, and shoes that look okay, everything Gale selects seems to be a statement. My decisions on the other hand, are much less complex: a pair of slacks, the first dress shirt I come to that isn't wrinkled, and comfortable loafers. My only rule for myself is no sweater. Every time I wear one to a party, I feel like a polar bear in a sauna.

We stop to give our names to a security guard before driving into the champagne and caviar enclave. This is the kind of place where nobody puts up their own Christmas decorations; they simply pay someone else to do it. I see that Evan Casey has parked his corvette in the center of the chief's driveway—another message to the rest of us *commoners.*

The party is nice, a lot of food and drink. Mostly the upper level of the police department and a few couples that I presume are Bradford's personal friends. I do my best to mingle, introduce Gale, and avoid Casey. I also go very light on the drink, partly so I don't make a fool of myself but mostly because it's a long drive home. Others seem to be enjoying the bountiful bar set up in the corner of the living room, the most notable being the chief's wife. *Why not? It's her house and her party.*

I wait until nobody's around the bar then take the opportunity to go over and pour Gale a glass of white wine. The chief's wife suddenly appears next to me, adding a generous splash of scotch to her nearly full tumbler.

"Congrats on being the latest victim," she says with a chuckle.

We have met before, but I wouldn't say I know her well. I laugh off the comment, as I would hope someone would do when I've had too much to drink. I ask about their kids and complement the house, but she seems to have an agenda that I'm not following.

"So, do you know Denise Freeman?" She gulps an inch off her drink.

"The state senator?" It seems a random question if there ever was one. "Well, I know who she is. Never met her."

The wife tosses out an exasperated huff. "Well, Carl knows her."

Carl's the husband—my boss. I nod as I'm pouring Gale's wine. "I imagine he knows a lot of politicians, what with being police chief and all."

"Whatever." She takes another swig. "You know the senator's little assistant? Tammy something or other?" An ice cube clicks behind her words.

"Don't know her." I'm not sure where this is heading, but it's nowhere good. I raise the wine glass, like, *cheers! Gotta go now.*

She doesn't get the clue. "Yeah, well that little bitch calls Carl all the time on his cell. You sure you don't know who she is? Ever heard Carl talk about her?"

"No. I mean, yes. I'm sure." I start to leave and then turn around. "Come to think of it, Evan Casey might know something. He spends a lot more time with the chief than I do."

I meet back up with Gale and roll my eyes. "Let's make this a short night," I whisper. Her smile tells me that she's ready to go whenever I am.

We stay another thirty minutes or so, just long enough to get introduced around as the new captain. I manage to steer clear of Casey, and avoid any further conversations with Bradford's wife—almost. We've just finished wishing everyone happy holidays and saying our goodbyes. The chief and his wife walk us to the door, and he thanks us for coming. She wishes me luck in the new position. Then over my shoulder I hear her add, "Just don't fuck it up!"

"Did she just say what I think she said?" Gale asks, looking back as I hustle her to the car.

Once we're safely out of the affluent commonwealth, I tell her what else the chief's wife said—about the senator's assistant.

"Do you think it's true?"

"You mean, do I think Bradford's having an affair?" I shake my head. "Highly doubt it. He doesn't really seem like the type."

"What type is that?" she asks. "He's a man, isn't he?"

My first few days as a captain are tainted with sadness. A young patrol officer in my division lost his two-month-old son. The baby had been born with a serious heart defect, and after surgery and a couple of hopeful, prayer-filled months, the boy passed away.

The service is packed with police employees. Like family, they've come to show unity and their support. The command staff decides to go as a group, all in our Class-A uniforms. At the last minute the chief decides to take his own car, but the rest of us wait for him outside the church so we can all walk in together.

The officer's father is there, too. I remember him fondly as one of my first sergeants, back when I was a rookie working the night shift. I'm sitting there thinking what a great guy he was and what a wonderful family he's raised. Then the tiny casket is wheeled into the church and my eyes fill with tears.

Most of us are barely keeping it together, but not the chief. He's checking his cell phone, which thankfully is on vibrate, and then he's looking around for the exit. Halfway through the mass, Bradford slips out the back door and isn't seen again for the rest of the day. Curious about what critical incident may be happening back at the department, I phone in to the watch commander after the services are concluded. There is nothing going on. I figure it must be something else of importance—perhaps some political emergency at city hall. Thankfully, those types of things are above my pay grade.

I'm settling into my new office, another wood-paneled job on the second floor—right across the hall from the deputy chief's and the chief's offices. Casey's division, and thankfully his office, is on the other side of the building—which from the way he's buzzing the hallway outside, must bug the shit out of him. I know he'd like nothing better than to curl up on a little sofa-bed right there next to Bradford's desk.

Anyway, I'm getting used to the job. It's a load of personnel: seven patrol teams, fourteen sergeants, seven lieutenants and a handful of miscellaneous evidence technicians and other civilian positions—which, I keep track of on a six-foot status board on my wall.

Danny Jenner, who held this position before me, is right across the hall in the deputy chief's office now. The other guy, Preston, left for a better title somewhere else. Anyway, Jenner is a huge help, and takes time every day to check in on me and go over the nuances of the patrol status board.

By about my third week I'm starting to feel pretty good. I've held a couple of meetings with my watch commanders and outlined some goals for the division. It's late Monday afternoon when the chief walks into my office and stands there awkwardly, checking out a couple of photos I've put up of my wife and daughters.

"Wow, cool." That's all he says about them before turning back to me. "Hey, I won't be able to attend the council meeting tomorrow night. So, can you sit in for me?"

"Sure." I grab a pen and a pad of paper. "What do I need to do?" I've attended a few city council meetings in the past, but mostly as an observer. A couple of times when I was a young beat cop, I had to stand guard at the door when they expected some rowdy attendees. But I've never represented the police department—especially in lieu of the police chief.

"Yeah," Chief Bradford says as he thumbs a text message into his phone. "There's really nothing you have to do. I don't know what they'll be discussing, but it's nothing about the PD. You just need to sit there and be seen. My secretary will give you an agenda packet."

"Oh, okay. Well that sounds easy enough." I set down my pen. "I guess I should wear my uniform then?" I usually wear it to work, but the chief usually wears a suit.

"The uniform is fine. It makes the mayor and council feel safe, so go up and say hi or something before the meeting."

"Sure." It almost sounds too easy. "So that's it?"

"That's it." He walks back to his office.

LESSON 10

"The most important quality in a leader is that of being acknowledged as such. A leader whose fitness is questioned is clearly lacking in force."
~André Maurois

Lillian Behrman is clacking the gavel against the sounding block, which used to be made of matching wood until it broke in two during an unruly council meeting some years ago. Now it's just a coffee coaster bearing the city's odd-looking seal.

"Your mayor looks like someone who backed into the job," my buddy, Terry, always tells me. "It's like she was baking an apple pie for her grandkids one day and somebody told her, 'I bet you'd make a good mayor.'" The notion must have appealed to Behrman, because she is now the elected leader of our fair city.

I'm sitting near the back of the council chambers, as relaxed as one can be in a police uniform. Everybody who comes in spots me first, then picks out a seat as far away as possible. I always wonder why that is; do they think I'll smell booze or pot on them? Are they worried that if shooting starts, anyone sitting near me will be in the line of fire? Whatever the reason, I pretty much have the whole back row to myself.

Meanwhile, it's nearly ten minutes into the council meeting and Mayor Behrman is still rambling on and on about how today is her 50th wedding anniversary. She even acknowledges her husband, who she's apparently invited to be here with her tonight. The poor old guy looks pretty feeble—swollen ankles, a walking cane and one bad eye. He's seated in the second row, right below the dais where his wife and the rest of the council are lined like bowling pins.

Everyone in the council chambers applauds the touching tribute, and some in the audience even stand—which I figure I should also do. The mayor's husband starts to stand as well, but falters on his cane and settles for a robust wave from his seat.

The council meeting finally gets underway and I settle back into my chair. As I scan over the agenda, I see it's likely to be a short and easy night. Most of the issues are on the consent calendar—which usually means just a single action approval. Since nothing there appears controversial, I'm thinking that the public comments might be the only area of concern. If there are any whiners and gripers in the room, that's where they'll come out of the woodwork. But only three audience members have requested to speak, so I'm feeling pretty good about getting out of here before 10 p.m.

The first to address the council is a round guy wearing bifocals. He waddles up to the podium then runs a hand over his hairless head before speaking. They're only given a couple of minutes to talk, but this guy's reading from several pages of a printed speech. As he gets into it, I see that it has to do with the city's eminent domain action on his family home—apparently the city has offered to buy him out so they can widen Duncan Street. The chubby guy's mother has lived there most of her life and doesn't want to move.

Mayor Behrman tries to correct him on one of his points, and he talks over her. He's getting louder and I see two of the councilmen exchange uncomfortable glances. The guy drops a few of the pages from his script, and rather than pick them up, he goes improv—calls the city council a bunch of "crooks," and then leans across the podium towards the mayor. "And you, Mayor, are the ringleader!"

At that last comment, Stanley Behrman, the mayor's husband of fifty years, yells to the guy, "Shut your mouth, you!"

Mayor Behrman ignores her husband and tells the speaker, "Thank you Mr. Richards, but your time is up. You may sit down."

Richards wants to get in a last word. He's wagging a finger at the mayor. "You and your band of hooligans are all corrupt!"

Now Stanley Behrman struggles to get to his feet. His wizened legs wobble under the weight of his body as he holds the seatback with one hand and his walking cane with the other. "Why I oughta punch you in the nose!" he yells to Richards, who's gathering loose pages of his manifesto off the floor.

"That's quite enough, Mr. Behrman!" A shrill feedback over the amplified microphone accompanies the mayor's admonishment to her husband. "Now sit down and behave yourself."

Stanley flails a hand through the air, and I can't tell if he's trying to catch his balance or waving away his wife's warning. Not that it really matters, because he's already fully under the influence of old man chutzpa and the kind of chivalrous bravado that happens when someone disrespects your wife on your anniversary.

The speaker, Richards, has to pass by the mayor's husband while making his way back to his seat. And though I see it coming, I'm too far away to do anything about it. So I just cringe.

"You son-of-a-bitch!" Old man Behrman lunges into the aisle, swinging his cane like a swashbuckler. Luckily, Richards steps back and Behrman stumbles against the empty seat at the end of the row.

"That does it!" screams the mayor. She stands and scans the audience. Finally her eyes lock onto me. "Officer, will you please eject Mr. Behrman from the council chambers?"

Let me see if I understand this correctly—it's the mayor's fiftieth wedding anniversary, and she wants me to physically throw her husband out of the council meeting?

The rest of the council glances back and forth with nervous grins, but she's not kidding. "Out!" she points to the door.

As I help the old codger back onto his feet, I whisper that I'm sorry for having to do this. We walk arm-in-arm out of the room and I seat him on a couch in the anteroom. Figuring the council meeting is nearly over anyway, I sit out there with the guy until people start filing out a few minutes later. All I can think about is that the police chief is never going to believe this one.

I get home and run the story down to Gale. She laughs, but can hardly believe it. "How embarrassing," she says. I'm not sure who she's referring to—the mayor, her husband or me.

The chief already knows about the council meeting debacle by the time he gets in the next morning; it's made the front page of the local paper. He thinks it's a hoot. *Hardy-har-har.*

On an early June afternoon, I monitor a radio broadcast of an incident occurring in the field. Sounds like whatever it started out to be has escalated into an armed standoff in an apartment complex off of Mission Street.

Dispatch keeps me updated, letting me know that responding patrol units have surrounded the target apartment—which is on the third floor—and they've begun evacuating neighboring units.

I head out to the scene, and I take over command as soon as it's clearly a critical incident that requires SWAT. Like most tactical incidents, this one is slow to unfold. Given the fact that we have no hostages, no neighbors in danger, and no shooting, yet, we can take our time with it. The goal is always to talk the guy down rather than amp him up. But this thing drags on all afternoon as the suspect drinks beer, becomes more belligerent, and refuses to answer calls from the negotiators.

Even though management of the incident is my priority, I'm also concerned that it's nearing the end of the school day. The place will be packed with curious kids soon, and then adult workers will be coming home—trying to get into their cordoned-off apartments.

Bobby Roselli and Don Nakamura are supervising the incident, so I have no worries. My place as a captain, though it's difficult for me to stay out of the action, is at the command post a block away inside the apartment manager's office.

"Nakamura to command." The sergeant's words come across the air in a whisper. "We've got the passkey and less lethal options stacked at the door."

"Good," I respond. "Standby one." The brief update from Nakamura tells me that we have ready access into the apartment if and when we decide to go in. He's also moved a gunner with a shotgun equipped to fire beanbag rounds, to the front of the line of entry team members. It's a good option, as long as the suspect isn't armed with a gun, because in most cases the beanbag round will temporarily stun the guy and only knock the wind out of him."

I meet briefly with Roselli—the new team commander—to weigh the pros and cons of the plan. We're both in agreement that if the entry team can sight-verify that the suspect is unarmed, we move in.

My cell phone rings and it's the chief. Surprising, given the fact that he's out of town.

"Evan called me," he says, referring to Evan Casey. "What are you planning to do? I don't want to escalate this thing into a shooting," he says, without giving me a chance to answer his first question. "We don't need to shoot this guy. Just wait him out."

He's the chief. I get that. But he's there, wherever, and I'm here. "Yeah, of course," I say, swallowing my balls in the process. But I'm a new captain and he is my boss, I console myself internally.

Bobby looks pissed as I finish the call. "Are you kidding me?" He turns away, shaking his head. I hear him mumble, "What kind of leader is Bradford?"

I immediately apply the question to myself. *What kind of leader am I?* Sure, I'm following directions, but I know exactly how this thing *should* be handled. I also have ample confidence in myself and in the skill-level of my team. *So now what?*

"We've got the door unlocked," whispers Nakamura over the air. "Suspect is standing near the open sliding doors to the deck. He's got a glass in one hand. Can't see the other hand."

One of the negotiators comes over the radio. "Negotiations to command, we've got him on the phone now."

If one hand is holding a glass, I reason. The other hand must be holding the phone.

I turn to Bobby. "Let's do it, now." I start through the maze of buildings toward the target apartment. Bobby is right behind me, giving Nakamura the *go* order.

I hear a deafening explosion of the flash-bang grenades as I round the corner where armed sentries demarcate the scene's inner-perimeter. I've been on enough entries to know and visualize exactly what the team is doing and when. Aware that the first cops in the door will be entering right behind the concussion, I wait for the next report—the sound of either the beanbag shotgun or of a fusillade of bullets.

The single crack of gunfire sounds, then a *whump* as the shaded silhouette of a man slumps to the planks of the patio deck above me. A dark liquid spills through the slats, a big gush followed by a dribbling line visible from beneath. His blood, I think. They must have had to shoot him."

I'm so screwed.

"Nakamura to command," says the team leader, no longer whispering. "Suspect in custody, and the rest of the apartment is all clear."

No call for an ambulance? Definitely a good sign. "What am I seeing?" I ask. "Dripping from the deck."

Nakamura answers in his classic unemotional voice. "Chocolate milk, sir. Nesquik, I believe."

The next call from Chief Bradford comes minutes later, in a frantic high-pitched yelp. "What happened? Evan told me that you forced entry and shot the suspect."

"No, no," I assure him. "The front door was unlocked and we could see that he had no weapon in his hands. It seemed the perfect opportunity to end this thing safely, so we disabled him with a beanbag round. Clean shot, no injuries."

"Oh." Silence for several seconds. "Well then, I guess that's good. Okay, good. Nice work."

I take a breath and let it out slowly. The chief ends the call and I'm feeling a great deal of relief. Technically, the door was *unlocked*, as I reported to the chief. I just left out the part about how it got unlocked. I drive back to the station thanking God that the entry team didn't shoot the guy. I'm also wondering why the chief ever listens to that idiot, Evan Casey.

* * *

A few months go by and I hear from one of the secretaries that Bradford's mother passed away. I met the woman once a few years ago, and I know she and Bradford were very close. I remember Jenner telling me awhile back that she used to babysit Bradford's young daughters—her grandkids.

When the time is right I walk across to the chief's office to offer my condolences. The office door edges open a crack and Evan Casey squeezes out.

"Carl can't see anybody right now," he says with a palm to my chest. "It's just not a good time."

I take in a deep breath and let it out slowly, looking at his hand the whole time. Casey takes a step back, securing his position in front of the chief's office door, and I turn and leave without responding. *It's almost time for another trip downstairs to the heavy bag.*

A couple of weeks later, when Casey is away at a conference, I take Chief Bradford out to lunch. I'm able to tell him how badly I feel about his mom's passing, and I also offer my daughters up for babysitting services, if he's ever in a pinch for childcare. Our time away is a nice respite from the police building, and I see flashes of the friendship that we once had as patrolmen.

When we get back to the office he asks me if he can take a look at my patrol status board. "Of course," I say. "You're the police chief. You can look it over whenever you want to."

His mouth morphs into a goofy grin. "It's just that Evan thinks you're hiding people."

"Hiding people." I repeat it back, but I have no idea what it even means.

"You know. He thinks you have more personnel in your division than you are letting on." Bradford shakes his head and chuckles a little, yet stands squinting at the board.

I point out each of the patrol teams—listing each officer and sergeant by name. I show him the canine units, the civilian crime scene techs and community service officers assigned to each of the seven squads. I run my finger down the list of the rookie officers who are in field training but not yet on their own; the injured officers on worker's comp, those who are working the desk or dispatch on limited duty, and at the top right of the board, in orange labels, the newly hired cops who are still in the police academy.

"Not sure where I would be hiding anyone," I say. "Or more to the point, *why.*"

The chief shrugs. "You know how Evan is. He probably suspects you're doing it because it's just the kind of thing he would do."

I couldn't agree more. But I have to wonder then, why Bradford relies on the guy so much. Can't imagine a worse person as a trusted confidant.

My wife and I attend the annual police union picnic, my first since being promoted to captain. It's always a fun day, lots of kids and families, and many retirees come—some from out of state.

While waiting in line for my ribeye steak, I overhear a couple of PBA board members grousing about the chief's non-appearance at the event. The two guys make reference to the "RC"—a hallway nickname recently bestowed on Evan Casey. The apparent meaning of RC is *Real Chief*. It seems that I'm not the only one who has noticed the level of influence that Casey has on Bradford.

" . . . It isn't like Bradford couldn't bring his kids," one of the board members says. "And he only lives a mile away from here. Probably busy vacationing with the RC."

"Or getting advice from him," says the other. "Bradford was also out of town when Linda Cabrara got into her shooting."

My memory about Linda's shooting is that she was attempting to arrest some guy who had assaulted his girlfriend. He escaped by jumping into his car, and then went for a gun under the seat as the officer tried to stop him from leaving. The suspect tried to drive off with Linda hanging half out of his window, so she let him have one in the gut. The suspect managed to escape, but we were able to locate and arrest him later.

Aside from their impressions of Casey, which I tend to agree with, I'm not sure if all of the PBA's criticisms of Chief Bradford are fair. After all, the police chief can't be around for everything—nor should that be expected of him. Bradford manages a department of over 400 employees, which undoubtedly comes with some heavy obligations.

September 4, 2001 (Tuesday)

The week following my vacation to look at potential colleges with Megan, I'm called into the chief's office. Bradford laughs as he fans himself with a typewritten sheet of paper. "What is this?" he asks through his grin.

I smile, too. Then shrug. "I give up. What is it?"

"You and Nye are going to Alabama for *anti-terrorist* training?"

"Huh?" I suddenly remember the application I sent off several months back. I explain to the chief that the feds will reimburse the city for all the costs of the course, and that it will be advantageous for the department to have two certified first-responder instructors."

"For what?" he asks. "In case the terrorists attack us?" He laughs again. "Like that'll happen."

I shrug again. "Might."

His expression abruptly changes to a more serious one as he sets the paper down. "Do you really think so?"

"Well . . ." I ease onto the chair across from him. "When my daughter and I were going through an orientation tour of NYU last week, I wouldn't stay at any of the hotels in lower Manhattan."

Bradford leans back. "Why not?"

"Terrorists tried to blow up the World Trade Center there."

"That was, like, seven years ago," he says.

I shake my head. "I know. But they never give up. And I don't want my daughter and I to be anywhere around when they try it again. Anyway, I just thought this training might be a good thing for us. Just in case."

Chief Bradford laughs again, handing me the acceptance form. "I guess, if you really want to go to Alabama in September."

One week later, to the day, Bradford summons me into his office again. A rolling TV stand has been brought in, and the monitor is tuned loudly to a news station. Horrific images of the unfolding attacks in lower Manhattan flash on the screen—the firefighters, the police, the smoke, the collapsing buildings, and all of the panicked workers running for their lives.

The chief's eyes dart between me and the TV screen. "Is there any way we can get more people into that class?" he asks.

A few more months pass and I don't see much of the chief. Not that I mind the autonomy, but it would be nice to know if I'm on the right track—especially since I'm in charge of the largest division in the department. Several important emails I've sent him have gone without a response, and I'm wondering why. I talk about it with Deputy Chief Jenner, and I mention how busy the chief must be. He gets an embarrassed look on his face.

"The chief isn't all that busy," he says. "Bradford and his wife are having problems, and I think that's taking up a lot of his time."

We both feel badly for him, but it's not like there's much we can do to help.

Jenner and I are at a countywide commanders meeting not long after that, and we run into a captain from another local city. He brings up Bradford and his marital problems, and then rolls his eyes. "You guys must be having a hell of a time holding that place together," he says.

Jenner and I feign ignorance; we react as if everything is fine. But the guy dismisses our act with a shake of his head, and he proceeds to tell us a story.

"We got a domestic violence call a couple of weeks ago—your chief and his wife. Some kind of fight between the two of them going on inside their car," he says. Whatever transpired, the wife gets arrested for spousal abuse."

Jenner and I are dumbfounded, and our faces show it.

"It's true," says the guy. "But your chief started flashing his badge around, ordering our beat cop to let his wife go. Told him not to write any report. Warned him not to breathe a word about it to anyone."

I can't even believe what I'm hearing. Jenner's face turns ashen with disgust.

The guy continues, "Next day one of your captains, guy name Casey, calls our chief and tries to get the whole thing buried."

Now that part I can believe.

Jenner has heard enough and finally cuts the guy off. "Chief Bradford has had a rough year," he says. "We're all pitching in to help him through it."

Without actually saying the words, Jenner lets the guy know that he ought to do the same and keep his mouth shut.

That night after work I enjoy a nice dinner with my family. I've just taken out the garbage and I'm settling into my recliner to watch the second quarter of the Monday night game—Ravens vs. Vikings. The house phone rings and I grab it.

I can barely make out the watch commander's rapid-fire words; they're dwarfed by an eruption of gunfire in the background. I grab the remote and shut off the TV so I can hear him.

"It's the street crimes unit," he says. "They're in a shootout with a parolee down on St. Marks Street. It's the suspect's girlfriend's house and it sounds like we found the guy hiding in a closet. He opened fire when the cops came in."

I still hear gunshots over the phone. "Are you there on St. Marks now?"

"No, you're hearing what's coming across my radio." He says something to someone in his office then comes back to me. "We've got at least one officer down, and another pinned inside the house."

"Do we know who's been hit?"

"Can't tell," he says. "But we've got two SWAT sergeants at the scene—Nakamura and Hayden—so I think it would be better if I manage this thing from here."

"Yeah, I agree." But my compass is still set with a tactical bent, and what am I going to do? Hang out at the station? So I tell him, "I'll go ahead to the scene and handle things there."

I see Gale's silhouette standing in my side view.

"Gotta go," I say as I grab my jacket and keys.

She holds the front door open for me. "Be safe."

I pull up behind a fire engine. A shroud of smoke hangs over the street, and though the gunfire has ceased, the air is still thick with the silent recoil of what has just happened. The firefighters are tending to a uniform, laid out on the dried grass in front of the house. Leaning over the top of them, I see that it's Gil Hayden who's been shot—a SWAT sergeant, and supervisor of the street crimes unit that had initiated the house search. He's conscious and talking, but he's clearly in a lot of pain.

I've experienced these types of situations over the years, to one degree or another, and there's a sense you get. Aside from the fact that Hayden's been shot, the body language and tight faces on all the cops tell me that this one was pretty hairy.

Nakamura shows no emotion. He's giving orders in his quiet but purposeful voice, and walking through the scene to get a sense of where and how this thing transpired. He was working uniformed patrol when it happened, and took charge of the scene when Hayden went down. I follow Nakamura toward the back bedroom where the shooting began, and I see him pause to look at the dead suspect inside the closet. I'm in the hallway and I'm unable to see the body, but the expression on Nakamura's face is no different than if he were taking casual inventory of his dry cleaning.

I get a few facts from him before I leave, and then I follow the ambulance to the trauma center. I call the watch commander on the way, just to coordinate and give him an update—which he's already gotten. My next call is to the chief, but after several rings it still hasn't gone to voicemail, so I hang up. I can't imagine where he could be at a time like this. But with his mother gone, two young kids, and his marriage in shambles, I can only assume that he's got his hands full.

Deputy Chief Jenner is my next call, but he's already gotten word and is on his way to meet me at the hospital. He tells me that he was able to contact Chief Bradford—who is at a conference in Bodega Bay.

It takes an hour or more for the doctors to stabilize Hayden, and then take x-rays to assess internal damage. A lot of cops are hanging around the hallway, and the nurses are getting a bit annoyed with the crowding and the noise. I clear them all out of the ER, which earns me some goodwill with the head nurse.

Hayden is loaded up with painkillers while they prep him for surgery, but the nurse lets me in for a second to talk with him. Still in pain and a little angry, probably with himself, Hayden thanks me for coming down. He asks if the other cops are okay, and also wants to know if I'd keep an eye out for his brother—a cop with another agency. Hayden had one of the nurses call him, and apparently he's on his way here.

Just as I'm about to leave the room I hear a commotion in the hallway behind me. It's Chief Bradford arguing with a nurse. "Don't tell me I can't go in," he barks. "I'm the chief of police. I'm Sergeant Hayden's boss!"

Not that police ranks mean much to head nurses anyway, but now Bradford's attitude seems to have really pissed her off. "Only one visitor is allowed in the room," she says.

Attempting to head off the situation, I back my way out. "No, no, it's fine. I was just leaving."

But the injured Hayden wants no part of the chief. "I don't want him in here!" he yells to the nurse.

I cringe, and the chief's face suddenly looks as tight as a balloon. Bradford storms past me into the room, but Hayden turns his head away and closes his eyes—completely ignores him.

Later I try to tell the chief that Hayden was pretty heavily sedated, and close to hallucinations. In truth, Bradford is not seen as a true leader and people see his overtures as insincere. Even though I feel the same way sometimes, part of me wants to let Hayden know what the chief's going through at home. *We all need to cut the poor guy a break.*

LESSON 11

"To avoid criticism, do nothing,
say nothing and be nothing."
~Elbert Hubbard

I realize I've been a little critical, though only in thought, of the fact that Chief Bradford has seemed disconnected and ineffective of late. A karmic incident puts me in my place a few weeks later.

Another middle-of-the-night call forces Gale to shake me awake, and this time it's a lieutenant buddy who I worked with years ago in narcotics. As hard as I'm trying, I can't seem to clear the fog from my brain. I understand most of what he's telling me; there was a police officer-involved shooting, nobody was hit or hurt, and he's just calling to let me know about it.

"Nobody was hit and nobody was hurt?" I force myself to repeat the question, making sure I got it right.

"No," says the lieutenant. "No injuries."

"Do you need anything?" I ask, garbling the words. "Do you need me to come in?"

"Not necessary," he says. "We've got it all under control."

That last line is the one that rings clearest in my mind, as I fall back onto my pillow. It isn't until I get into work the next morning and read the watch commander's log that I realize how badly I've screwed up. Until that moment, I didn't even remember the middle-of-the-night call. Now I can think of about two dozen questions I should have asked while I had the lieutenant on the phone, and a number of steps that needed to be taken, and weren't.

Sure, the wily old watch commander intentionally downplayed the whole shooting to me—probably to protect his guys—but it's my responsibility to sift through the bullshit and make certain that the right decisions are made. I didn't do either. No excuse really, I was just too exhausted to focus the way I'm supposed to. Now I'm feeling like I was unfair to judge Chief Bradford so quickly. Who knows what that poor guy is going through?

I'm looking at the shrinking list of names on my status board, thankful that the chief is swearing in a bunch of new rookie patrol officers at two o'clock this afternoon. Even though they'll be in training for a long time, it will be great to start beefing up our ranks.

The *swearing in* ceremony has evolved into a pretty big deal; families of the new hires are invited, and most of the employees turn out. A lot of our retirees show up, the department's honor guard marches in and posts flags, photos are taken, and there's a cake and coffee reception afterwards. It's also an opportunity for the chief to boast about his department, and a chance for the command staff to mingle with the new officers and their families. This will be my first such appearance as a captain.

By about 1 p.m. the place is buzzing. A dozen retirees have shown up, and through my open office door I see clerical personnel escorting family members into the assembly room. Meanwhile, the chief's secretary is pacing nervously in the hallway, checking her watch and glancing in at me. Finally she steps into my office.

"Do you know where Carl is?" she asks.

My face goes numb. "The chief isn't here?"

She shakes her head. "I've called him on his cell, left messages, but he's not picking up."

"He knew about the swearing in, right?"

She rolls her eyes. "Of course he knew; it's been on his calendar for weeks. Can you step in and do it, if he doesn't show up?"

"Me?" My voice is an octave or two higher than normal. I look at the clock, and now it's only twenty minutes until showtime. "I've never . . . I mean, what do I do? What am I supposed to say?"

The secretary runs back to the chief's office and returns with a script of the sworn oath. I look it over. This part I can do. *But what about all the other parts? The improvised talk about the police department's illustrious history, welcoming remarks to the families, inspirational comments to the new cops? What if I forget someone's name? What if I screw up and everybody laughs?*

"Keep trying Carl's phone!" I tell her.

I put on my tie, formal jacket and hat. My stomach is pulling me backwards as I make my way down the hall toward the assembly room. I peek in, as nonchalantly as a groom peeking into the church before his wedding. The place is jam-packed. There must be two hundred people in there, and it seems like they've all spotted me.

The secretary rushes out to meet me in the hall. "He's still not answering."

I close my eyes. "Shit!"

100

A minute later I'm standing before a hushed crowd, sweating like a llama in my full regalia. "Ladies and gentlemen; good afternoon, and welcome to the swearing in of the newest members of our police family."

I make an excuse for the chief's absence, which sounds reasonable enough, but I can see from faces of some employees that they're not buying it. My personal comments to the families and the cops come off okay—not great—but not bad for my first time. And the actual oath and swearing in goes off without a hitch. The other captains and I are asked to pose with the young cops while their families take photos, and I finally begin to breathe a little. Though my stomach is still way too jumpy for the cake.

My secretary signals me from the doorway, motioning that I have an urgent phone call. It's Cari, my oldest daughter, calling from her job in downtown Oakland.

"Someone broke into your truck, Dad." Her voice registers fear, but I don't think she's afraid that I'll be angry. It's the idea of someone pilfering through the truck and her having to report the crime to the police. And just knowing some dirty criminal had been inside there—it's freaking her out. Unfortunately, Cari's little car—the one she bought for six hundred dollars—stopped working a few days ago, so she's been driving my Tacoma.

I ask if anything was damaged, and if she's okay to drive home. The back window was broken out, but otherwise she's able to drive it. As far as Cari can tell, the only thing taken was a small amount of change from the glove box. I remember that I used to keep an old pair of handcuffs in the side pocket of the door. She checks for me and those are gone, too. No big deal, except that the guy who did it probably knows now that the truck belongs to a cop.

I don't see the chief for the rest of the day, and I never hear what happened to him, where he was, or why he missed the swearing in ceremony.

Lieutenant oral interviews are coming up, and for the first time I'll be sitting on the easy side of the table. Along with Deputy Chief Jenner, another captain and a civilian commander, I'll be talking with and assisting in the selection of my next watch commander. Although I already know the candidates—all of them sergeants—the orals provide an interesting perspective not always seen at work. The grueling process plays out over the next few weeks and we're finally nearing the end of the two solid days of interviews.

One of the candidates is in the middle of describing a recent staff study he prepared when the door swings open, knocking into the back of his chair. The room goes silent and the bewildered candidate turns in his seat. Chief Bradford squeezes his head and torso in.

"Oh, sorry." He looks past the applicant to the deputy chief and asks, "How much longer will you guys be?"

Jenner's face flushes red. "I'm not sure, we still have two more candidates to interview."

The chief glances nervously at his watch then wrinkles his nose. "No, I don't have time." He looks down at the candidate and motions with a hand. "Go ahead. I'll just stand back here while you finish."

The poor guy nervously brings his interview to an abrupt close, while the panel members exchange grimacing looks. As soon as the candidate leaves, Chief Bradford rushes to the board at the front of the room.

"Okay, so who do you like?" He picks up a marker from the tray.

Jenner's face is still red. "Carl, we haven't interviewed all of the candidates yet. In fact we haven't even had time to discuss our individual rankings."

Bradford swipes the air with the pen. "Fine, fine, then just tell me who you like so far."

"Carl . . ." Jenner starts to protest again, but is cut short by an intense glare from the chief.

"W-h-o looks good so far?"

In nervous bits and pieces, each of us offers up observations on those we've interviewed to this point. The chief scribbles names in random order on the board, and then starts ranking them by numbers while we all stare down at our notes. One candidate that I marked pretty high—my old academy roommate—isn't even on the chief's list.

"Timmy was higher in my ranking," I say cautiously.

Bradford whips his head around. "I don't like him," he growls. "He doesn't have enough confidence to make good decisions."

"Okay." I hadn't intended on debating it; I just felt obligated to at least mention another perspective.

But the chief is obviously steamed now. He points a red marker at my face. "You name one time, just one, when Timmy took it upon himself to act without someone telling him to."

"Well," I pause. The others on the panel glance sideways at me without looking up. "The night of the Sacramento Street shooting, when three cops were shot and the suspect was still firing at us from the third floor apartment balcony."

102

Bradford glares, but says nothing.

"Timmy was only a patrol officer at the time," I continue. "Yet without being told to, he unlocked the sergeant's car, took the rifle from the trunk, climbed to a rooftop across the courtyard and took the suspect out with one shot."

After a long silence Bradford says, "Yeah, okay." Then he uses his palm to smudge the name of one candidate off the list, replacing it with Timmy's.

"Okay, who else?"

We all look back and forth at each other in disbelief. Bradford is obviously agitated, and it's quickly apparent that he's only here to give us his own assessment. That's when we all kind of clam up.

The lack of interaction squeezes the chief's face even tighter, as if the tension has depleted the room of oxygen. He glares around the table, pointing at each panelist, baiting for an argument. Bradford's bearing is aggressive, almost bullying, and none of us want to challenge him. After a few minutes of a mostly one-sided rant, the chief shakes his head and huffs out. We each exhale, long and slow.

Another five or ten minutes pass and we hear a timid knock on the door. The next candidate, dressed in his pressed suit, tie and tie bar with the city seal on it, leans his head in. In a tentative voice he asks, "Are you guys still going to interview me?"

Relationships between the chief and his command staff seem more strained during the months that follow, especially between he and his deputy chief, Danny Jenner. Not that any of us are angry with Bradford, rather we just don't really know which way to go. It's like we're trying to manage the castle despite a maniacal king.

Then one night I get a call from the watch commander—the same guy who put one over on me with the on duty shooting. Only this time I'm going to make sure I'm awake. He tells me that a few of his midnight shift officers were called down to the Motel Six on Industry Road, and ended up arresting some combative crackhead.

I'm already reading between the lines, having been party to enough of these to know what happens: The guy fights, and the cops beat the living shit out of him. As far as I'm concerned, that *could* be a problem, but it probably isn't a huge problem—so long as our response was within reason. It's sort of what happens when you fight the cops. Anyway, the watch commander tells me that the suspect stopped breathing and now he's dead.

Now that *is* a huge problem.

On my way in, I skip calling the chief and phone Jenner instead. I tell him what's going on, figuring he can deal with Chief Bradford. Turns out that it doesn't matter; Bradford is out of the country—on vacation. Jenner leaves him a voicemail message anyway.

I also phone the investigations captain and request a call-out of the officer involved shooting investigators. Even though there was no shooting, common sense dictates that this incident should be investigated similarly. After all, it's a death that occurred while the suspect was in our custody. Jenner agrees, and that's how we proceed. The PBA attorney is involved in all of the officer interviews, and the district attorney is notified as well. We handle the entire investigation by the numbers—protecting the city and the officers who were involved in the arrest, as much as ensuring that the crackhead's rights weren't violated.

Chief Bradford must have finally listened to his voicemails, because he calls Jenner a few hours later in a state of outrage. I'm twenty feet away from Jenner, yet I can still hear the chief's voice yelling through Jenner's cell phone. "You're not going to treat these officers like suspects!" the chief screams.

To Jenner's credit, he keeps his cool. Stepping away from earshot of the officers at the scene, Jenner calmly explains that the protocol we're following is in the best interest of everyone. The chief disagrees but the deputy chief doesn't back down. End result is we're here and he isn't, and we handle it the way we feel is best.

By the time the chief returns, preliminary results of the autopsy are in. The suspect probably died of heart failure, or possibly from positional asphyxiation—a condition brought on by restricting the movement of someone high on stimulants. No injuries were found on the suspect's body and toxicology results confirm the drug usage. The city attorney's office is complimentary of the investigation's thoroughness, and since the dead guy is Caucasian, there is no community outrage. The press loses interest after the initial article.

Praise from city hall takes some of the gusto out of Bradford's anger, yet he's now drifted farther away from his deputy chief and closer to his confidant, Evan Casey. Up to this point, I've been seen as Switzerland—a neutral country. And why not? I just want to mind my business and do my job, which is plenty busy without all this drama. In private however, I'm increasingly annoyed at how much the chief panders to the PBA. His aversion to investigating the in-custody death is but one example. Bradford doesn't operate with the conviction of doing the right thing, but instead his decisions appear as if he's in a popularity contest.

The chief makes another such decision soon after the prisoner's death, when a complaint is filed against a veteran motorcycle officer—one who has already received dozens of citizens' complaints for rudeness and foul language. But since Bradford has never confronted him, the officer has never changed his behavior. Only this time it is a superior court judge who files the internal affairs complaint, claiming that after losing a traffic citation case in court, the motorcycle cop stormed off the witness stand and out of the courtroom, slamming the door on his way out. This latest outburst is more than I can stomach, and I recommend to the chief that we send a strong message: pull the officer off of his motorcycle and kick him out of the traffic unit. But Bradford only agrees to call the officer in to "have a talk with him."

A week later the chief sheepishly mentions that the cop had been so arrogant during their talk, that he leaned back in the chair and actually kicked his feet up to rest them on the chief's desk—dirty motorcycle boots and all. Yet Bradford, still afraid to ruffle the union's collective feathers, tells me, "He's too popular and he's got too much of a following. I just don't want to fight that battle, so I've decided not to discipline him for going off in the courtroom."

I would really like to offer the chief some advice: The cops don't necessarily need to like you; they just need to respect you.

My division has been greatly impacted by a lot of promotions in the past year, mainly because newly appointed sergeants and lieutenants return to patrol for their probationary period—which means I've got a lot of new people to keep my eyes on. In addition, a contract agreement with the city a few years ago now allows for sworn ranks to draw their pension as early as age fifty. That has led to an onslaught of retirements, the need for aggressive recruitment, and the infusion of a whole lot of new people at the officer level, as well. So, I've found myself looking at a very inexperienced patrol force where about 85% of my personnel are still on probation and have less than two years on the job.

One of the more seasoned people is a woman I call Scooter. She and I worked together on a midnight shift when we were rookie officers. I remember once when I was assigned to work inside on the desk—the duty nobody wants—and Scooter volunteered to do it for me. I went up to her after briefing to thank her for taking the desk.

Scooter said, "You're competing for a sergeant spot, right?"

I told her that I was.

"Well, just in case you do halfway decent in the rankings," she said with a grin, "I figure I might as well just start kissing your ass now."

We both laughed, but it was the beginning of a good friendship. As one of only a handful of black women in the department, I've seen her deal with her share of challenges. What I liked was that she always put the job and the community before her race or gender. And she did her job well.

So Scooter is now under consideration for one of the new lieutenant positions. If promoted, she would be the first African American woman in the history of our department to attain the rank. It's an attractive incentive for Chief Bradford, and he talks about it in our command staff meeting in terms I don't like. Things like, "We'll get a lot of mileage with the council for promoting her," and comments of that nature.

Evan Casey is not a fan of Scooters and tells the chief, "Even though there are better male candidates, you may just have to bite the bullet and promote her."

After holding my tongue awhile, I finally speak up. I tell Bradford that the council's political likes and dislikes shouldn't carry any weight in our decision, and that the promotions we make should be based on a candidate's abilities, their fit, and what they bring to the table.

"So what are you saying?" the chief asks. "You think we should go with someone else?"

"Not at all," I say. "I think she brings a unique perspective that I would love to have in my watch commander group. She's creative, her cops will follow her anywhere, and she's highly regarded in the community. I'm just saying, those are the reasons, the only reasons, we should promote her."

About a week after the promotion is announced, Scooter taps on my open office door. I push my paperwork away and lean back as she walks in and closes the door behind her. But instead of sitting down to talk like she usually does, Scooter walks to the far wall, glances up at some photographs I have hanging there, and stands with her back to me.

"Everything alright?" I ask.

When she turns back, I can see she has tears in her eyes. I've seen her in a lot of rough situations, but never like this. I'm trying to read her face, but I don't see these as tears of joy.

"What is it?"

106

Finally she sits in the chair on the other side of my desk, and I come around to take the seat next to her.

"I should have come to you earlier," she says. "I should have come to you when I first heard it. I'm ashamed that I've spent the past three days doubting your friendship."

My mouth is open, but all that comes out is a weak, "Why?"

Scooter's head drops. "Somebody told me that you were against my promotion."

My mind races in a dozen directions. Was there something I may have said to somebody that could have been misinterpreted?

"No way," I say. "You can ask anyone on the command staff."

"This person," she pauses. "The person who told me this *is* part of the command staff. He said . . . *he* talked the chief into it."

I feel weak and sick and angry at the same time. I'm trying to remember everyone who was in the command staff meeting when we discussed it. Then I stop suddenly and my eyes narrow. "Evan Casey."

Scooter raises her hands in front of me, as if to push my anger down. "I talked to my husband about it, told him what I heard, and I asked him what he thought."

I'm listening to her, but all I can see is myself strangling the life out of that snake, Casey.

"Anyway, my husband asked what the point would be for him to tell me that, even if it were true. 'What would he have to gain?'" Scooter drags a sleeve across her eyes. "That's when I realized, it's just the type of thing Casey does to make people feel that they owe him. I was wrong to even listen to that jerk."

I nod. My own eyes are watering up, and I don't understand why. Could be the anger, but more likely it's just frustration. There's just nothing I can do about Casey—he's a fellow captain and he's got the ear of the chief. I guess I should just be glad that Scooter saw through his bullshit.

We hug each other and Scooter leaves my office. It takes me a long time to cool down.

* * *

Manuel Guardado lives in a second floor apartment with his mother, her boyfriend, and a younger brother. It's Sunday and the six year old is excited about his friend's birthday party. Manuel rides his bicycle past his friend's apartment, which is in the same complex, and sees they're already starting to erect an inflatable jumping house.

107

At 4:30 p.m., after the birthday party, one of the neighbors sees Manuel in the parking lot, heading back toward his apartment. It's the last time anyone sees Manuel alive—except for Darvin Talina, a neighbor who lives in the unit downstairs from the Guardado family, on the other side of the stairway. He's watching the boy from his living room window.

The 28-year-old Talina is alone in the dark apartment, where he's been drinking and smoking cigarettes all day. His roommate is still at work and won't be home for hours.

Talina makes sure nobody is around to see, then opens his door and lures the boy inside. Even at his young age, Manuel senses a discomfort with Talina. But the boy's internal warning comes too late. As he tries to leave the apartment, he's yanked backwards onto the floor and dragged into the bedroom. Talina covers the boy's mouth so nobody will hear his screams. Not even his mother, who is less than thirty feet away, holding her toddler and glancing out the window for Manuel to return for dinner.

An hour has passed and it's getting dark. Mrs. Guardado walks through the complex looking for her son. Kids are everywhere, yet nobody seems to remember seeing Manuel since the birthday party. Through the corner of his front window blinds, Talina watches the boy's mother calling out for him. He looks at his hands—the hands that have just strangled the little boy to death. The terrifying reality of what he's done has a somewhat sobering effect, and Talina's blood stokes him with fear. He's got to move the dead boy out of the apartment before someone finds him there.

It's nearly dark outside, but it's a warm summer night and there are too many children playing in the parking lot. Besides, the kid's mother is still perched on the stairway just above his front door, nervously watching for her son. So while Talina passes the time, waiting for the complex to quiet down, he uses a clear plastic drop cloth and duct tape to wrap the boy's body like a mummy. He opens a bottle of vodka and sits behind the blinds, trying to drink some calm into his body while he watches and waits for the right moment.

A lone police car pulls into the lot, shining a spotlight on the apartment numbers as it moves slowly toward the back of the complex. Talina's head buzzes and his body is wracked with panic. A young cop walks up the stairway just outside his door, and Talina presses an ear to listen. Mrs. Guardado speaks in broken English, telling the officer about her missing boy, Manuel. They go inside the Guardado apartment and Talina darts back to the window.

108

After an excruciating hour, the policeman comes down the stairs and walks around the complex. Talina sees the reflection of the flashlight's beam in the parking lot, between the buildings, and in the gated area where the garbage dumpsters are kept. When the cop gets back into his car and starts writing up his report, Talina decides that this is the time to move the boy's body.

He slides open his bedroom window—which faces the rear of the apartment—and removes the screen from the frame. The area behind the building is tight, about a three-foot space before an ivy covered fence. But it's dark and as long as he's not seen, he can drag the wrapped body to the end of the building and load it into the trunk of his car.

Talina props the bundle against the windowsill, feet first, and climbs outside. With his bedroom lights off, it's difficult for Talina to see what he's doing. There's little give in the wrapped body because he's taped it so tightly in a prone position. As Talina angles it out the window, the dead boy's feet bump up against the fence and get tangled in the ivy. Talina has frightened himself by making too much noise, so he sets the body down, in the dark space beneath his window, and makes his way to the far end of the building, alone. Talina had hoped the cop would be gone by now, but he's still sitting in his car.

Knowing he can't leave the boy out in the open, Talina moves back along the length of the apartment building and shoves the body back through his bedroom window. He then climbs back in and rolls the bundled corpse under his bed, shoving it as far back as he can.

Rather than go out the front door, Talina climbs back out the window and goes around the side of the building to his car. He sits in the car awhile, waiting to see if the cop is going to leave. Talina then circles the lot, seeing that all the kids have gone inside now, and the complex is empty. All he'll need is a couple of minutes once that cop leaves. Then he can back his car into a space at the far end of the building, retrieve the body from under his bed, carry it out the window and along the back wall to the end of the building, and then load it into the trunk of his car. Talina drives slowly through the lot again, waiting for his opportunity, but now a second police car has come. They're inside the manager's office at the front of the complex.

LESSON 12

"Trust your instinct all the way to the
end, though you can render no reason."
~Ralph Waldo Emerson

I've rented *My Big Fat Greek Wedding*, and the main character's father just found out that his daughter was secretly dating a non-Greek guy. It's 9:40 p.m. when my phone rings and I hit the pause button on the VCR.

I hear a sigh and I recognize it as my buddy, Timmy, the night shift watch commander. Since we roomed together at the police academy as rookies, I've known that sigh. "Sorry to bother you, Phil. We have a missing six-year old boy down at the Cypress Woods Apartments."

I'm familiar with the complex. With lots of Section-8 housing, it has always been a haven for single mothers on welfare and their kids. Aside from the custodial disputes inherent in such families, it wouldn't be out of the realm of normalcy for a parent to lose track of a youngster there. "How long has he been missing?"

"Last seen around 4:30 p.m., at a kid's birthday party in the adjoining building. Nothing particularly suspicious about it, the boy is known to more or less have the run of the place."

Remembering a similar situation in another complex, where we eventually found the child asleep on the floor of a vacant apartment, I ask how well we searched the area.

"Pretty well," says Timmy, though his tone tells me what I already know—that no matter how well we search, a small child can crawl into the most unlikely of spaces.

"What about the parents?"

"Lives with his mother and her boyfriend," says Timmy. "Doesn't look like a custody issue, though. The real dad is out of the picture, living back in Mexico."

"What do you think?" I ask.

The line is quiet, and Timmy lets out another sigh. "We've done just about everything we can for now. Two cops are still on scene, but it's a busy night and we could sure use them back on the street."

I look at the clock; it's been five hours since he was last seen. "He's six years old?" I say to myself, still trying to decide.

Neither of us speaks for several seconds. "So, I'm seeing we have two options," I rub my forehead and lean into the phone. "We either pull the cops out and give it a few more hours to see if he shows up, or we ramp it up now and call in every resource we have."

Timmy sighs again. "Odds are the kid lost track of the time at a friend's house, and he'll probably come back on his own."

Now I sigh. Something bothers me about this, but I don't really know what it is. "I don't want to take that chance," I finally say to Timmy. "Let's go ahead and pull out the stops. SWAT team, CHP's helicopter, reserve officers, and see if we can get the county's search and rescue team. And as far as investigators, let's get whoever's on-call in here, too. We'll set up the command post in the manager's office at the front of the complex. In the meantime, make sure we search everything again—the laundry rooms, garbage dumpsters, utility rooms. And let's double check if there are any family members who may have grabbed him up without the mom's knowledge."

Fifteen minutes later I'm standing in the Cypress Woods parking lot, watching a simple lost kid call become a huge and costly logistical operation. I can't help but second-guess myself as I see vehicles from several other agencies arriving.

I'm talking to one of the SWAT sergeants, Mark Fowler—a good guy who has a son the same age as the missing boy. Although we've never used SWAT for this kind of thing, they're a capable unit with plenty of equipment, and we can deploy them at a moment's notice. They are exactly what we need right now, and I can tell by Fowler's intensity that he's in complete agreement with the decision to use his team for this.

Another guy who shows up is Rich Harris—a detective sergeant who oversees a group of investigators. Although he works for Evan Casey, he's not one of Casey's handpicked boys and he's been treated like shit since he was assigned there. In fact, I'm surprised he got tapped to come out tonight. Casey usually saves the face time for his favorites and keeps Harris buried under a pile of auto theft and fraud cases. I figure that Casey probably didn't want to bother *his* guys with something as petty as a missing kid.

"I'm glad you're out here," I tell Harris. "Surprised, but glad."

Harris smiles. "The only reason I'm here is because Casey and his minions are out of town. Otherwise, I'd be his last choice."

I brief him on what's going on and what we need from his inspectors. Harris suggests running a list of all registered sex offenders living in the area, which he assigns right away to one of his people.

I've also called Deputy Chief Jenner, just to let him know what's going on. He wants to make sure I have all the resources I need. The guy has got a knack for being supportive like that. Though he doesn't say it, I know he will show up as this thing progresses. And even then, he'll be a huge help rather than a hindrance.

Meanwhile, Timmy's patrol squad is finishing up with a recheck of the entire complex. SWAT coordinates with the county's search and rescue team, which includes bloodhounds that can track a scent.

CHP's helicopter is using their spotlight to search along San Antonio Creek, running north-south behind the Cypress Woods complex.

It's early morning now, still dark, and we've got nothing. No new witnesses, no word from any of the local hospitals, and no sightings reported to our dispatch or to any of the neighboring jurisdictions.

Suddenly a transmission comes across the radio. "One of the bloodhounds is alerting on something behind the missing boy's apartment building."

Rich Harris and I stand anxiously, our ears tuned to the radio. Deputy Chief Jenner nods as he joins us at the command post. We're all praying that the dog has tracked Manuel's scent to a play area or a hidden space where he will be found unharmed.

After a few moments of radio silence my cell phone rings. It's Sergeant Fowler, who's leading the search with the tracking dogs. His call is not a good sign, as I'm sure whatever he has to say to me is something he doesn't want broadcasted over the air.

"Go ahead," I say into the phone.

"The dogs hit on a shoe," says Fowler. "It's a blue tennis shoe—little kid's size—and it's in the ivy behind the building where he lives."

"Anything else?" I ask, just as a couple of news vans pull up on the main boulevard out front.

Fowler pauses. "The shoe is right outside a first-floor window. It's opened a crack and there's no screen on it, but nothing's visible inside—just an empty bedroom."

"Go ahead and check it out."

112

The searchers climb through the open window while we wait in the office on the other end of the complex. Less than a minute later my phone rings again.

"Go."

"It's him," says Fowler. "Dead. His body is wrapped in plastic under the bed."

"Okay. Keep everything off the radio from here on out. After you clear the rest of the apartment, keep one guy there inside and have the rest of the team assemble out in front. The inspectors will be there to take the scene in a minute."

Jenner and Harris hear enough to put the rest of it together. Harris is already pulling two of his investigators and a crime scene tech so he can brief them. Within seconds, they join us in the office, and it crosses my mind that neither of the inspectors are the department's premier homicide guys.

Harris is about to walk with them down to the apartment when he glances back at me. "Thought it would be nice to give someone else a chance for a change."

"Where are Casey's boys?" I ask.

"Where else? They're off somewhere with Casey."

Harris and the investigators head to the scene while I try to get my head into a different gear.

What am I going to do about the Guardado family?

By this time the day shift has come on duty. I call the incoming watch commander and tell him what we need. Within an hour I have a Family Services counselor and a patrol officer with me—both Spanish speakers. I explain that the Guardados barely speak English and haven't got much in the way of money or resources. Then I give them the unenviable job of breaking the news to the boy's mother and her boyfriend.

I tell them that once the death notification is accomplished, and the family has been given time for it to sink in, we'll offer to temporarily relocate them into a motel room down the street. I know we have a few hours, since it's likely we'll have to write a search warrant for the collection of evidence in the suspect's apartment. And I don't want to worsen the family's grief by subjecting them to the hours of impersonal bustling in and out of the neighboring unit, or worse, the cold inevitability of the deputy coroners removing the boy's body. I ask that both the counselor and the officer stay at the family's disposal, and do their best to see to all of their needs—food, transportation, notifications, whatever.

A resident of the suspect's apartment suddenly arrives, claiming that he has been at his job all night. He's cooperative and identifies his roommate as Darvin Talina, a heavy drinker who is currently out of work. He describes the car Talina drives, which one of the officers remembers having seen slowly circling the complex earlier in the evening—just prior to the arrival of all the extra police personnel. The car is gone now, and so is Talina.

I notice Danny Jenner sitting in his car with the door propped half open, talking on his cell. He doesn't look too happy. When he's done with the call I walk over to him.

"Everything alright?"

"Yeah." He raises his eyebrows and does a slight eye roll. "It's the chief; he's calling from Las Vegas . . . not too happy about how the investigation is being handled."

I drop my shoulders. "You gotta be kidding me. How does he even know how it's being handled?"

He shakes his head. "Evan Casey. They're together down there, and Casey's telling the chief that we're doing everything wrong."

"They're together? In Las Vegas?"

Jenner nods.

"And Casey's got all his homicide boys with him," I say.

"Except one," says Jenner. Then he motions with his chin toward an inspector who's been given an ancillary role.

"That's where they're getting their information." I say. "But now I'm really curious. What the hell is the chief doing in Vegas with Casey and his boys?"

Rich Harris walks up, hearing the end of the conversation. He smiles. "I don't know for certain what they're all up to, but I know what the scuttlebutt is in the bureau."

The deputy chief and I look at one another—not sure we even want to know. "What is it?" says Jenner.

"Rumor is they're down there doing a surveillance of the chief's wife, to see if she's cheating on him."

Harris and I meet in my office at noon to coordinate aspects of the investigation and decide on a strategy with the press. The roommate's alibi about being at work has checked out, and Talina has not shown up at any of his relatives' homes. We decide to put out a Western states wanted bulletin with Talina's photo and a description of his car.

Meanwhile, Jenner receives two more phone calls from the chief. "He and Casey are trying to run this thing from Vegas," Jenner tells me. "The chief is critical of everything we're doing—says we're screwing up the whole investigation."

I'm feeling the exact opposite. Between Jenner, Harris, and me this thing has gone about as smoothly as one could hope for. Every employee here, even the ones who picked up the slack on the street, have gone above and beyond. And with the exception of not yet finding and arresting the suspect, I think the investigation has been flawless—especially since so many resources responded to the scene so quickly. It's probably what prevented Talina from discarding the body. Had that happened, the case might have gone unsolved.

By the time I get home that night, I've been at it almost 24 hours straight. I have some leftover spaghetti with Italian sausage and zucchini, a piece of French bread and a glass of milk. This thing is so sad that I don't even want to tell Gale about it, and she doesn't ask. She's already seen it on the news.

At midnight, the phone rings next to my bed. It's Timmy, the night shift watch commander. "Thought you'd want to know . . . they just caught Talina in Nevada."

Apparently a gas station clerk—a young woman—had seen the bulletin on the news and remembered the license number. When Talina stopped for gas off Highway 95, the station clerk called the local police.

I sleep well after that call.

Two weeks later I arrive at work to find several news vans in the parking lot out front—usually not a good sign. Although this time a gas station clerk from Lovelock, Nevada is at our police department, along with a dozen local politicians and even more media people. The clerk is the sharp young woman who spotted Darvin Talina making his getaway after murdering Manuel Guardado.

Chief Bradford stands at the podium, atop a dais bathed in spotlights. He's dressed in his uniform, and wears a proud smile. Cameras roll and lights flash as the chief hands the clerk a two by four foot cardboard check—a reward from the area Crime Stoppers.

Bradford does his spiel, talking of the importance of community partnerships. "You are the eyes and ears of the police department. We couldn't have done it without you."

The deputy chief and I exchange glances, the obvious question discernable in his eyes: *We? Who the hell is we? You were following your wife around Las Vegas!*

Our command staff has been invited to attend a Drug Court graduation. One of the local superior court judges is heavily involved in the program, in fact she's become nationally recognized in treatment approaches to those arrested on charges of substance abuse—an intervention she calls *Therapeutic Jurisprudence.*

It's another opportunity for Chief Bradford to support a good cause and cultivate a powerful ally at the same time. Other local police chiefs are there, but Bradford never shows up. It's no real surprise to Jenner and me, and out of habit we try to cover for him as we so often do nowadays.

But the judge is irritated at the chief's absence, and takes it out on us. She recites a list of the program's benefits, and all but accuses our police department of encouraging a *devil-may-care* attitude.

Moments later the police chief from a neighboring city walks up wearing a sarcastic grin. "How's Chief Carl doing these days?"

"He's good," says Jenner. "He had a scheduling conflict, and--"

The other chief holds up a hand to cut him off. "Yeah, yeah, sure. He hasn't been attending the county chiefs meetings either. But hey, I was lucky enough to have actually had a Carl sighting about a month ago." He then bursts into hysterics. "A Carl sighting," he repeats, as if we hadn't gotten his clever joke the first time, then walks away laughing.

My only bright spot of the summer is sitting downstairs. Megan, my youngest daughter, has landed a summer clerical job at the department before she starts the fall semester at NYU. Seeing my little girl at her desk in the front office, a cup of tea next to her as she works her way through stacks of papers, does my heart good. We take our breaks together during the day, and she stops by my office to say hi whenever she's upstairs.

To Megan, mine is probably a piece of cake job—big office, a secretary, everybody calling me *sir*, and no stress. I don't bother letting her in on the bad parts, but it doesn't take long before she witnesses it for herself.

I'm in bed, enjoying a summer morning—one that followed my first full night's sleep without a call from work in quite awhile. No sooner does that thought cross my mind when the phone rings. I glance at the clock, realizing that Sunday's day shift has just begun their tour.

"Ryan Madsen was involved in a fatal crash on his way home from work last night," says the watch commander. "I just got the call from the Highway Patrol."

116

It takes me a second to process his words. Madsen is, was, a young rookie cop, one of my favorites. His image flashes in my blurred field of view, a call I backed him up on a year ago. I was driving home and heard Madsen ask for a supervisor, so I stopped by. Madsen's eyes registered shock as I pulled up in my unmarked sedan. Poor kid probably wished it were anyone other than the captain of his division. And worse, he was trying to find the proper section to cite a woman riding a horse in the middle of the street. I can see him clearly in my memory, standing there with the vehicle code in his hand and a sheepish look on his face—the big tan horse standing there beside him.

"What happened?" I ask the watch commander.

"They're still trying to figure it out. Sounds like someone dumped a stolen car in the middle of the freeway, and Ryan crashed into it. Took awhile for them to figure out who he was, because he was driving his mother-in-law's car and it wasn't registered to him."

"Has his family been told yet?"

"Uh-huh." the watch commander pauses. "And, there may be an issue with the crash."

Now it's me who says, "Uh-huh."

"Ryan had stopped off at a choir practice with his squad before heading home." Choir practice being a euphemism for drinks with the squad after work.

"Was he drunk?"

"CHP says no, but it looks like he had polished off a beer or two before he hit the road. Haven't been able to confirm anything with his squad yet—they're all home in bed."

"Wake up his lieutenant and sergeants, and let them know what happened. I'll be in shortly."

Again, I forego calling the chief and dial Danny Jenner's phone on my way in instead. When we meet at the station Jenner tells me that Chief Bradford is on vacation in Florida. Jenner's call went unanswered and he had to leave a voicemail message alerting Bradford to the death of one of his officers.

A lot of planning needs to be done in a short period of time, and the circumstances of Madsen's death plunge the deputy chief and I into a murky paradox of protocols, decorum and legal opinions. We both recognize the potential minefield where not everybody will agree. The PBA and the rank and file naturally want Madsen honored as if it were a line-of-duty death.

But the litigious interests of the city will want to separate, with clear distinction, Ryan's after work activities, including his drinking with his squad and his subsequent fatality, from beneath their umbrella of culpability. The more we try to make it a police thing, the more the city's attorneys shudder about a legal action.

And then, overlay all of that with Chief Bradford's propensity for Monday morning quarterbacking. But the deputy chief and I proceed with a strategy we can both live with, while we await the chief's inevitable frantic phone call from Florida.

In the end, we do what we believe is right. Madsen's funeral is planned as a hybrid of sorts, including the customary uniformed tributes, which seems to aptly show the deference that the young officer deserves. Services will be scaled back a bit in terms of involvement from other police agencies, and handled more as if it were a private family interment—our department being his extended family. Whether or not the city attorney's office has a problem with it is a lesser consideration—one that we figure Chief Bradford can deal with when he gets back.

Megan has checked in a few times, but we haven't been able to enjoy our breaks together. She can see the group of planners in my office preparing for the funeral, and through that and the long hours I've put in, she's able to witness the other side of the coin.

Services are held on Friday morning, and Megan attends along with the rest of the employees. As it turns out, the memorial is right on the mark in terms of appropriateness, and it reflects well on the police chief—as few know that he had little to do with the planning. For that reason, the deputy chief and I are spared an upbraiding upon Bradford's return from yet *another* vacation.

But reading between the lines, I get the feeling Jenner is becoming really irked that the chief is gone so often—especially since his decisions are the ones most criticized by the chief. And I would have to admit that I'm just as annoyed. It seems as if we've been pulling on the rope all the harder in order to support the chief through a tough time and a crumbling home life. Meanwhile, he's relaxing on some tropical beach every time we turn around.

In addition to all that's amiss within the command ranks, I'm also starting to think there might be something wrong with the department's email system. I can't seem to get a response from Bradford about anything I've sent him, even when he's here.

118

Megan and I pull up to the house that afternoon, having spent most of the day at Madsen's services. I'm physically spent and emotionally exhausted from the hectic week I've had.

"Look Dad, the backyard gate is open." Megan motions to the side of the house. "Do you think somebody broke in?"

"No," I say with certainty. "Mom probably forgot to close it."

"I don't think so, Dad. I can see my clothes basket lying on the ground outside."

I have always taken great pride in my daughters' confidence and discerning intelligence. But this is one time I hope that I'm right and Megan's wrong. After all, I'm the decorated police commander and she's a report reproduction clerk.

LESSON 13

*"Never grow a wishbone where your
backbone ought to be."*
~Clementine Paddleford

When we get inside the house I see that Megan is entirely correct—
we've been burglarized. I ask her not to touch anything, and then I
go through each room making sure whoever did it is gone. As I do
so, I can't help but notice the lack of an obvious entry point—no
broken or open windows and no forced doors. It doesn't take me
long to put it together: the burglar got in through the garage door.
Which means, he (and I'm assuming it's a male) had somehow
managed to get the garage door open.

I slap myself on the forehead as I walk out to my truck. Inside
the glove box—where I probably put a remote garage door opener
years ago, before I stopped parking my truck in the garage—there is
nothing but my registration papers.

The guy who broke into our house is the same guy who broke
into my truck in Oakland a few months ago—the guy who took my
old pair of handcuffs and knew I was a cop. As I put the pieces
together now, I'm figuring out that he also took the garage door
remote, along with an old vehicle registration form—which had my
address on it—and then he waited. He waited until he read in the
newspaper that a police officer had died, and he knew I'd be at the
funeral.

Son-of-a-bitch!

Gale and Cari get home to find a crime scene van and a police
car in front of the house. Megan has already printed out a matrix-
like form listing each of her missing music CDs, with their original
cost in one column and their *fair market value* in another. The cops
laugh, having never seen any victim so well organized. Apparently
the burglar wasn't interested in any of Cari's things, as her room is
relatively untouched.

The rest of the house had been ransacked, though. But oddly, the burglar has taken several other items that make absolutely no sense to me: a gallon jug of liquid dish soap, our vacuum cleaner, and my bedroom slippers. *What? Not my good L.L. Bean slippers!*

I'm almost embarrassed to tell the cop taking the report. Then Gale remembers that she left her cell phone charging on the dining room table, right next to where she had been working on our monthly bills. The phone is gone, along with some cash and checks.

I call the cell service provider and learn that the phone has been active within the past few hours. I give that information to the cop, who contacts the detective sergeant, and the case is assigned to an investigator right away—a benefit, I suppose, of living in the city in which you are a police officer. The downside, of course, is getting ripped off in the first place.

The inspectors track the cell calls to a home about a mile or so outside the city limits. They set up surveillance on the place and wait. An hour or so later, the guy and his girlfriend come driving up. The cops make their presence known, the guy takes off, and the chase is on. He screws himself by driving into a regional park, just below the residential neighborhood where they first spotted him.

He dumps the car and now he's making his escape by running through the bushes. Within minutes, a police helicopter is overhead and a police canine is in hot pursuit. Meanwhile, the girlfriend is detained with the car, and some of my stolen property is found inside it. The girlfriend gives up the fact that they had just moved into an apartment in Oakland together, and were stealing supplies and furnishings for their new place—which included, apparently, a pair of men's bedroom slippers.

The suspect is eventually dragged out of the bushes in handcuffs and is now walking with a pronounced limp. I'm not told the particulars, but I'm enjoying a fantasy where the guy was chewed up by the dog and then got his ass kicked on top of it. At any rate, he is sent back to prison—from whence he came.

The inspector writes a search warrant for the couple's Oakland apartment, and there they find Megan's CDs, our vacuum cleaner, and my treasured slippers.

The investigators all take turns wearing them at the scene, while posing for photographs. The pictures end up in multiple copies, which adorn the walls of the police building by the time I get to work the next day—playful humiliation it seems, being yet another perk of my job.

* * *

I'm on Bryant Street in San Francisco, taking Megan to one of her favorite restaurants before she heads off to college. My ringing cell phone interrupts our day together.

I answer the call to a squelchy voice, bordering on sobs. It's one of the sergeants, a woman who is a friend and a team leader on the hostage negotiations team. She launches into an emotional account of her recent effort to become a lieutenant.

"I went through the whole testing process," she tells me. "And I got word that I came out number two on the list."

I glance at my daughter and shrug, whisper, "Sorry."

"And then I just received a letter from the city's personnel department that there had been a mistake; a miscalculation of the numbers. I had actually scored the highest, and I'm number one on the promotability list."

"Congratulations," I say weakly, knowing that there's going to be more to this story.

"Thanks, Phil. But when I talked to the chief about it, he said that he's already promised the position to Mark—the guy he thought was number one, but turns out is actually number two."

More conversation takes place between us, mostly me asking questions and making sure I have the facts right before calling Chief Bradford. I end the call by telling her that I'll see what I can do.

My phone call to Bradford goes well in the sense that I'm able to reach him on the first try, though he's dug into his position. "But I've already congratulated Mark," the chief says. "The poor guy was so happy that he had tears in his eyes. What am I supposed to do?"

"Well, shouldn't we just be honest about it?" I ask. I know I'm not the chief, but in my opinion the guy needs to see this thing from a different perspective. "Mark is a big boy," I tell him. "He may not be happy about it, but he'll understand."

"I wish Human Resources hadn't screwed up the results," says Bradford. "This is all their fault, not Mark's. Why should he be the one to suffer?" The chief lets out a sigh. "What if I don't promote her? What if I just leave it as it is?"

I pause, squeeze my daughter's knee and smile. "I guess it depends on what kind of message you want to send, Chief. Mistakes happen; everyone knows that. But when they do I think we should try to fix them—you know, do what's right. Now if she had some performance problems, or if she wasn't ready and you weren't going to promote her anyway, regardless of her place on the list, then I'd say you need to tell her that and then leave things as they are."

I switch the phone to the other hand as I merge onto the freeway. "But if the only reason you're promoting Mark over her is because you mistakenly congratulated him and he got tears in his eyes? I'd say we're sending the wrong message."

When I get off the phone, Megan asks if that was some guy who works for me. "No," I tell her. "That was my boss."

Ultimately Bradford makes the right call. He apologizes to Mark and promotes the person who rightfully earned it.

* * *

One afternoon I'm working quietly in my office. The chief is not in, but I think he's around, somewhere—perhaps a meeting at city hall. I'm listening to the police radio at my desk when a call goes out that a man has taken a hostage in an industrial area office building. I listen for a few minutes to make sure it's a legitimate incident before making my way down to the lot and getting into my car.

Today happens to be a SWAT training day, and I hear them notify dispatch that they are already responding directly to the scene from the firearms range.

As I head for the back gate, Evan Casey sprints from the building, waving his arms and blocking my way. In a queer moment of weakness, I actually stop to pick up the son-of-a-bitch. He's acting like we're buddies as he jumps into the car, and all I can think of are his words: "I don't think you're a piece of shit or anything—I don't."

Whatever; off we go toward the scene of this unfolding incident.

Casey talks to me excitedly, like this is the first time he's been on a "real" critical incident call. And it probably is; the guy has lived his entire police career without getting his uniform dirty. In fact, I can't remember ever even seeing him in a uniform.

He's asking me stupid questions like, "What are *we* going to do? Shoot the guy?" I'm wishing he would just shut up so I can hear what's going on over the radio.

We've trained on this type of call for years—an "active shooter" who goes into a school, mall or office with the intent of taking as many lives as he can. By all accounts, this guy may be the real deal.

"Apparently the suspect's girlfriend is an employee there," says the dispatcher, adding more information to my planned response. "We have a co-worker on the phone who says the suspect has been abusive in the past, and the victim has a restraining order against him. The suspect is releasing everyone else from the building, and now he's threatening to kill the girlfriend. Apparently he's tying her up with tape."

Casey claps his hands like a little kid at a birthday party. He's clearly overjoyed that he will not have to make any decisions at this scene—only the usual cameo appearance with the chief at an after-action press conference.

I hear the spotters, already in position next to the snipers. "We have a male suspect duct taping a woman into a rolling chair. He's in the front portion of the building, behind a plate glass window. And he's armed with a handgun."

"Are the snipers in place?" I ask.

"Longmeyer is set up on the rooftop across the street," one of the sergeants says. "He's got an unobstructed view of the number one side."

My mind settles on the fact that Longmeyer has already been in a couple of shootings, and now I'm about to order him to take another life. Just then Longmeyer comes on the air.

"Suspect has placed tape over the victim's mouth, and he's rolled her, in the chair, right up to the window." Longmeyer waits a beat. "Black handgun. Right hand. He's holding it up to her temple."

Casey's cell phone rings and he answers it. His eyes are bugged out as he talks excitedly into the phone. I hear the chief's voice over the speaker, and he sounds worried—undoubtedly listening to the radio traffic from wherever he is, and having a fit. I know that his direction is going to be to hold off and do nothing. But the last thing I want to do is let this nutcase of a suspect blow away his girlfriend while we stand around waiting.

"Confirm, he's got the gun up to her head?" I ask over the radio.

"Longmeyer's response comes back clear as day. "Affirmative."

Casey, eyes still wide, holds his phone out to me.

"You've got a green light." I say. "Take the shot." Only then do I take the phone from Casey's hand. By the time the order to stand down leaves the chief's mouth, it's too late—Longmeyer drops the suspect with a shot to the chest.

"Yes, sir?" I answer.

The chief flusters on the other end of the line, most likely listening now to the radio traffic of a "suspect down."

"Nevermind," he says. "So they opened fire on the guy?"

"I'm just pulling up to the scene now," I tell him. "But yeah, I gave the order for *us* to take the suspect out."

"I wish you hadn't . . ." Bradford sounds resigned to the inevitable. "I guess there's nothing we can do about it at this point."

I hand the phone back to Casey.

If the chief was trying to stop this thing before the tipping point, he missed it by several minutes. As far as I'm concerned, the suspect was fair game the minute he forced his way into the building with a firearm. Either way, what's done is done.

After Casey disconnects, he tells me that the chief was concerned that we might accidentally hit the victim instead of the suspect.

I nod, less than surprised by the lack of confidence.

We spend the next couple of hours at the scene—me overseeing the SWAT team debrief, and Evan Casey organizing his group of investigators. It's an unusual occasion where we both work together in relative harmony. When a news van pulls up, I see Casey stop what he's doing and hustle over to the reporter. One can only imagine the General Patton picture he'll paint of himself, leading *his* troops into battle.

On the way back to the station, I suddenly notice that Casey's brown eyes are now green. They've literally changed color. When I bring it up, he gets a sheepish expression on his face. "They're contact lenses," he says, admitting that he bought greens ones, "mainly to wear during press interviews."

I'm trying not to laugh, and Casey abruptly changes the subject. "Bradford should have shown up at the scene," he says. "It's his job to support the cops and to get involved once in a while."

Casey is preaching to the choir, but I'm still surprised to hear the words come out of his mouth. Right away I wonder if it's a trick. This could be Evan's way of getting me to say something that will come back to haunt me.

"I get that he's only doing the chief job for the money," says Casey. "He's told me that before. But . . ."

I'm still reluctant to say anything critical of the chief, though I'm definitely keeping a mental note. "What do you think it is?" I ask.

"Carl hates this place, can't stand it here," Casey says. "He told me once that if he even has to drive within ten miles of this city, he counts it as a full day worked."

Damn! I wish I had a little voice recorder right now. This is the last thing I'd expect Casey to share with me, but a few minutes later I find out why. He's ready to check out.

"I'm filing my retirement papers," he says.

It comes as a surprise to me, but like always, Casey's got more up his sleeve.

"I've talked Carl into letting me stay on per-diem for another six months," he says, referring to what is essentially a double paycheck for any time worked after his official retirement date.

125

I'm not aware that it's ever been done before—certainly not at a captain level, where we have a legitimate promotional list from which to fill the position. But rather than take the bait that Casey has cast out in front of me, and point out the absurdity of the per-diem concept, I just smile.

A week later, Evan Casey is driving a brand new BMW. So confident about the extra sixty grand he'll be earning, thanks to the sweet deal he managed to cut with the chief, Casey's already spent the money on a new car. More arrogant still, he's going around the building boasting about it. "Carl wants me to stay on for another six months to help out," he tells anyone who will listen. "But it's cost him a new car."

Rumblings around the department already reflect a growing loss of respect for the chief due to his chronic absenteeism—in fact, the rank and file has started referring to him as "Bradford's Ghost." And on the few occasions when Bradford actually shows up at the building, people joke openly in the hallways about having made a "chief sighting." But this latest deal to keep Casey here, supposedly to train the new captain, has got everyone steamed up. The decision is seen as another sign of Bradford's weak grip on the department, abdicating what little influence he has left to Evan Casey—a guy that most employees regard as a conniving weasel.

I'm sitting in the chief's conference room on Monday afternoon. It's 2 p.m., time for our weekly command staff meeting to begin. Although "weekly" has been hit or miss during the past year, the chief has promised that we would all meet today. Also in the meeting are Deputy Chief Danny Jenner, Claire Melville—the civilian commander, and the new captain, Miguel Zavala. For whatever reason, neither Bradford nor Casey have shown up.

As we sit waiting Zavala asks, "Are the staff meetings always like this?"

The rest of us chuckle. "This is the first time we've even met this month," I tell him. "But it's looking like it might just be us four."

"Yeah, get used to it." Claire walks to the coffee pot and pours herself another cup. "The chief had me set up a mandatory meeting last week between him and all the civilian employees. About fifty people had come in—a lot of them on overtime, and a lot on their days off. Anyway, Carl didn't even show. Called at the last minute to cancel the meeting. And that was the second time we tried to set it up; he had cancelled the first one, too."

"Happens all the time lately." Jenner says to me, "Tell him about your supervisor meeting."

"You remember that," I say to Zavala. "Our meeting last month with all the sergeants and lieutenants? A lot of you guys had worked all night."

"Yeah, same thing," Zavala says. "We were all sitting there in the meeting room at city hall, and the chief was late." He turns back to Claire. "He kept us all waiting for about a half-hour, but at least he showed up for our meeting."

We all laugh again, but it's tinged with bitter disappointment.

"Why is it so hard for Carl to be on time?" asks Zavala.

Jenner shrugs. "People have heard him say that he doesn't like his job, and that he doesn't want to be in a leadership role."

"It's pretty obvious he doesn't want to be here," I say. He's never lived in the city, and he's openly made fun of us for living here. Carl calls this place a ghetto and an armpit."

"Oh, worse than that," says Claire. "Once I was telling him about the school my sons go to, and he said 'I'd never send my kids to school here, in fact, you guys are crazy to live in this shithole.'"

We wait in the conference room for another ten minutes or so, and the chief's secretary pops her head in. "Carl just called to say he's tied up at a meeting. He wants to know if you guys can reschedule for tomorrow at 10 a.m. instead."

"Yeah, whatever." I gather my folders.

Claire gets up with her coffee. "I've got work to do."

Jenner and Zavala check their schedules. They tell the secretary that they'll be here in the morning. I will be too, but I leave the room without answering her—too tired of the wasted time. We all feel the same way.

Bradford's reason for the meeting the next day is to tell us to make sure that all of the departments' employees use their allotted vacation leave time by the end of the calendar year. "It's city policy," he says, "They either use it before January, or they lose it."

He passes around an employee leave balance printout from the city's payroll department. As I glance over it to see who in my division is in danger of losing leave time, I realize that Chief Bradford's name is blacked out. Nobody mentions it, but Jenner notices it, too. He glances at the chief and then at me.

"Something isn't right," Jenner says to me after the meeting. "And I'm going to find out what it is." He goes into his office and shuts the door.

The chief's secretary scampers into the hallway behind me, as if she'd been chased from her desk. I nearly jump out of my skin. "Carl wants to see you!" she says.

I just left his meeting not ten seconds ago. But I swallow my frustration and follow her back into the chief's office. "You wanted to see me, Chief?"

He hands me a crudely printed flier. "The MA gave me this."

The chief's handwritten notes are scribbled across it, but the flier appears to be an open invitation to some sort of demonstration or rally at the next school district meeting. I know that the municipal administrator's wife is a public school principal, so any gripe she has takes a direct route through her husband's office, straight into the police department. But why this was handed to me, I don't really know. The school resource officers and district issues are run out of the investigations division, not patrol. And what with both Evan Casey and Miguel Zavala in there now, you'd think . . .

"They're worried about violence and damage to the city hall," says the chief. "I'm giving it to you because SWAT has crowd control capabilities, and they're under you."

"Sure," I say. "But what does city hall have to do with it? This flier seems to be about the school district board meeting."

Turns out that the district uses the city hall council chambers to hold their meetings. Chief Bradford goes on to say, "The school district doesn't want to see a bunch of commandos, either. I think sport coats and ties are more appropriate for your guys." I'm making notations on the paper as he speaks. Then he leans across his desk, his narrow eyes pinching the bridge of his nose as if he's suddenly angry. "This is a public meeting, you know. There *is* such a thing as free speech!"

"Uh, yeah, I think I've got it." Sometimes it's like the guy is hearing voices. Anyway, it's now my assignment to put together a crowd control plan to handle the demonstration—while striking a delicate balance between preventing property damage and violence, and pacifying the school board's fragile sensitivities.

And where will the chief be during all of this? He finishes the conversation by telling me that he will be gone on vacation all next week. *Shocker!*

The tactical plan comes together quickly, thanks in large part to Bobby Roselli and Don Nakamura—the guys running SWAT now. Though nobody is really happy about the sport coats and ties, I think they all understand the politics.

The superintendent comes out before the meeting to lay out *his* expectations for our conduct. In addition to a heavy, yet invisible, presence, he wants us to keep all of the protesters and troublemakers outside of the school district's meeting. I guess we're supposed to somehow know which ones are legitimate public audience members and which are supposed "activists" who have come to *legally* express opposing views.

Just then, before I can even object, out come two school board members. "We've decided to allow some of the demonstrators to speak," one of them says. "But not too many."

"Maybe the police can just let a few of them in," says the other guy. "And you can, you know, evaluate them beforehand. So we can keep the real trouble-makers outside."

"I know what you could do," says the superintendent to me. "You could set up some kind of lottery system for speakers."

I look at all three of them, swallowing down the nauseating taste of such utter stupidity. Then as they each start providing me even more direction, talking over one another, I hold up a hand to politely quiet them.

"Excuse me," I say. "Let's get a couple of things straight here, shall we? This is *your* meeting, not mine. You can allow whomever you want into it, and you can allow whomever you want to speak. That's your business. Our business is to keep everyone safe, and protect the property from being damaged. And that's what we plan to do. That's *all* we plan to do."

It turns out to be better for us, because as the school district people began to pick and choose who gets in and who speaks, other demonstrators become more and more pissed off. But for once, they're not angry with the police. In fact, one well-read gentleman wants to press charges against the entire school board for violating the Brown Act—a government code requiring open public meetings. Of course, we direct him to contact the attorney general.

But no violence occurs, no property damage is sustained and no arrests are made—a win-win as far as I'm concerned. The experience also reaffirms an important practice that I learned a long time ago in this job, about asserting myself: Sometimes educated people, community leaders, and elected officials don't have the slightest clue. In situations such as these, even the so-called pillars of society need to be corralled, directed and managed, no different than a bunch of hysterical witnesses at a crime scene.

After the event, I run into Russ Emory, a business owner whom I came to know during my stint as a community-policing lieutenant.

Not only is he a bigwig in the chamber of commerce, but he's also very involved in the school district. He talks about issues in the city as if we have the special bond of residency. He likes me, and likes the fact that I'm home grown.

Odell Graham comes over to join us—one of my favorites on the city council. I'm surprised that Councilman Graham not only knows that I live in town, but he even knows where.

Graham congratulates me on my promotion to captain—even though it's now been well over a year. They both ask me about the FBI National Academy, an intensive program in Quantico, Virginia offered to only a handful of police executives each year. Smiling back at them, I'm surprised again that they are familiar with the program.

"The chief has recommended Deputy Chief Jenner, myself and Captain Zavala to attend the course whenever they have the openings," I tell them. "In fact, Chief Bradford sent our application packets to FBI headquarters several months ago. We've just been waiting to hear back from them."

"I don't think the city has sent anybody back there in quite a while," says the councilman. "At least not since Carl's been chief of police."

Emory says nothing and I just shrug. As much as I'd love to attend the three-month program, I wouldn't want the councilman to say anything to the chief that would make it appear as if I went over his head. So I just smile, "I think there's a pretty long waiting list, and an agency our size can only send one commander per year. I'm sure we'll get word soon."

* * *

The girls are finishing up their homework and getting ready for bed when I get home. They remind me that we were supposed to get our Christmas tree tonight. Gale nods her concurrence, and I see all the boxes of decorations stacked in the corner of the family room. I feel like a chump for having forgotten about it. Not that I could have gotten out of the school district meeting anyway.

"Tomorrow night," I say with a clap of my hands. "For sure, we'll pick out a good tree when I get home tomorrow. I promise."

We hold a disciplinary review board in the afternoon, and as patrol captain, the majority of internal affairs investigations before us are out of my division. Besides my fellow captains, the others in attendance are the IA lieutenant and the PBA president. He's there to represent the interests of the accused officers.

130

Checking my watch, I'm encouraged that we're moving through the cases pretty quickly, which is good since tonight is Christmas tree night. With only three cases left, I check my watch again. It's 4:40 p.m.

I present the IA case of Mildred Moss vs. Officer Ken Heath. There is really no dispute of the facts; Officer Heath had been investigating a serious car accident on Mission Street, and had blocked off two traffic lanes. Dear Mildred, driving her 1977, mint condition Chrysler LeBaron, and her head securely up her ass, must have missed the half-dozen lit flares blocking the roadway. Heath waved his hands and screamed at the top of his lungs to get Mildred's attention, but to no avail. Finally, in an act of desperation and hot-tempered tantrum, the officer threw a flare at the side of her prized LeBaron. The good news is that the flare was not lit. The bad news is that Mildred's driver side window was open and the road flare sailed in, hitting the woman in the head. No injury—thankfully—just some minor dizziness. And yet she managed to drive herself straight to the police internal affairs office.

The cop, Heath, came to us eight years ago from the South Lake Tahoe police department, and has a clean record—no history of excessive force, or any other citizen complaints, for that matter. But while his frustration was understandable, even a tad humorous, we still have to do something to the poor guy. A letter of apology to Mrs. Moss, we decide, and twenty hours *on the beach* (suspension without pay).

The PBA president wants to weigh in on the proposed discipline before the final decision is made. "It's not all the officer's fault," he says. "Mrs. Ross endangered herself and others by driving into the scene. Kenny Heath was trying to prevent another accident."

"Mrs. Moss," I tell him. "Moss, not Ross."

"Yeah, whatever."

I look at him and can feel myself starting to chuckle. He and I are good friends, and I know he can argue passionately sometimes. Because of it, I love giving the guy a bad time. But it's all in fun.

He's hiding his own grin as he addresses the group. "Besides, they taught Ken to do that in Tahoe, where he came from."

I cock my head. "They taught him to hit a driver in the head with a road flare?"

Now everybody in the room is laughing, even the PBA president. "Well, no," he says. "But they taught the cops to get the attention of a driver who is running into an accident scene."

"Well, he got her attention alright." I close my file. "I'll let Kenny know that we're not mad at him. He just needs to understand that it could have been worse. A lot worse. For Mrs. Moss and for him. The twenty hour suspension stands."

The next complaint is out of Evan Casey's division. Not even a sworn officer, but a family counseling supervisor. He was called in from home to help with a death notification; a teenage boy had been killed in an accident. The large extended family of Hispanic descent had gathered at the house, awaiting news on their missing loved one. The unfortunate counselor had forgotten to turn off his cell phone, and it went off right in the middle of telling the family that their son was dead. To make matters worse, his ringtone was the Mexican Hat Dance. *Don't ask me why.*

The counselor felt terrible and had apologized immediately. We decided to handle that one with an advisement that he changes the ringtone to something more generic, and make sure he shuts off the phone during death notifications.

The last one is a pretty easy case of misconduct. The cop lied about using sick leave when he wasn't ill, and he was caught. Not the worst thing in the world, but enough that he's going to be facing some trouble. The IA lieutenant asks to postpone this one because the union's attorney is representing the officer, and they want more time to prepare.

After the board of review, Bobby Roselli, the new internal affairs lieutenant, catches me in the hallway. "Do you happen to know where these IA cases are?" He hands me a list of about two-dozen names.

I frown at the paper. "These are old cases that we've already recommended discipline on. You can't find them?"

"No. I conducted an audit of all the files when I transferred in," he says. "There are nearly thirty cases that I'm unable to locate."

"The board passed all of these on to the chief for a decision." I look at the list again. "No way he'd still have them. I'd check with the lieutenant you just replaced, first. He's probably just filed them in another location."

Bobby loiters there as if he's got something else. "You know, any one of these cases could get a little sticky for us. Especially if they ever go to arbitration."

I ask him what he means.

He stretches his neck, trying to find the words to express what's on his mind. "The chief has lost a lot of credibility with the street cops."

I frown. "Why's that?"

"They're beginning to ask questions about him being gone so often. It's like, who's running this place?"

I nod my concurrence. His nexus to the disciplinary hearing involving leave usage is not lost on me either.

"There's something else," he says. "You know the chief teaches a law enforcement ethics class out at the police academy, right? And he gets paid for it."

I've heard that Bradford teaches at the county's training facility, but I never knew any specifics. "It's a paid teaching gig?"

Bobby nods. "I know the guy who runs the academy. Anyway, the chief teaches during his work hours, and a lot of people are asking if he gets paid for both or if he's taking time off from here to teach there."

I think about Bobby's words on my way home, and I feel torn. The chief picked me to be his captain, and he trusts me with Patrol. His reputation, and even mine and the rest of the command staff, is suffering because of the lack of leadership. His leadership. Morale has been impacted, and even worse, the convoluted message of what is right and wrong is weakening the standards that we're insisting everyone measure up to. I'm not convinced that the chief is doing anything illegal, but it bothers me that others believe he is.

I can't just stand by and watch our police chief self-destruct. And I'm not about to let him take this place down with him; I'm thinking that I have to find a way to help—Bradford as well as the police department.

I make it home with ample time to eat dinner with my family and make a fun night of Christmas tree shopping. We're halfway through the meal—pork chops, mashed potatoes and zucchini—when my cell phone rings.

"Captain? We have a shooter barricaded inside a house near the Mall." The watch commander goes on to tell me that what began as a domestic dispute ended with a victim shot in the ass as he ran out of the house. Patrol units have secured the perimeter with the armed suspect still inside, and a full SWAT team call-out has been initiated.

I turn away from the dinner table, shielding the phone as if that will cleverly conceal the nature of the call. Even though I am no longer a team member, the patrol captain is expected to assume command of these types of situations. I mumble into the phone that I will be on my way to the scene, but as I turn back to the table my mind races: *Is there any way to take Gale and the girls to buy a tree, then I can make it to the shooting . . . if we take two cars . . .*

Gale picks up my dish and puts it in the sink. "Better get a move on," she says. Not in a mad or sarcastic way, just matter of fact. She's seen me take enough of these calls that my body language has already told her all she needs to know. "Don't worry about the tree, we can get it tomorrow. Just be careful."

"Yeah," Megan adds. "Be careful, Dad."

Cari has a sad look. "Poor Dad," she says.

Apparently they have also witnessed their share of these calls. It would have been easier on me if they were all angry. Now I feel like even more of a jerk. "Hopefully, I won't be gone long."

It's beginning to rain, so I put on an overcoat before heading out the door. The coat is long and gray, and it doesn't make me look the least bit captainly.

I pass by the police station on my way to the scene. The tactical equipment van and the armored truck sit idling in the back lot, and the logistics and equipment guys are loading them up with weapons, ammunition, tear gas, etc. But other than those two officers, and a few more SWAT guys who were already on duty and have responded to the shooting, the remaining members of the team are still driving in from their homes and have yet to arrive. Rather than wait at the station, I continue on to the scene.

The shortcut around the back of the crowded shopping mall drops me right into the neighborhood of single-level homes off Alabama Avenue. Orange cones, road flares and flashing lights guide me to the scene. An ambulance is just leaving as I pull up. Nobody recognizes my vehicle, because I'm in my personal truck rather than the city-issued sedan. And the overcoat doesn't help either.

"You look like a flasher," says an evidence tech as she passes me with her crime scene kit. Then, with a grin, she adds, "Sir."

The lieutenant on scene briefs me on the situation. The shooting victim will live; he staggered across the street and took refuge behind a tree. Responding units covered the front of the house while they evacuated the victim from the threat zone. It took a while to get him safely out of the line of fire and into the ambulance. Although we still believe the suspect is contained inside the house, we haven't made voice contact with him yet.

I figure it will take the tactical team about thirty minutes to get geared up and drive out here, and the hostage negotiators even longer. In the meantime, the uniformed cops on-scene have got the place pretty well covered. "Stay with it, and I'll be back in just a bit," I tell him.

It's raining pretty hard now, and I need to move fast without getting into an accident. I pull into a Christmas tree lot just off 95, and grab the first decent Douglas fir I find. My hand-held radio is tucked into my pants, and though my coat covers it, the squawking banter over the air gives me away to a few people in the tree lot. I pay the man, while covering the speaker with my hand, and then I zip back through the city and up into the hills where I live.

When Gale and the girls open the door, all they see is a huge evergreen with a sap-covered man buried beneath it. I set it down in the corner of the living room and head for the door. "Gotta go!"

I'm listening to the radio as I drive back to the scene. Bobby Roselli and Don Nakamura are there, which is a big relief. They are the team's commander and assistant commander, and I have ultimate confidence in both of them. I show up at the Alabama Avenue command post and then make my way up to get a look at the house. Bobby meets me there and we talk briefly. He plans to replace the beat cops on the inner perimeter with SWAT team members, and then give the negotiators time to talk the guy out.

Suddenly there's a commotion outside the perimeter, a horn honking, people yelling, cops diving out of the way, and a pair of headlights bearing down on me. The car isn't trying to get away, but instead it's heading straight for the front of the house. I have a momentary urge to pick up a road flare and beat the driver senseless with it, but I'm too busy avoiding the charging car. Instead, I pancake myself behind a tree in front of the target house.

The beat-up Chevy skids to a stop right next to me. I see the driver—an older man with a beard, and he's yelling something out of his open window. On instinct, I lunge toward him—yanking the door with one hand and grabbing the guy by the throat with the other.

As his body slowly follows his head out of the car and onto the wet street, I hear him cry out, "That's my brother in there!"

A couple of uniforms run over and quickly snatch him up, dragging him out of the line of fire and back towards one of the patrol cars. I'm suddenly feeling pretty good. *Like, yeah, I may be a captain, and I may work behind a desk, but the old man still has it.* That is, until I get a better look at the guy. He's got no legs. The poor son-of-a-bitch is stumbling along on prosthetics—one of which is now mangled and bent awkwardly backward, thanks to yours truly.

"Nice work, Captain," Nakamura says with a quick grin.

I run into Deputy Chief Jenner at the conclusion of the incident, and he compliments us on the handling of the situation. He's been at the scene for a while, and true to his style, never interfered.

"So, I found out a little more about that vacation leave printout," Jenner says. We walk to a dark area, away from the command post and the rest of the cops. "I spoke to Pam Ackers in the city payroll department."

We stop talking as a crime scene tech gathers more gear from her van and hustles past us toward the suspect house. I nod for the deputy chief to continue.

"Anyway, Pam says . . . ready for this? Carl has a surplus of 372 hours of vacation leave. That's more than nine weeks."

I stare into space. "Danny, he's never here. The guy has taken more vacation than any other employee in the department. How can he still have that much time on the books?"

"There's only one possible way." Jenner slowly shakes his head in disbelief. "He's been marking himself down as working."

LESSON 14

"You can get discouraged many times, but you are not a failure until you begin to blame somebody else and stop trying."
~John Burroughs

Hallelujah! Evan Casey is finally gone. The rank and file was so pissed off at the sweet deal the chief cut him that they went to their union. When Bradford caught wind of it, he was dumbstruck. In our next command staff meeting he asked us, "Don't people around here know how valuable Evan is? How many connections he has? How loyal he is to this department?"

Then we were dumbstruck. We all just stared back at the chief in silence—including Captain Zavala, the guy who is replacing the supposed irreplaceable Evan Casey. The question on all our minds was; if Casey is so damn valuable and so damn loyal, why doesn't he simply postpone his retirement for six months, rather than stay around to bamboozle sixty grand out of the city?

Bradford must have finally gotten a clue that he is the only member of Evan Casey's fan club, because he rescinded his generous *stay-on-for-six-months-and-collect-double-paychecks* offer. Casey was pissed off and suspicious of everybody, but left, nevertheless. He turned his back on efforts to honor him with a retirement luncheon, and skulked away from the organization to which he was supposedly so loyal, without ever providing any succession training for his replacement. He sped out of the back lot in his spiffy new car—later arranging a private luncheon with the four or five lackeys he'd cultivated in the investigations bureau. Like an impeached politician or a defrocked priest, he was too humiliated to show his face around anybody else. *Anyway, good riddance!*

The chief meanwhile, looks like he's lost his best friend. If he wasn't around much before, now, without his advisor and confidant, he shows up even less.

The frequency of the chief's command staff meetings is even more sporadic now, and not nearly often enough to keep pace with the critical decisions that need to be made. When we do hold meetings, the chief is tired and distracted, checking his watch and texting, and always rushing through the agenda as if he's got someplace more important to be.

And I've become extremely frustrated at his lack of accessibility, email and otherwise. I finally went to the department's IT manager to find out what happened to all the messages I've sent the chief.

Then, out of the blue one afternoon, Bradford shows up as chipper as a songbird. He even orders in food for a meeting—our first one in weeks—and then hands each of the commanders a tiny black box. I'm feeling like a Holocaust prisoner being offered a gift by Hermann Göering, yet, out of sheer curiosity, I go ahead and open it. The chief has purchased—albeit with the city's money—gold plated badges for each of us. The strangeness of the gesture is only exceeded by Bradford's sudden interest in police department issues. It's short lived however, and after several interruptions by his buzzing cell phone, the chief starts gathering up his bulging folder.

It appears to be an unceremonious conclusion to our first decent meeting in a while, so Deputy Chief Jenner hurriedly brings up the topic of our pending FBI National Academy applications.

"I haven't heard back from the guy yet," Bradford says.

It's been nearly two years since we turned in our applications, and even a rejection would seem like the logical thing. But the chief insists that we're on track to attend and he promises to give the local FBI representative a personal call to check on the status.

Bradford's flash-in-the-pan interest dissipates like the effects of an anti-depressant, and his mood and attendance quickly return to the pre-gold-badge days. We try to maintain some sense of regularity and structure among the commanders, but the chief postpones or cancels our weekly meetings so often now that it is nearly impossible. Deputy Chief Jenner is reprimanded when he convenes the group in Bradford's absence, so Jenner has resorted to arranging informal, ad hoc meetings in alternating offices. This way the chief's secretary won't know, and won't snitch us off to the chief.

Somehow, Bradford still manages to make brief appearances at his meetings with the MA and the city council, but otherwise he's let go of everything around the police department and we're operating almost completely on our own.

The IT guy finally gets back to me with a tracking list of my sent emails, shaking his head as he hands them to me.

I thumb back through each of them:

- July 9th – Municipal Administrator's report the chief asked me to prepare – deleted 63 days later without being opened.

- August 2nd – Advisement about private armed security at a church-owned apartment house in the city – read 27 days later.

- August 5th – Potential PBA issues Re: scheduling and overdue selection of internal affairs lieutenant – read 24 days later.

- August 12th – Update about IA investigation into accidental police canine bite of innocent citizen, subsequent involvement by city attorney's office – read 17 days later.

- September 26th – Copy of patrol meeting notes – deleted 105 days later without being opened.

- October 2nd – Copy of my response letter to inquiry by mayor's office – deleted 98 days later without being opened.

- October 2nd – Information about mandated racial profile training for employees – deleted 98 days later without being opened.

- October 14th – My request to schedule a 1-week vacation – deleted 96 days later without being opened.

- October 21st – Update on disciplinary demotion of employee – deleted 89 days later without being opened.

- November 1st – Update from committee working on department budget objectives – deleted 70 days later without being opened.

Disappointing, but at least I now know the fate of all my emails. Quite simply, many of them have never been read. And here I thought that I was diligently trying to forewarn the guy about important issues, without overburdening him with day-to-day minutia. And this printout represents only my emails. What about the rest of the department? How many other important questions or notifications has the chief ignored? Clearly, he doesn't care to know any of it.

The police department has barely gotten through Ryan Madsen's death when I'm awoken around midnight. Gale's shaking my shoulder and trying to hand me the phone. The night shift watch commander tells me that one of the patrol officers was in a serious car accident while responding to a call. The cop, who has only been on the street for a year, is now on his way to the trauma center.

I ask how bad it is, and the lieutenant tells me, "It's bad."

"What about the other driver?"

"Okay," he says. "Treated and released at the scene. We took him into custody for DUI."

Chief Bradford's phone goes to message when I call to advise him of the injured officer. As I'm nearing the hospital, I get a hold of the deputy chief who answers on the second ring. I tell him what I know about the crash and he says he'll meet me at the hospital.

I'm going over operational protocols in my mind as I'm driving—arranging for CHP to investigate the crash, handling line of duty deaths, calling in counselors for the family and the officer's squad members. There's a lot to it, as I've already learned. All the while, I keep thinking that Chief Bradford needs to know about this.

I'm only in the ER a few minutes when the injured patrolman's parents rush in—eyes swollen red and faces full of fear. I'm struck by the fact that they look so young—about the same age as me. Then I realize that the officer is only a kid, about the same age as my daughters. I can suddenly feel everything they feel.

I escort the parents into a quiet room off of the busy hallway and assure them that the medical staff is doing everything possible to take care of their son. I'm trying to appear calm and under control, and at the same time preparing myself to help them if their kid doesn't make it.

"Your son will be okay," the doctor says, pulling the blue latex gloves from his hands. "He's got a serious head injury and we'll have to observe him here for a few days, but he turned out to be in better condition than it appeared."

The parents grip each other as their legs nearly buckle in relief. The young patrol cop is a big guy, and although he had lost consciousness, he had sustained the impact of the crash without suffering any life threatening injuries. Jenner steps in as I'm thanking the doctor, just in time to hear the good news.

A minute later the deputy chief and I find a spot in the hall, away from the noise. "Were you able to get in touch with the chief?" I ask.

Jenner nods. "He's at another retreat in Bodega Bay. Says he didn't hear his phone."

We've struggled long enough to support the chief through his personal problems, and with little or no effort coming from him. In my mind, the chief's health and wellbeing are going to have to be secondary to those of the police department.

I share my thoughts with Deputy Chief Jenner and he admits to me that he's already started recording how often Bradford is gone. He says, "It's way easier to just count the times he's actually here."

In the first three months that Jenner tracks it, the chief shows up at the police department eight times. Only eight visits in 90 days. Most of these are only for an hour or so—just long enough to be seen by employees and his staff in the building.

One of his tricks, we soon learn, is to park his city car in his assigned parking stall, then pull an officer off the street to drive him to the airport. It not only allows him to save money on long-term airport parking, but having his car parked outside gives the appearance to the employees that he's here at the department— working hard and burning the midnight oil.

Danny Jenner openly holds our weekly command staff meetings in the chief's conference room now, and pretty much takes charge of the day-to-day operations—regardless of the consequences. Joining us in the meetings are Bobby Roselli, the internal affairs lieutenant, and Gary Donahue, the personnel and training lieutenant. We're in one such meeting when Claire—the civilian commander—says, "You know that conference the chief told us he attended last month in Sacramento? He was actually skiing in Idaho."

"How do you know that?" Jenner asks.

"I looked at his cell phone records," she says. "The calls he made while supposedly at the conference were long distance, and were transmitted from cellular towers in Sun Valley."

Jenner's head drops down and he presses his palms into his temples.

"That's not all," says Claire. "His payroll records show that he was working the whole time."

Zavala looks like he's wondering what he got himself into, and the two lieutenants want to crawl under the table. Jenner is still massaging his head, and I'm scribbling notes on my pad. I'm happily surprised that Jenner and I aren't the only ones who are keeping track of this stuff. And it makes sense that Claire and the others are as concerned about what the chief is up to as Jenner and I are. The employees view the commanders—inclusive of the chief—as a single unit. What Bradford does or doesn't do reflects on all of us.

Claire smirks while stirring her coffee. "So I asked the chief's secretary how his leave time is recorded. She said, 'Carl told me to mark him as working every day, unless he tells me different.'"

"Well that answers one question," I say. "Now we know how he ended the year with more vacation time on the books than any other employee in the building."

"This is absurd," says Zavala. "We've got to do something," But none of us are sure what that would be.

There's a kind of code that we are indoctrinated with from day one: Police look out for our own, and we take care of our own.

Going to somebody outside would not only appear disloyal, but it would actually *feel* disloyal.

"Do you think we can still support Carl?" asks Jenner. "Find a way to prop him up and get him to engage back into his job?"

To this point we have yet to confront the boss. Knowing how unpredictable and volatile he can be, a move like that may just make things worse than they are. Regardless, we decide to speak with the chief as a group. Our hope is that hearing the same message from all of us, Chief Bradford may be open to some constructive advice. Now we just have to find a time when the guy is actually here.

A big event is on the horizon and we're certain the chief is planning to attend. The annual volunteer recognition dinner is one of the biggest deals in the city, and the police department has more volunteers than the rest of the city departments combined. Many, such as the reserve police officers, risk their lives during their duty nights without any compensation whatsoever. Traditionally, this has been our one opportunity to honor them for their service.

I try to meet with the chief about some patrol issues one morning, on a week leading up to the dinner. His car has been in the lot since early this morning, but his office door has been closed all day. Bradford's secretary stops me at her desk in the outer office, shushing me with a finger to her lips. "Carl can't be disturbed," she whispers.

An hour later, Bradford emerges from his office with clothes as wrinkled as a bed sheet, and a puffy face with eyes full of sleep. His hair is matted like a schoolboy as he hustles out to his car and leaves. I don't see him again until the night of the volunteer dinner.

I've brought Gale to the event and Danny Jenner has brought his wife with him. Zavala and Claire are both at our table as well. We're all dressed up, and some of the volunteers have actually rented formalwear for the affair. We keep two spots open at our table for the chief, but he's not here yet.

After an hour of cocktails, the ceremony gets underway. The mayor introduces the city council, and then the municipal administrator and his department heads; the director of public works, city facilities manager, library director, city clerk, finance manager, city attorney, fire chief . . . and . . . and . . .

Danny Jenner stands up, his face red with embarrassment. An uncomfortable murmur snakes through the crowd as the mayor acknowledges him. I'm checking out some of the expressions, but the most obvious is on the face of the fire chief. He's clearly disgusted, whispers to a couple of his underling battalion chiefs.

Later, as the salad plates are being cleared, a side door bursts open and the chief catapults in. He's wearing a coat and dress shirt with no tie—a bit more casual than everyone else—and he has one hand oddly buried in the pocket of his sport coat.

Bradford beelines over to the mayor's table and greets her and council members, then the MA. He finally works his way around the room to the honored volunteers, all of who are seated and now being served their main courses. Bradford presses between two servers, reaching awkwardly across the table to shake hands with the head of the police reserves—never taking the one hand out of his pocket.

While rushing past our table, and the seats we've saved for him, the chief offers a charitable wave to his commanders. A minute later I excuse myself to use the restroom, which is outside the main hall and down the corridor. I'm exiting the restroom a minute later and I see the chief zip through the doors, heading out to the parking lot— his hand still glued into his coat pocket. Hanging back so he doesn't see me, I wait before peeking into the lot. Bradford is getting into a black sports car—one I've never seen. As the car's interior light flashes on, I see a redheaded woman who I know is not his wife. The interior goes dark again and the car speeds out of the lot. Had I timed him with a stopwatch, it would be a stretch to say he spent all of five minutes at the event.

A week later I run into a community service officer friend of Bradford's. They had just returned from lunch together, and the chief's dash back to his own car and out of the lot is the first time I've even glimpsed him since the volunteer dinner. I ask the friend if the chief hurt his hand recently.

"I don't know," he says. "But he's been on vacation the past few days, skiing in the mountains."

I check the payroll records and they are marked as if the chief had worked the entire week.

Chief Bradford actually attends the next staff meeting, and Jenner asks if we could all speak with him privately afterwards. Bradford's face registers skepticism right away. Lieutenants Roselli and Donahue swiftly pack up and leave, while Jenner, Zavala, Claire and I stick around to attempt our intervention.

As Jenner begins to talk, the muscles in Bradford's neck and face draw tighter with each word.

"We've all noticed how often you're gone from work," Jenner starts. "And we understand that things have been really difficult for you since losing your mom." Thankfully he leaves out any reference to Bradford's screwed up marriage.

The chief leans forward in his chair. "What are you saying?" His voice is loud and aggressive. "Are you trying to tell me that I'm not here enough? Huh? Is that what you're saying?"

Jenner pulls back. "Carl, I don't know if you realize how you're viewed by the employees. They've all noticed--"

Bradford cuts him off, his face red and eyes bulging. "If I need to be around here more often, that means you commanders aren't doing your jobs!" He shoves a pointed finger at Jenner's face, and then sweeps it around the room to the rest of us.

With that, the chief storms out of the room. The door closes with a thud and we all sit in shocked silence.

Claire gathers her folders. "Okay then, I think that went well."

At the end of summer, one of our former chiefs dies—a guy who started with the department in 1943 when only seven officers were on the force. Another huge and involved funeral is planned, and because of the old chief's history, it generates a great deal of media coverage.

The day of the services begins with the command staff escorting the former chief's family on a tour of the police building. Flags are at half-staff at all city facilities, dozens of streets are blocked off around the church, and several other agencies have gathered to help with the massive traffic control plan.

All of the local dignitaries attend the mid-day services—city department heads, local and state politicians, and chiefs of other agencies throughout California. Our police honor guard leads the procession at the church, along with the sheriff's bagpipe corp. But a glaring vacancy on the attendance roster leaves all the employees and other dignitaries whispering among one another. Our own police chief is a no-show . . . vacationing in Boston.

* * *

My wife's birthday and our wedding anniversary are both at the end of January, but it's always difficult to plan anything. The PBA usually holds an annual retirement dinner, and then there's the Martin Luther King Jr. holiday the same weekend. The latter generally involves community events in which we are all expected to participate.

Both Jenner and I spend the day at work on Monday, and then stick around to attend the evening MLK observances. Chief Bradford is gone all day, only coming in for a two-hour evening celebration—the one held at city hall, where the council and MA will be sure to see him. I later find out that the chief is compensated for working the entire day, and since it's a federal holiday he's paid at 1.5 times the normal rate.

It's Tuesday, not much more than a week later, and the chief simply doesn't call or show up at work. His secretary is frantically going from office to office asking the commanders if any of us know where he is. He doesn't attend a city council agenda review meeting at city hall, and then finally contacts his secretary in the afternoon to reschedule four meetings he had calendared for that day.

Two separate homicides occur in the city later that same evening. Our investigative resources are stretched between the two scenes, and then bad turns to worse. A supervising sergeant from the investigation bureau arrives drunk to manage one of the crime scenes. He's removed from duty and driven home, and other members of the command staff handle the situation in the chief's absence. We later learn that although the chief was a no-show all day, he is paid for working his full eight-hour shift on that occasion as well.

Chief Bradford is in and out for the next few months—mostly out. He's claiming more teaching stints at the county sheriff's academy, but still collecting full pay from the city on those days. It's late afternoon at the end of the week when the chief's car pulls into the lot. We hadn't expected to see him, especially on a Friday. He's only in the building for ten minutes—long enough to pick up his paycheck. Bradford tells his secretary that he's going to Las Vegas, but tells another employee that he's headed to Tennessee. In any case, he calls a uniformed officer in from the street to provide him with a ride to the airport.

That night a patrol officer is seriously injured when an escaping suspect rams the officer's patrol car. Several calls to the chief's phone go unanswered.

Things are getting to the level of absurd, and as a command group we're wondering how nobody at city hall has noticed what's going on. We discuss it in one of our meetings—another in which the chief does not show up.

Claire, who oversees many of the secretaries, fills us in on the scam as she's heard it from her subordinates. "If the municipal administrator calls for Carl when he's away skiing or wherever, his secretary is instructed to say that he's tied up in a meeting. Then the secretary calls Carl on his cell phone, and he calls the MA back from wherever he is—acting like he's here at the department, working. That's why nobody in city hall knows."

Our previous effort to talk with Bradford about his attendance was a disaster; he simply blamed everyone else, and then showed his distrust by lying even more about his whereabouts. And since our little attempted *intervention,* he's shown up even less often.

We discuss going to the municipal administrator, and someone suggests contacting a few of the city council members. We trust all of them, and are confident that they would be mortified if made aware of the situation here at the department. I'm sure that the municipal administrator in particular, would want to be told about Bradford's issues; after all, his job is to oversee the chief. But it still feels disloyal to go to any of them, even after our own failed effort to talk with the chief.

"What about the county sheriff?" I ask. "He's a law enforcement icon. Carl would have to listen to him."

In fact, the man was our police chief before being elected county sheriff, and he was the one who hired all of us. It seems like an idea that would accomplish both objectives: helping Bradford get some fatherly advice, and not airing our problems outside of the law enforcement family.

I call the sheriff's administrative headquarters in Oakland and the sheriff's secretary transfers me directly to him. I invite the sheriff to meet me for a cup of coffee, and tell him that I'd like to discuss a situation at the P.D.

"Sure," he says. "I'd be happy to meet with you. How about I come down to the police station, have a look around, and then we can walk across the street for coffee?"

This guy's no dummy. He knows something's up, and he wants to see if this is above or below board. My response tells him the answer. "Well, I'd rather we just keep this meeting between you and me for now."

146

The sheriff and I meet across the street, but even with the close proximity to our police building, I'm not too worried about Bradford seeing us; he hasn't been around for a couple of days.

We get our coffees and exchange a few pleasantries. The sheriff lives about two blocks from me, and I ask him about the little dog that I always see him walking. The sheriff laughs and tells me that his wife makes him take a baggie with him. "So," he says. "If you find any dogshit on your lawn, it isn't from my dog."

Once we get through the small talk, I present a brief summary of the problems going on within the department. Without going into a whole lot of detail, I describe how Carl's absences are affecting the entire agency.

The sheriff hangs his head. "You know how much I love that police department," he says. "I still have a big place in my heart for you guys, and I hate to hear this. It doesn't surprise me though; I've noticed Carl missing a lot of county chief's meetings. And you know that I hear things. I've heard he's lost touch."

At the conclusion of the talk the sheriff thanks me and shakes my hand. He says he'll get in contact with Bradford and invite him to lunch. "I'll talk to him about the things I've heard, without letting him know where I heard them. The bottom line is, he's got to come to work. He can't turn his back on his organization."

Only a few days pass before Bradford shows up at the police department just before the lunch hour. He dashes through the first floor, making sure he's seen around the building, then upstairs to let his secretary know that he'll be meeting with the sheriff. The chief doesn't check in with any of us, and then he's gone the rest of the day.

The next morning Chief Bradford is in early, passing me on the stairs with a face that looks like he's been holding his breath since the day before. I suspect it has something to do with his meeting with the sheriff, but I don't know for sure. Waiting in the stairwell a minute before racing back upstairs, I find the chief's conference room door closed—his shrill, demonic voice vibrating through it, echoing about the entire second floor.

LESSON 15

*"To know what is right and not do
it is the worst cowardice."*
~Confucius

"You went behind my back!" the chief bellows. "I know it was you!"

I hear a muted response, but the words are so softly spoken that I'm unable to make them all out. It sounds like Danny Jenner's mollifying denial, and my heart sinks.

"And who the hell does the sheriff think he is?" Bradford continues. "Telling me I have to spend more time at work. What the hell does he know? What did you say to him?"

Deputy Chief Jenner again refutes the allegation.

"Don't give me that shit," bristles the chief. "I know you're the one who did this!" Bradford is like a steam turbine with a blocked valve, about to blow sky high. He's going to take it out on someone—even if it's the wrong someone. I feel terrible for Jenner, being that I'm the one who actually did what he's being accused of. But the notion of going into the conference room now and throwing myself on the grenade, well, I see no value in it. What's done is done. So, I have to admit that I take the chicken's way out and head straight for my office. Justifying it, I remind myself that the plan to go to the sheriff was hatched by all of us, and fully endorsed by the deputy chief, too. Any one of us might have been suspect, and any one of us would have endured the chief's wrath.

Bradford leaves early, telling his secretary that he's got some sort of important meeting for the rest of the day. It's just as well, as it gives Jenner some time to decompress after the lambasting he took from the chief. We talk behind closed doors, and I can tell Jenner is still very upset, though not so much by the chief's anger—that was pretty much to be expected. What bothers him most is Bradford's incrimination of everyone else, taking no personal responsibility for any of it. He completely dismissed the sheriff's message.

"I'm not sure what options we have left," Jenner says. "The guy isn't listening to anyone."

That evening I have occasion to talk on the phone with my sister. Her husband, Tom, used to work with me before he retired on a knee injury. In fact, I fixed the two of them up on their first date many years back. The problem is that Tom is a good friend of Chief Bradford, so now I have to choose my words carefully whenever Tom or my sister asks me about work.

Just by coincidence, my sister tells me a funny story involving Bradford, which had just happened earlier in the day—the same day the chief had left work for an "important meeting."

"I was in my backyard this afternoon and noticed an airplane circling overhead," she says. "And when Tom came home, he told me that it was he and Carl Bradford."

Apparently Bradford had not attended any meeting, but instead spent the afternoon taking my brother-in-law up in his airplane. And of course, the chief was compensated for a full day worked while doing so.

A week later the chief shows up again, but goes into his office and stays in there with the door closed. I suspect he's sleeping, because his secretary shushes me again when I stop by to talk with him. The deputy chief thinks Bradford's arguing on the phone with his ex-wife, because he hears yelling and cursing when he refills his coffee in the adjoining conference room.

Bradford leaves around lunchtime, telling his secretary that he's teaching ethics at the police academy all afternoon. He misses a scheduled meeting with the assistant municipal administrator and the IT director, which is unlike the chief—seeing as he's usually on his game when city hall folks are involved. Jenner comes by my office to tell me that the missed meeting caused the municipal administrator to come sniffing around. It brings about a momentary hope that the gig might be up—that Bradford's boss might finally figure out the ruse and step in to help. But the chief's secretary covers for Bradford, and the MA goes on his way, none the wiser.

After that, the chief is gone the first part of the week for a three day California Chief's Conference in Oakland. He stops by the police department briefly around lunchtime on Wednesday, wearing Levis and a tee shirt. He tells his secretary that he's just now heading to the conference. That same night he fails to show up at an animal shelter volunteer's meeting that he had scheduled. Over twenty volunteers have driven in for the meeting, which had already been rescheduled twice to accommodate Bradford's calendar.

Curious, I telephone a friend who also attended the Oakland conference. I learn from him that Bradford was never seen at the conference on the first two days, and only showed up for lunch on the final day. He had not signed in or attended any of the conference workshops. But again, his payroll records reflect that he was compensated for working all three days.

An academy graduation is on the books the following week. It's a big one for us because six of our officers are in the graduating class. The event is held at the sheriff's training center, which may be a little awkward given the sheriff's recent talk with Bradford. That is, of course, if Bradford even shows up.

To all of our surprise, the boss arrives at the training center dressed in his Class-A uniform. Although I never actually witness any interaction between he and the sheriff, Bradford behaves as sheepishly as a teenage kid whose dad is keeping a close eye on him. That, I surmise, is the only reason the chief even came to the event.

I'm standing with Zavala, just behind Jenner and the chief, as the room goes silent. The three hundred or so in attendance quietly stand at attention as the honor guard marches in to post the colors. Suddenly, just as the sheriff steps up to the podium, Bradford's cell phone goes off. It's a goofy ringtone, set on high volume. We all cringe as Bradford fumbles the thing from his pocket and tries to mute it. The sheriff glares at him and then locks eyes with me. His expression says that he sees exactly what I've been talking about.

At the conclusion of the graduation, our command staff mingles among our graduates and their families. I happen to overhear an interesting conversation between the father of one of our new cops and Chief Bradford. They know one another already, because the kid's father is Bradford's dentist.

"Finally," says the cop's father. "I get to see the police chief in uniform. From what I hear from my son, you're the invisible man. You're never around."

Bradford's face turns red, and he attempts to treat the comment like a joke. He holds a finger to his lips and looks around, like it's our little secret. The kid's father intends no malice, but he has no idea that his comment hit the bull's eye. It must have struck a huge nerve in Bradford, because he flies out without a word to any of us. Zavala, Jenner and I talk about it on the way back, unable to imagine that even a new hire, a kid who hasn't spent a single day in the building yet, already knows that the police chief is MIA most of the time. So obvious is it that even the kid's father knows about it.

Bradford is gone Wednesday and Thursday of the following week. According to his secretary, the chief is attending the attorney general's symposium in Sacramento. We all have our doubts.

He's acting paranoid now, calling in to check on things when he never would have before. Whether the municipal administrator said something, or because of the sheriff's little chat with him, we have no idea. It could simply be that Bradford no longer trusts his deputy chief, and now he's nervous about leaving him in charge. Regardless of his discomfort, Bradford still stays gone for the two days.

On Friday he finally comes in, but he's wearing a stained tee shirt, work Levis and tennis shoes. Bradford runs upstairs to pick up his paycheck, and then meets with his community service officer buddy who drives him to lunch. When they return, the chief gets back into his own car and leaves.

"Do you know if the chief is going to be around later?" I ask the community service officer friend.

"I don't think so," he says. "Carl's in the middle of a construction project."

"Construction project," I say back. "I understood that he's been at a work-related symposium in Sacramento."

"I don't think so." The guy shakes his head. "Carl's on vacation this week. He's been remodeling his girlfriend's kitchen."

Jenner and I talk about this most recent revelation and decide to check into it further. Turns out that the chief's payroll record reflects that he's been working all week, with no time deducted for vacation. We check the chief's cell phone records and find that he made 48 calls while supposedly attending the symposium; and none of them were from Sacramento cell towers.

Two weeks later I'm surprised to see Bradford's car pulling into the parking lot at 9 a.m. But he's only there long enough to catch a ride to the airport. He's compensated for the full day, but his cell phone records show he's making calls from Portland, Oregon— where his sister happens to live.

Shortly after his return from Oregon, Chief Bradford shows up to work one day claiming to have an important meeting with the assistant municipal administrator. But from a second floor office window, the chief is seen walking to a secluded section of the courthouse parking lot next door. There, he meets with an on-duty employee and loads his suitcase into the employee's car. Having left his own car parked in his designated spot, the chief orders the employee drive him to the airport in secret. Bradford then flies off to another ski vacation out of state.

At city hall later in the day, I happen to run into the assistant municipal administrator. He says he did not have a scheduled meeting with the chief and hasn't seen him all day. Bradford calls his secretary later in the afternoon, still pretending to be in the city hall meeting. He speaks with some urgency, wanting Deputy Chief Jenner to immediately hand-carry an important internal affairs disciplinary document to the city attorney's office. Apparently it was something he had forgotten to do before leaving.

Jenner and the chief's secretary search for the document in the IA files, on the chief's desk, and all around his office, but are unable to locate it. Bradford is livid, yelling over the phone about the incompetence of his staff. When the chief returns from his ski trip, he finds the "important document" still inside his own briefcase, which he had left locked inside his car parked in the back lot.

During the search for the missing documents, Jenner got a close and personal vantage point of the chief's lack of organization. He wants to meet me for lunch somewhere outside the building, so that we can discuss the chief's declining behavior.

"I came across at least a dozen missing IA files," Jenner says. "They're all of the old cases that we've already made disciplinary recommendations on; the ones the PBA and the rest of us have been searching all over for. I found one case that's over three months old."

I shake my head in disbelief. By contract, we're supposed to get them back to the accused officers within thirty days. "The cops have been waiting all this time to hear back on the official dispositions."

"And the union's attorneys, too. It makes us all look like a bunch of idiots." The deputy chief pauses, glancing around the dark Chinese restaurant. "And I stumbled onto something else . . ."

I close my eyes, not even sure I can handle this.

"Our FBI applications."

I nearly spit out my pot sticker. "What the hell?"

"Yeah, all three of them." Jenner glances around again then leans in close. "They were crammed into a folder under Bradford's desk, with his kids' coloring books on top of them."

"He never sent them in . . ." I'm talking more to myself now, thinking back to all the bullshit the chief laid on us about still waiting to hear back from the FBI. "I can't believe that he looked you right in the eye and told you that he had sent them in."

"Yeah, said he'd personally give the guy a call." Jenner looks exhausted. "There's something seriously wrong with Bradford."

"There are a lot of things wrong with him." I say, leaning back in my chair. "And one of them is that he never went to the FBI academy, so he probably doesn't want us to go."

"Right," says Jenner. "Carl's frail ego would never let us get training that he hasn't had; he's probably afraid that we'd end up knowing more than him."

My dad's expression is beyond anger when I tell him what's been going on at work. I know it's difficult for him to listen to all of this and not be able to help.

We look over the breakfast menu and he sips his coffee as we wait for the server to take our orders. Dad is a guy who really enjoys his coffee in the morning. "Nothing like that first sip," he says.

I watch him as we sit there. He always loved his job as a teacher. I wonder how much misconduct he witnessed in his career, and how he managed to keep such a positive outlook on life. He's a funny guy, because money and power don't matter to him like they do most men. He values family and friends first and foremost.

"What about karma?" I ask him. "Don't you believe that people who cheat and hurt others will get what they deserve someday?"

His face takes a doubtful twist. "Not really. I've seen a lot of guys do some pretty rotten things." He takes another sip of coffee. "Some of them end up getting theirs, but others end up sliding through life—no price to pay at all."

I slump back. "That's not what I wanted to hear, Dad."

He laughs. "Yeah, I know. But it's kind of the way it is."

"So then, what's the point?" I ask. "What's the use of working hard and doing the right things in life?"

Dad smiles. "It has to be enough to know that you are an honorable person. If you can look at yourself in the mirror and know that you've done the right thing . . . then it won't matter whether or not the other guy gets his. Guys like you and me will still be pissed off and want to get even, but it won't matter as much."

The next day I'm in my office with the door closed, still trying to process everything that's going on around me. This situation, this dilemma, a boss who not only neglects his job but lies to cover it up. How could he not care about the employees and the citizens who put their trust in him? This is not what I expected when I was promoted to captain. Not in my worst nightmare. And I've had a gnawing premonition that my career and my life are heading for a crossroads—one so momentous that I can't even bear to look at it.

But the pity party for myself is cut short when an attorney for one of the cops we're firing has shown up for a scheduled meeting with me. It's not a formal appeal just yet, but I'm guessing the attorney wants to feel me out as to whether or not there's room to negotiate. We're meeting in the chief's conference room—which has a separate entrance. Not that it matters, because I don't expect Bradford to come in this close to the 4th of July holiday.

The attorney and I sit down, and I get each of us a cup of coffee. I'm trying to keep it cordial, and for the most part it is, except for his *I'm holding the ace card* attitude, which seems to be a characteristic of most lawyers I've ever known.

We talk casually about the case, and for some reason the guy keeps bringing the conversation back to Chief Bradford. Mostly he's asking questions about the chief's management style, his opinions about discipline, and his relationship with the PBA.

I'm wondering if he's gotten an earful about Bradford's lacking work ethic, or if he's just fishing around to cut a deal for the cop. In either case, I'm not about to speak for the chief or comment on his behalf. And I tell the attorney just that. "I'm meeting with you because you requested it," I say. "It's not part of the formal appeal process, but I thought I'd agree to it in the interest of open dialogue, with you and with the PBA."

"You seem like a no-nonsense type of guy." He grins and takes a sip of his coffee. "So let's clear the table and get down to it."

Even though that's much more my style, I suddenly feel as if he *is* holding the ace card. "I'm listening."

The attorney takes the Styrofoam cup all the way to his lips then lowers it. "Carl's reputation with the rank and file is that he doesn't give a shit about this police department or the people who work here."

I guess you could call that clearing the table. Without even hinting at a reaction, I just look straight into his eyes. I figure that this is his discourse, not mine. So I'm just listening.

When I don't jump to the chief's defense, he keeps going. "Your chief has been derelict in just about every aspect of his job, and everyone in this building knows it."

Finally I cut him off. "Is there a question for *me* in any of this?"

"Sure." The attorney pauses, turns his cup in a circle on the table. "My question is, how are *you* going to discipline this employee for being untruthful, when your own police chief is the most dishonest employee in the entire police department?"

154

His question is a fair one. Sadly, he's not telling me anything that I don't already know, or presenting me with an ethical paradox that I haven't already been wrestling with. But it also feels a little like extortion. The implication is that if I keep pushing the discipline against his client, he'll bring up the chief's misconduct in an appeal. And maybe that wouldn't be such a bad thing. But the bigger issue, his actual question, is a morality issue that feels more about my character than about Carl Bradford's.

How am *I* going to hold employees accountable when I haven't held my own boss accountable?

I realize that to actually do something about it would change everything for me—in my job and in my life. I know in my heart what I have to do, but I also know that once I do it, there will be no turning back. *This is that crossroads that I've been avoiding.*

I'm in my office, remembering back to when I was a street cop. We used to watch the captains with a lot of judgment—privately joking among ourselves that they were all spine-donors, and that castration was a requirement for promotion. I had promised myself that I would never follow that lineage of career climbers, that I would always do what's right, and fair, and just.

With the realization that the chief's conduct has bottomed out, I feel like he's now dragged his entire command staff down to an all-time low. And he's bringing the entire police department, and all its employees and their reputations, down with him. I'm wondering if things can get any worse than they already are, when there comes a knock at the frame of my open office door.

Claire Melville steps in holding a sheet of paper, and then closes the door behind her. "My secretary found this on the printer and didn't know what to do with it."

I hold out my hand and Claire walks it to my desk. She stands there while I read it, and then I glance up at her face. I can't tell if she wants to laugh, cry or find the closest bar. Finally she says, "Not only is the guy a liar, but he's a fucking pig."

We call over to Jenner's office, and when he answers I hear a rattling echo on the line that causes me to stop. I was going to have the deputy chief step across the hall to my office, but instead I'm only making small talk on the phone. Quickly throwing open my office door, I see the chief's secretary hastily hang up her desk phone. Instead of saying anything to Jenner, I motion for him to come over.

After hanging up my phone I ask Claire, "Is Bradford's secretary able to listen in on our calls?"

Claire nods as Jenner walks across the hall to my office. "She could if she wanted to," Claire says. "All of the secretaries have our lines on their desk phones; all any of them would have to do is pick up the receiver and listen."

I give the chief's secretary a nasty glare as I close my door with a bang.

"What's she up to now?" Jenner asks, referring to the secretary.

"I thought I caught her listening in," I say. "But that's not why we called you over. Take a look at this."

Jenner reads the printed sheet that the other secretary found. His ears turn red, and the rest of his face quickly follows them. When the color reaches his neck, Jenner sets the paper down. "Match-dot-com?"

"It's an online dating website," says Claire. "This is his personal profile."

I pick it up and see Bradford's name and photograph, then read aloud some of the highlights: "Professional single white male, very flexible schedule, can meet virtually anytime . . ."

Jenner turns to Claire. "Where did you get this?"

"My secretary found it sitting in the printer tray," she says. "Poor girl didn't know what to do with it. Apparently, Carl printed it out on the group printer instead of the private one in his office."

Jenner rolls his eyes. "Dumb ass couldn't even get that right."

"Enough," I say. "This is enough!"

The deputy chief agrees and so does Claire.

"Let's all meet after work," Jenner says. "Somewhere no one will recognize us, where we can figure out a game plan."

"The whole command staff?" asks Claire.

"Yeah, all of us." Jenner glances at the phone, then at me. "Can you set it up? And make sure Miguel can make it, and Bobby and Gary, too."

"I'll talk to them in person," I say. "And then we have to do something with the phones."

"I'll talk to Kay in IT," says Claire. "She's the one who dug up the chief's cell phone records for me. We can trust her."

It's late on Thursday afternoon, the day before July 4th. The chief is long gone, has been for a few days—though I suspect he'll pop in for a minute or so tomorrow, just so he can then claim the full day at holiday pay.

156

The command staff meets in the back of a small office in Alameda, where my father and brother run a financial advisors business. While everyone else is driving home to start the three-day holiday weekend, the six of us are nervously planning a move that will alter the course of Carl Bradford's professional career.

As a group, we immediately agree on four things:

1) We can no longer just stand by and allow the chief to continue in this reckless manner. We owe it to the other employees in the organization to hold the chief accountable, at whatever the cost.

2) Since the chief has rejected all of our attempts to get him back on the right course, the time has finally come to reach out to someone higher in the food chain for decisive help.

3) As a command staff, we all have to be in agreement. Any one of us can offer ideas, suggestions, or veto any part of the plan. In other words, for our purposes there is no rank in the group. And nobody is obligated to participate in this.

4) As much as possible, we need to contain this information among only our command group. Publicly criticizing the chief or instigating gossip around the building will only cause further damage to the department. We want whatever action we take to mend this place, not fracture it further.

The commanders are all fully committed, but we struggle over who to approach and how best to expose Bradford's misconduct. Some feel that individual city council members would be our best bet. Most of us have relationships with a couple of them, and trust that they will act in the best interest of everyone involved.

A couple of us, including me, feel that we owe it to the municipal administrator to go to him first. He's Bradford's boss, and we believe he'll handle things swiftly and fairly. The MA will also be able to protect Bradford's public reputation, and allow him an exit strategy that will cause the least disruption in the department.

We have all been victim to, and witnessed Bradford's instability and outrage, and for that reason we understand that this move will be a game changer. Under no condition will we be able to work for him or with him once we come forward.

The commanders ultimately agree to meet with Hector Lara, the municipal administrator. In the meantime, Danny Jenner and I will draft a memo to him from all of us, outlining the specific allegations of misconduct. Once this is compiled, we will all meet again to go over the memo, gather input, and then secure everyone's approval and signatures.

Danny and I spend the entire holiday weekend at my mother's house, which is just outside the city. It's quiet and she's gone for the weekend, and her kitchen table has plenty of room for all of our records, files, and notes.

By the following Monday we have a seven-page memorandum covering the last eighteen months with specific detail. Once it's all written down on paper, it looks even worse than it did before. Even a liberal accounting of the chief's payroll records show him gone 631 hours during the past six months—over 60% of the time. We found that he had credited himself for working 443 hours of that time. That attendance pattern, if played out over a year, would equate to 111 workdays missed, or over $60,000.00 in salary paid to the chief of police—the city's top law enforcement official.

We've cited five separate violations of departmental rules and regulations—all of them termination of employment offenses, had they been sustained against any other employee.

The commanders hold a few additional meetings at the Alameda office during the first two weeks in July. Small details and typos are corrected, and points that each member finds significant are moved around the document to make it flow better. The end result is a daunting final draft. It's sad in one respect and terrifying in another. Besides changing the course of Bradford's career, the gravity of our allegations suggests that it will change the course of our careers as well. Thankfully, we are all respected executive level managers in the city, with long and proven ethical careers behind us.

Our expectation is that those in city hall will act with the same sense of principled integrity that we have exhibited in bringing this to their attention. The municipal administrator will appreciate how we privately approached him with the facts of the situation, rather than go to the district attorney or the media. And the mayor and councilmembers will know that we did right by the city and its employees.

LESSON 16

*"If you go after the king, you better make sure
you kill him."*
~*Ernest F. Ribera*

"I'll have the Moons Over My Hammy," my dad says to the waitress, trying his best to make a ridiculous menu item sound serious.

I chuckle for the first time in a week. But my stomach is a mess, and even my plain wheat bagel just sits on my plate.

I feel fortunate to have my dad to talk to about all this stuff, though. He's the kind of guy who listens without judging, and offers ideas without making it sound like advice. I can see the disgust and anger in his eyes as I recite even more details about the chief's misconduct. When I tell Dad what we've decided to do about it, he stares down at his scrambled egg sandwich without saying anything.

After a few seconds he looks back up at me. "Well, you know what your grandfather used to say: 'If you go after the king, you better make sure you kill him.'"

Bobby Roselli and I are driving to Oakland later that morning to meet with an attorney, Mark Fereday. The union lawyer agreed to the informal meeting as a favor to Bobby, since they have enjoyed a good working relationship ever since Bobby was the PBA president. I've met Fereday before and he seems like a squared away guy. We want to have him take a look at the memorandum before we present it to the municipal administrator, on the slight chance that it contains anything that could get us into trouble. That is, besides the fact that we're accusing our boss, the chief of police, of gross misconduct.

Fereday shakes his head ruefully while reading it. When he gets to the signatures at the end, he sets down the memorandum and stares off. "You're giving this to the municipal administrator . . . Lara?"

We nod.

"You know that he'll have no choice but to get rid of Bradford," Fereday says. "But you're on solid ground. Lara might not like it, but you're definitely on solid ground."

"You're positive we're okay?" asks Bobby.

Fereday grins. "Do you want to know who I met with just prior to you guys? It was the president of your department's police union. The PBA board of directors and the rank and file are as fed up with your chief as you are. That's why they came to me."

It's a bonus that Bobby and I hadn't expected.

"Usually the union is at odds with the management," Fereday says. "But this is one of those times when everyone sees eye-to-eye. As far as Hector Lara goes, the only thing that you and the other commanders will have done is brought a problem to his attention. And that's what you're sworn to do, right?"

My head bobs up and down, but I know deep inside that it can't be as simple as that. We're somewhat relieved though, until the attorney asks if he can keep a copy of the memorandum. Bobby and I look at each other.

"I'll keep it locked up in my office," Fereday says. "Even though this meeting between us is unofficial, anything you show or tell me is still under attorney-client protections and privileges. It's not a bad idea for someone outside your group to have a copy, just in case."

I should ask, *just in case of what?* But I don't.

When we get back to the police department there is a second phone on my desk. Bobby has one too, as does Gary Donahue, Claire Melville, Miguel Zavala, and Danny Jenner. These new phones, thanks to the quick work of Kay Owens in IT, have unpublished numbers and cannot be monitored by any of the clerical staff—not the chief's secretary, and not the investigation division secretary, who has a long history of working closely under the retired Evan Casey.

Paranoid? Maybe, but I'm always about precautions now.

Our commanders group is of one mind when it comes to how and when to approach the MA. We want to do it early in the day, before the chief or anyone else at city hall will see us there.

With the stress of what we're doing beginning to wear on our group, we finally put our plan into action. It's a warm morning in the middle of July, yet for us it feels as grim and colorless as the coldest of winter days. Bradford has marked himself out of the city all day, so hopefully it will give us a little breathing room to work through the whole memo with the MA.

We know where Lara lives and we know his car, but we don't know his morning routine. And since we can't chance word getting back to Chief Bradford, we have Bobby and Gary take a post in an unmarked car and follow Lara from his house to city hall. That way they can radio ahead by way of a private police frequency, alerting us of his approach. The rest of us are already inside the parking garage at city hall, waiting in near the elevator next to Lara's parking space.

Gary Donahue advises us that the MA is turning into the garage now, and I feel the air leave my lungs. Zavala, Jenner and Claire Melville all have expressions on their faces that must mimic mine— as if we'd rather be anywhere but here. If any of us has second thoughts, it's too late. Hector Lara's sports car pulls into his space, and I immediately see his eyes fixed on us in his rearview mirror.

As he gets out with his briefcase, Bobby and Gary drive in and park nearby. They walk over to the elevator to meet us, getting there a few steps before Lara. His calculating mind is visibly ticking through the scenarios, but seeing the police command staff, sans Carl Bradford, must be a huge clue.

The deputy chief steps forward. "We'd like to talk with you, Mr. Lara. It's about some urgent issues at the police department, and we thought it important that you hear this from all of us."

Lara eyes us. "I'm assuming this has something to do with the chief, since he's not here with you."

"Can we talk in your office?" asks Jenner, sidestepping the comment. "We'd like to keep this meeting confidential."

I can see Lara's mind still processing as we ride silently to the top floor. He ushers us into a glass conference room, and has us wait while he steps into his office next door. It goes through my mind that he may already be telephoning Bradford or perhaps activating some kind of listening device or recorder in the conference room. It's just how I think.

When Lara returns to the room five minutes later, he's visibly calmer. His secretary has come in to the outer office, and Lara leans out to tell her he'll be in a meeting with the police commanders. That's another red flag for me, and I wonder if his secretary will immediately phone over to the PD and ask the chief's secretary what is going on.

Lara seems relaxed as he pours himself a cup of coffee and then sits at the end of the table. As Danny Jenner begins to explain why we are here, Lara interrupts to ask if we had followed him to work this morning.

"Yes," says Jenner. "We didn't want to be seen hanging around city hall, and we wanted to time our meeting with you as soon as you got in."

But as Jenner continues with the purpose of our meeting, Lara's irritation is apparent. He keeps returning to the topic of us following him. It seems clear that he finds it insulting that he was the subject of a police surveillance—which wasn't our intent, exactly.

Anyway, we finally get past that, for the time being. Jenner hands Lara the signed memorandum, but Lara only glances at the first couple of paragraphs and sets it down. The way the document is structured, he's seen enough to know the bottom line—we can no longer work with Chief Bradford due to a pattern of misconduct. But the way he tosses it aside gives me a bad feeling.

"I'd like to hear from each of you," he says. "How you became involved in this."

We glance back and forth between ourselves, wondering what that could possibly have to do with anything.

Lara leans forward, his eyes narrow and black. "Isn't it true that some of you have recently been promoted?"

It seems like an odd question, and right away I'm thinking that it sounds like a subtle threat. At this point Lara has been successful in derailing our presentation of the facts, and we're now playing by his rules. He further puts us on the defensive by asking, "In fact, weren't each one of you *given* your promotions by Chief Bradford?"

The top of my head is hot and tingling as I lean forward in my seat. "We weren't *given* anything by anybody, Mr. Lara, I believe that each one of us has earned our positions."

He bristles at my answer and waves it off with another of his questions. "Has anyone else seen this memorandum?"

"No," a couple of us say. I see no reason he needs to know that we consulted with an attorney, and judging from Bobby's silence, he feels the same. And Lara's next question makes me certain that he doesn't need to know.

"And there are no other copies?"

"We have a copy," Jenner says. "But we don't plan on letting anyone else see it."

"I'd like you to destroy all copies of this." Lara's seems to be immediately focused on containment of the information and control over the situation. And even though I understand that, I wonder why he isn't more interested in the facts and specifics of the chief's misconduct. Still hasn't looked at the document or asked us more about why we have come to speak with him.

After some more cat and mouse conversation, Lara asks us what we expect to come of this.

"We can't work for Carl anymore," says the deputy chief. "None of us can. He's lost our trust and respect, and he's unfit to lead the police department. And once he learns that we came to you, he'll be furious and vengeful. It will be impossible to even be in the same building with him."

"We're not trying to hurt the chief's reputation," Gary says. "In fact, however his departure is framed or made to appear publicly is fine with us. Nobody outside this room even has to know."

Lara ignores that. "Seems that the promotional domino effect of the chief's departure would potentially benefit several of you."

"This isn't self-serving," says Miguel. "If you read our memo, you'll see that we've tried to get Chief Bradford to become more engaged. We've made efforts to help him."

"I'm only suggesting that your timing is suspect," Lara says. "The entire command staff is in here, supposedly in full agreement about the chief. What would Evan Casey have said if he were still here?"

"Who cares?" I hear the words escape from my mouth. But the others are equally disgusted by the question.

"Evan would say whatever you wanted to hear," says Claire.

"Casey was a big part of the chief's undoing," Jenner says. "Everyone in the department distrusted Casey, yet they could see that *he* was the chief's sole advisor. Once Evan left, the chief nearly stopped coming to work altogether."

Lara asks a few more probing questions, as if trying to find a chink in the armor. His line of inquiry hints at Jenner and me having concocted a coup d'état, and the others of simply falling into line. They feel it in his questions, too—devaluing their roles in this. I see it as another thinly veiled effort to divide our group.

"I'll need some time to review this," says Lara, indicating we've run out of time with him. "I'll meet with you again at the same time tomorrow morning, and we'll talk some more."

Jenner has the presence of mind to add an important warning. "The chief is volatile and at times can be very aggressive," he says. "That is why we took so many precautions when coming to you. I hope you won't betray our confidences by telling him anything. At least not without warning us beforehand."

Lara gives us his word that he won't say anything to Bradford without first telling us that he plans to do so. The meeting is clearly over, and the MA exits the room without so much as a handshake.

We return to work, occasionally comparing notes and thoughts with one another about the meeting. We're trying to remain hopeful, even with the defensive overtones in the municipal administrator's questions. And though I'm sniffing the air for any scent of a double-cross, I detect nothing out of the ordinary. The chief's secretary is cordial, Evan Casey's former secretary is doing her own thing, and the chief doesn't come in at all. Pretty much a normal day.

Next morning is July 18th—my birthday. The atmosphere in the MA's conference room is completely different—I sense it in his tone, his mannerisms, and even in the way he walks into the room. He's like a dog that until now has been held back by some invisible leash. And in the time since we last met, Lara has had ample opportunity to digest the memo, gather his thoughts, maybe even talk with Bradford. Lara no longer has a leash restraining him.

He runs through a façade of questions about the memorandum, though never once asking anything specific about the chief's false work claims, unreported trips out of town or shoddy management. Never asks about his holiday pay, the cancelled meetings or the money he's collecting from teaching at the academy while simultaneously working for the city. Instead, Lara wants to know which one of us actually wrote the memorandum, and whether or not the others even read it.

"It seems like you were lying in wait," Lara says, directing this question to Jenner and me. "As if the two of you were keeping book on the chief."

No shit! Did you think we would come in here and accuse the chief of misconduct because he was mean to us and gave us dirty looks?

"This whole thing seems like something of a mutiny," Lara says. "I find this memorandum disloyal and perhaps even libelous. Carl could very well sue you for what you've written about him. In fact, I would strongly advise each of you to get legal representation."

With the table completely turned, we all sit numbly in our seats. Before any of us can gather enough composure to mount a counter argument, Lara continues with what is clearly a scripted exposition.

"From now on, I'll only be meeting with the deputy chief. The rest of you can leave now. You can get your information from him. In the meantime, you are prohibited from discussing this with anyone else, and none of you are allowed into the chief's office. That includes you, Deputy Chief Jenner."

"We had hoped you would be appreciative that we brought this information to you," says Bobby. "It's not like this is an easy thing for any of us."

"That's right," says Gary. "We're not used to doing this sort of thing."

"You should have thought about that before you put your names on that document. You're all way out of your league," says Lara with a demeaning smirk. "You may think you can play in the majors, but you're all just a bunch of minor league players."

We wait downstairs in the parking garage for a few minutes, muttering among ourselves about the things Lara had said. Now that we're away from the guy, each of us is able to come up with sharp, witty lines and great comebacks, but the passage of time has rendered them cold and irrelevant. So we drive back to the police department and wait for Jenner to return. When he does, we all meet downstairs in Bobby's IA office.

Jenner's face is red with rage when he walks in. Bobby nervously wipes his desk with a cloth, and Claire is too anxious to even sit down. Zavala and Donahue are slumped in plastic chairs, their chins pressed against their chests, and all I want to do is hit something.

"He's not getting rid of Carl," says Jenner. "At least not right away."

"What?" We all yell at the same time.

Jenner leans a shoulder into the wall for support. "This is Lara's exit strategy for the chief, which he insisted is '*non-negotiable.*' He's keeping Bradford here for six months, so that he can get his city retirement when he turns fifty. In the meantime, Lara will put him on some sort of medical leave for part of the time. But even when Bradford's gone, he'll still be in charge and we'll still have to consult him about all decisions."

"That won't work in a million years," I say. "Bradford will make your life miserable. He'll make all our lives miserable!"

"No," Jenner's color deepens. "Lara wants me to announce my retirement and file my papers immediately."

None of us can even believe this; it feels like a bad dream. We're arguing back and forth—*He can't do this! What about Whistle-blower protections? We need to get ourselves an attorney.*

The mention of an attorney sparks an idea in Bobby. While the rest of us lament about our dismal predicament, he phones Mark Fereday, the union lawyer we spoke with before submitting the memorandum. Bobby puts him on speakerphone, which hushes us.

Bobby provides an abridged account of our meetings with Lara, including his separate meeting with Jenner. Fereday groans when Bobby gets to the part about forcing Jenner to retire.

"He actually said that?" Fereday asks.

"Yeah," says Jenner. "Basically, Bradford stays and I go."

"Does he know you guys came to me?"

"No," says Bobby.

"So he doesn't know anyone else has seen the memo."

"No."

"Lara thinks he can contain this thing," Fereday says. "He's protecting himself."

"Protecting himself from what?" asks Zavala. "Our complaint is about the chief, not the MA."

The lawyer's chair squeaks in the background. "Lara handpicked Bradford for the chief's job. When he fucks up it looks like Lara was asleep at the wheel. He doesn't want the council to know how bad things got down there on his watch. So he's going to try to spin it."

"How's he going to do that?" asks Gary. "By getting rid of the deputy chief?"

"I don't know." The attorney is quiet for a second or two. "Maybe that's Lara's backup plan in case this thing comes out down the road. He can lay all the problems at the department off on the deputy chief—who'll be retired by then. Whatever the case, the little weasel has you guys over a barrel now. And he knows you'll do what's best for the department and keep to your word about staying quiet. That's why he wanted to know who else has seen the memo. He's going to bury this thing."

None of us say a word. We don't have the energy to even be angry right now.

"Well, just keep me posted." The lawyer disconnects and we all just stay in the office. Nobody talks for several minutes, and then, one by one, we leave.

In the afternoon, Danny Jenner comes into my office. He looks like he's about to burst with anger. "I just came from a department heads meeting at city hall. Carl and I were at the same table, and he just sat there staring down at the floor."

"Do you think he knows?"

Jenner nods. "I'm sure Lara told him. Carl's eyes were red and he had some papers rolled up in his back pocket. I think Lara gave him a copy of our memo."

I drop into my chair.

"I went up to the municipal administrator's office after the meeting and confronted him." Jenner takes a breath. "He admitted that he told Carl. Said he felt it was 'unfair' to keep him in the dark about this."

I shake my head. "Bradford is so loosely wound, it's a wonder he didn't pull out his gun and shoot you right in the middle of the conference room."

"Don't think that wasn't on my mind throughout the entire meeting. Carl looked like he was about to come unglued."

My desk phone rings after Jenner leaves. It's my secretary, letting me know that a call is holding for me. I answer the line to an East Indian woman's voice. "Hello Captain. It's me, Shanti Patel. Remember? I am owner of the sari shop on Mission."

"Yes Shanti, I remember." I roll my eyes. This isn't what I need right at this moment. "How are you?"

"Good, well actually not so good." She lowers her voice, as if she's in the store and doesn't want anyone to hear. "Our front window was smashed last night."

"Of the store?" I ask. "Sorry to hear that. Did you file a police report?"

"Yes, but I thought you would want to know about it."

Not sure why, but okay. "Yeah, I'll see if we can increase patrols of the building." It's a stock response, but what else can I say?

"Oh, thank you so much." I hear her groan and cover the phone, and now I'm not so sure that she's calling me from her shop. "I have a watery stomach," she says. "I'm home in bed today."

"Okay then, I hope you're feeling better soon."

"Thank you, Captain. I'll talk with you later."

I can't eat or sleep that night. My head spins with snippets and sound bytes from the meetings with Hector Lara. I have a real problem with people getting over on me, and when I have underestimated them or wrongly placed my faith and trust in them, it bothers me even more.

I lie in bed, staring up at my bedroom ceiling and thinking about my grandfather's words. I may have heard the saying before, though I'm not sure I ever understood it. But its meaning is clear to me now, even more so than when my dad said it to me at breakfast a few weeks ago. *When challenging an opponent of the police chief's magnitude, I should have struck a blow sufficient enough to permanently end the confrontation. Inflicting a lesser injury on the king causes the aggressor to stand in constant fear of revenge.*

167

It is only now that I realize the sad reality of the battle I've gotten myself into: Carl Bradford was *not* the king, but merely a pawn. The king I needed to kill sits in a corner office on the fourth floor of city hall.

I wake up on Saturday morning feeling more tired than when I went to bed the night before. I slog over to the couch and set my mug of coffee on the end table next to me. Opening my morning newspaper, I look down and literally have to blink the sight into my head.

It feels as if all the blood is running out of my body as I stare down at the headlines of the lead story. There on the front page, for the entire world to see, is an article outlining the command staff's allegations against their own chief of police. An unnamed source, according to the story, had faxed a copy of the seven-page memorandum to the newspaper's editor.

LESSON 17

*"We leave unmolested those who set the fire to the
house, and prosecute those who sound the alarm."*
~Sébastien-Roch Nicolas De Chamfort

"Everyone knew the commanders had to do something about the chief," says Scooter, one of my lieutenants, as she tosses the morning paper onto her desk. "But did you have to chop off the guy's balls and run them up a flagpole?"

My shoulders slump as I feel the last few drops of conviction trickle out of me. I fall into the chair across from her in the watch commander's office. "Assuming it was one of us who contacted the press," I say.

Scooter tilts her head, as if to ask *who else could have done it?*

It's a really good question, but one I have no answer for. How this happened and who was behind it is a complete mystery to me. After reading the article, I immediately suspected one of our group had panicked and went to the newspaper. Regardless, is this the way it goes? Everyone in the building gripes and moans for two years about the do-nothing, worthless chief? And then, when we finally take action, they complain that it was too harsh? *I'll hold your jacket while you go and fight.*

"You know what, Scooter?" I'm now feeling a little indignant. "The chief chopped off his own balls!"

I leave her office and walk out to my car. Gale and the girls are there, waiting for me. We'd been on our way to a family birthday barbecue at my dad's house, and I just needed to stop in to the department and take the pulse of the place. Big mistake.

My dad and brother have both seen the front page. They give me an extra tight hug when I see them, but say little about my work situation. "Try to relax and enjoy the day," my dad says. But I can tell that my vibrating cell phone isn't going to let me.

I answer to the nasally voice of a chubby city councilman. He starts with an accusatory tone, asking me why the command staff went to the press instead of the city council.

"I'm not sure who talked to the newspapers," is all I can say.

"My constituents are very upset with the six of you," he says. "They think you went after the chief so you could move up in rank."

I glance at my watch. The Sunday paper has only been out for a couple of hours. I'm not buying that the councilman was up early speaking with all of his "constituents" about the scandal down at the PD. More likely it was Hector Lara, frantically calling around to all the councilmembers—scrambling to put his spin on the whole thing.

But the conversation serves as my indicator to what the MA's spin will be: There is no substance to the allegations, and the police commanders only did it to benefit our own careers.

"Have you actually read the allegations?" I ask him.

"Well, no."

I tell the councilman, "Then before you jump to any conclusions, you and the rest of the council probably need to read the memo."

"The municipal administrator says it falls under the privacy of personnel records," says the councilman.

"Oh, is that so?"

"Yes, but I assure you that he's summarized it over the phone."

"Really." I pause, hoping even he will hear the impotence in his logic. "I thought that the municipal administrator worked for the city council, not the other way around."

The councilman has nothing more to add, and neither do I. We end the conversation, and I go back to *enjoying* my birthday party. It's shaping up to be the most memorable on record.

I receive several more calls during the remainder of the day—all from the other signatories of the now infamous memorandum. They each swear on their lives that it wasn't them who tattled to the press. The only other possibility is Mark Fereday, the attorney friend who wanted a copy of the memo for "*safekeeping.*"

By Monday morning every employee in the building has seen the headlines. Opinions are flying, lines are being drawn, and sides are being chosen—all of the destructive consequences we had hoped to avoid. Most, even the chief's closest friends, believe he had become ineffective and disengaged. But they feel sorry for the guy, and some see our actions as disloyal and contrary to the unwritten police code of protecting one another. None of them know the whole story, or even one tenth of the story, but I still can't fault them. They are his friends, and I actually see their loyalty as an admirable quality.

As much as the commanders and I would love to leak the memo's contents and tell our side of this thing, we don't. We have given our word to do what is best for the police department, not what is best for us. That means keeping quiet about exactly how bad the chief's conduct had become.

Sometime during the day Bobby phones Fereday. The attorney admits to faxing the memorandum to the local newspaper. He had taken it upon himself to do it, unbeknown to us, but explains it to Bobby over speakerphone with all of us in the room.

"Like I told you the other day," he says. "Hector Lara had you guys over a barrel. He was about to screw you, and there would have been nothing you could do about it. Your worthless chief would have stayed, and all of your lives would have been a living hell."

His logic makes sense, even though it goes against the way we had hoped to accomplish the chief's departure.

"You guys wouldn't have faxed it," the attorney continues. "Not without putting your jobs at risk. I did it without your knowledge or permission to insulate you and allow you to maintain deniability."

I take a deep breath and exhale it slowly, but it does nothing to lessen the heavy pressure on my chest. When the conversation with Fereday is concluded, we kick our thoughts around the small office.

"Nothing we can do about it now," Gary says. "What's done is done."

I tell them all, "Nobody will ever believe that we didn't leak the memo."

"This changes the whole game," says Claire.

"Has anybody seen Bradford?" Zavala asks.

Claire shakes her head. "And I don't think we will. I heard from one of the secretaries that he's been put on worker's comp leave."

"For what?" I ask.

She shrugs. "Apparently Lara just stormed into the human resources office at city hall this morning and ordered them to put Bradford off on 4850 leave. When the personnel director asked what job related injury or illness to list him under, he blew up at her. Lara said, 'I don't care what you list it as, just put him off duty!'"

A couple of the commanders hear from others on the city council, and it's pretty much across the board; Lara has painted us as a disloyal group of malcontents out to sabotage our good chief's reputation. Though Lara still hasn't shared the memorandum with any of the politicos, he's apparently convinced all of them that there's no wrongdoing on Bradford's part.

After some discussion among us, we decide to take Lara's advice and seek legal representation. Despite the friendship between Bobby and Mark Fereday, we all agree to look elsewhere. We settle on a well-known lawyer who has successfully represented higher-level police administrators in cases such as this, with political overtones.

When I get back upstairs to my office, the industrial shredder in the hallway is humming and crackling like a wood chipper. The chief's secretary has two wastepaper baskets full of papers and manila folders. She sears me with a pair of livid eyes, and then continues with her destructive mission.

Over the next two days the shredder grinds at high speed, as the secretary makes trip after trip into the chief's office to gather who knows what. Our guess is a couple of years' worth of neglected memos, emails, reports and studies, internal affairs investigations, personnel actions, and FBI national academy applications that had never been submitted. Along with other potential supporting evidence, I have no doubt that Bradford's revised dating profiles are also being turned into confetti.

The deputy chief and I believe that she is acting under the direction of Bradford or Hector Lara or both, but there is nothing we can do about it; we've been ordered to stay out of the chief's office. Meanwhile, the six of us continue to manage the nearly 400 police employees, their personnel problems, the city's neighborhood issues and the crime sprees that never seem to take a break—regardless of what's going on internally.

On Wednesday morning Claire comes into my office and takes a seat. "Bradford is announcing his retirement."

"What are you talking about?" I ask. "How do you know?"

"Just heard from his secretary. He's coming in today and he's called for a departmental meeting to announce it."

"You know he's going to be breathing fire. He'll blister the shit out of us in his little goodbye speech."

Claire nods. "That's why all six of us have to be in there. We've got nothing to hide or be ashamed of. We need to sit right there in the front row with our heads held high."

So that's exactly what we do. All six of us walk in together and take the row of seats directly in front of the podium. Carl Bradford looks like he's been punched out in a dark alley. His eyes are puffy and red, and his pasty skin hangs like melted wax on his cheekbones, yet he stands before a packed assembly room trying to exude confidence. I realize how difficult this must be for him. I even feel a little badly, that is until he starts thrashing us.

172

Like the mother of a bullied son, Hector Lara stands against the wall, glaring at us with his spiteful expression. He watches from the side of the room as the chief reads the tightly scripted statement.

Bradford lays his sudden departure off to a previously unknown and undisclosed mystery medical issue, yet he never actually says he's retiring. The clever wording confirms that he'll remain on the payroll as chief.

He says his goodbyes to the people who were his friends. He goes on to tell the department that he regrets trusting those who were "disloyal" and so forth, never even glancing down at his command staff, except when he makes that comment.

There are a few tears and hugs from some of the employees, but of course, none for us. The six Judases file past the sneering municipal administrator on our way out of the room, our heads held high—if anyone even cares to notice.

The next morning, a follow-up article appears on the front page: *Police chief to step down—announces retirement as top officers accuse him of absenteeism, incompetence.* The story, accompanied by a picture of the beleaguered chief, actually names each of us— referring to us as "the police chief's top commanders who lambasted him as an absentee boss and demanded his firing."

In addition to a few more specifics from the memorandum, the article includes comments from the mayor and other council members—all of them heaping praise on the chief while admitting that they still haven't even seen the memo. And though they all claim to stand behind the man, they also seem to distance themselves from the possible problems at the department by saying that they were "not aware of conflicts." Their statements tell me that they are covering themselves, just in case any of our accusations turn out to be legitimate. But in reality, they've all been as clueless as everyone else at city hall. I'm convinced that people only saw what they wanted to see.

The article's tone has me wondering if Lara has manipulated the newspaper editor, in addition to everyone else in the city. Some of the wording seems awfully close to the rhetoric that Lara has been spreading. I'm not sure if this thing has me so off balance that I'm paranoid, or if I'm actually seeing the guy for who he is.

Any hopes that the primetime scandal will die down and go away soon are snuffed when I wake up on Friday. Another front-page article—the second in as many days—features the same tired photo of the chief, beneath the headline: Plan for chief draws scrutiny from cop union.

This one appears to have been initiated by Mark Fereday, the attorney for the PBA. Thankfully, he admits to leaking the memo without our consent, saying he did it in our best interest. And he also questions Lara's plan to keep Bradford on the city payroll for a year—asking, "Had these same sort of allegations been made against a rank-and-file officer, would the police department management and city management be trying to find a way to allow that officer to remain on the payroll for another year in order to maximize retirement benefits?"

Lara's quote in response? "It's a function of the information presented and the nature of the representations made. We will look at some things if appropriate."

As many times as I read this news story I still can't make heads or tails of Lara's bizarre statement. It's like he had pulled a random collection of words from the dictionary and scattered them onto the paper. They mean absolutely nothing, yet his brain-dead council swallows them whole. One councilman, the guy with the pickled nose and bad breath, agrees with the MA. "This is not a council matter at all. These are nothing but allegations."

The more I read, the more I'm convinced we did the right thing by hiring ourselves an attorney. The six of us have arranged to meet the guy outside the city at the end of the week. So as the toxic brew of lies, deceit and politics boils over at home, the commanders drive to San Francisco for our first of many consultations with our new lawyer, Joel Ingerman.

By now he's read the memorandum, and he's seen all of the newspaper reports. Ingerman has also heard a rumor, from what source he doesn't say, that one of our group of six has "reached out" to Chief Bradford and expressed regret for their role in the incident. We glance around the table at one another, and our eyes settle on Claire—the only woman in the group, which I suppose in our minds makes her the most vulnerable to empathy and compassion.

She immediately glares back at us. "It wasn't me, you assholes. I never contacted him!"

Right away we feel badly for doubting her. Maybe that was the intent of the rumor in the first place—to generate suspicion among the group and try to divide us. After all, we've already seen Lara try that tactic.

In any case, Ingerman feels that we were diligent in going to the municipal administrator with our concerns, and that we are sheltered by the federal whistleblower protection act, from any reprisals from Hector Lara and the city.

First order of business, says the attorney, is to get that memo in front of the mayor and city councilmembers. But as hard as he works to make that happen, Hector Lara is working even harder to prevent it. He's even got the city attorney backing his play—convincing the council that it wouldn't be proper to share with them the specifics of a "personnel matter."

A flurry of additional newspaper articles and published letters to the editor ensue. It quickly becomes apparent that it's not only the police department that objects to the chief's continued payout, but many in the community find the city's handling of it reprehensible. Focus settles mostly on the mayor—who comes out as Lara's biggest supporter—and also on the other councilmembers, none of whom have publicly criticized Lara for not sharing the memo.

Somewhere in the midst of all this, real work still needs to get done. That painful reminder comes in the form of a phone call one afternoon that Marilyn Quintel, one of our new police officers, just sustained a serious injury at the police academy. I learn that Marilyn suffered a cerebral hemorrhage while lifting weights.

She's airlifted to a hospital across the bay where they prep her for emergency surgery. I'm driving over the bridge in rush-hour traffic, feeling badly that I've let this business with the chief and MA distract me so much. I pray that Marilyn makes it through this.

Several hours later I'm still in the hospital waiting room, sitting with the officer's husband and parents. I want them to know that this is considered an on-duty injury and that the medical bills will all be covered by the city. But to bring up such a thing as money, seems clumsy and insensitive. So instead, I just sit quietly with them and try to be encouraging and comforting.

Marilyn survives the surgery, but the doctors say that her recovery will likely be a long one. I hug the family and give them my cell number. "If you need anything at all, please call—day or night."

I get back home late in the evening, but for the first time in a while my mind isn't on *the scandal*. I call the hospital to check on Marilyn before turning in for the night. The news that she's doing well is a huge relief.

A phone message from Russ Emory awaits me when I get in on Monday morning. The business owner and bigwig in the chamber of commerce seemed like an ally in the past, but I know he's close with Councilman Odell Graham. I wonder if my recent involvement in the takedown of the chief might have changed his opinion of me.

Not knowing what to expect, I use the private phone to call Emory back. I'm guarded at first, especially when he begins the conversation by telling me how long he's known the chief.

"Carl and I went to the same high school," he says. "I've known the guy forever. But let's face it, anybody who's been paying attention can see that he's been checked out for the past few years."

I'm a bit relieved to hear his assessment, if it's an honest one, but still unconvinced. Subsequently, I say very little.

"You probably can't talk much over the phone," he says. "But I'd like to meet with you off-site. Maybe with both you and Danny Jenner, if you think he'd be open to it."

"What did you have in mind?" I ask.

"I have a few things to discuss with you . . . things you might find helpful. How about tonight at my house? Maybe around 9 p.m., if that works."

I'm not sure what Jenner is doing, but I accept the invitation on his behalf. "We'll both be there at nine."

Emory gives me his address before ending the call. I log his information on a sheet of paper and put it into the file folder I've begun to compile—just as I would when keeping track of any other major investigation.

Jenner agrees to the discreet meeting, and he's already parked across the street beneath a streetlamp when I pull up to Russ Emory's house. Jenner and I walk to the door together, both uncomfortable and a little bit apprehensive.

Without speaking, Russ lets us in and leads us down the hall to his study. He's a tall guy, just a little older than me, but he doesn't appear to be in the best of health. He walks with a hint of a limp, and moves like every bone in his body hurts.

Sliding the double doors closed behind us, he eases himself into an overstuffed leather chair and smiles. "Sit, gentlemen."

Jenner and I lower ourselves onto a couch across from him, both of us unnerved by the awkward silence.

"I see you've stirred up quite the hornet's nest down at city hall." He crisscrosses his fingers and rests them on his stomach. "I want you to know something, first and foremost. Even though I'm a longtime friend of Carl's—well, more like an old classmate—I'm on your side. What I mean to say is that I know you guys did the right thing, and now it's coming back to bite you in the ass."

"You know this from reading the papers?" asks Jenner.

"That," he says, "and talking with people."

Jenner and I glance at each other, not sure what "people" he's referring to.

"You guys aren't as alone as you think you are. A lot of folks in the business community see what's going on." Emory pauses to stuff a pillow under his lower back. "It's no secret that I have a couple of friends on the council, and sometimes they tell me things. Things that you guys need to know. That's why I wanted to meet with you. Because I support what you're doing, I want to open a dialogue and keep you up to date on what's going on behind the scenes."

"Okay," I say. "So why isn't the council pushing the MA to hand over our memo?"

Emory smiles again. "One of them *is* pushing, but he just hasn't gone public yet. The rest of the council are sheep, especially the mayor. Lillian Behrman will do whatever Lara tells her to do."

"But the municipal administrator works for her, works for all of them," Jenner says. "Isn't Hector Lara obligated to follow the council's directions—even if it's just the one councilmember who wants to see it?"

"It's a seven member council," says Emory. "As long as Lara has four of them in his pocket, he doesn't give a shit what the other three say. They need a majority vote to get rid of him."

Jenner's jaw tightens. "So since he's got four votes, he can do whatever he wants?"

"Pretty much." Emory ponders with his fingertips for a moment. "But the police department drama got away from him when your attorney sent that memo to the press. Lara wasn't expecting that, and he doesn't like surprises. Now he's found himself holding the pile of shit that he himself created; he knows he's got to get ahead of this thing before there's so much heat on the council that *they* turn on him."

"Heat about keeping the chief on the payroll?" I ask.

Emory nods. "So, Lara has decided to cut Bradford loose—in his mind it's the only way to assuage the community and lessen public criticism of the council."

"He hasn't told us that," says Jenner. "In fact he's said that Bradford is still in charge, even though he's on medical leave. My hands have been tied since Carl left the building."

"Lara is going to announce it this week," Emory says. "But all this bashing the council's taken in the paper has exposed them as weak and gullible, and I think because of it, more of them are asking to see the actual memo—not just hear Lara's summation of it."

"They haven't made their requests public," says Jenner.

"And they won't. That's not how they work." Emory shifts in his seat. "The MA doesn't want them to see the memo, but he also knows that none of this is going away anytime soon. So he's trying to get ahead of that, too."

"How?" I ask.

"He's looking outside for someone to investigate your claims against Bradford."

"Looking where?" The emotion in my voice is evident. "There's the district attorney, the county police chief's association, the state department of justice . . . all Lara has to do is pick up the phone. How hard can it be to find a legitimate . . .?"

Then the light comes on. I look at Jenner and he looks at me. Then we both look at Emory.

Emory waves his hand and laughs. "Now you guys get the picture. The MA doesn't want a 'legitimate' investigation. In fact that's just what he doesn't want—they'd find Bradford guilty on all counts, and Lara knows it. He's got to come up with an outfit he can control. If he can get a report in front of the council saying that there was nothing to your allegations, the council won't care anymore about seeing the memo."

This meeting with Russ Emory is enlightening, but it's got me feeling even more hopeless than I did before. I can see by Jenner's face that he feels the same.

"In addition to all that," Emory adds, "Lara still has to hire an interim police chief to run the department." He nods his chin toward Jenner. "And you can bet Lara has no intention of letting you manage things any longer than he has to."

As we walk down the hallway toward the front door, Emory tells us that he'll get back to us if he hears anything. "In the meantime," he says, "keep your heads down and watch your backs."

Jenner and I get outside and stand in silence next to his car. "We're so screwed," I say without looking up.

Jenner shakes his head. "Yeah. This is a shitty end to what was a good career."

I look at the glassy reflection of the streetlight in his eyes.

"I can't be in charge of the department, yet be required to run every decision through Bradford."

"You heard Emory," I say. "Lara's finally going to cut Bradford loose."

"Too late for me," he says. "I haven't told anybody yet, but I've decided to put in my retirement papers."

LESSON 18

"To know your Enemy, you must
become your Enemy."
~Sun Tzu

I'm sitting in my family room, gazing out at the aging wooden deck behind the house. I've been thinking about hiring someone to tear it down and build me a new one. But I don't have the energy.

As I stare mindlessly out at the warped and rotted boards, all I can see is a collage of newspaper articles floating by in front of my eyes. The heavy sense of regret, the feeling that I've misjudged everything since the very beginning of this mess, is swallowing me up. It embarrasses me to realize that at one time I actually thought the municipal administrator would appreciate our discreet handling of the chief's performance problems. And because we brought the issues directly to him, perhaps even admire our demonstration of loyalty.

What a chump I was to believe that we were all playing on the same team—Lara, the mayor, the city council . . . and me. That they, too, would see the difficulty in our situation—faced with a non-performing, unethical police chief and all—and that they would applaud the manner in which we dealt with it.

And now, with my partner leaving, I can't see a tomorrow; the rest of my career is just a black hole. *What am I going to do without Danny Jenner? Who can I even trust?*

The doorbell propels me out of the slump and out of my chair. A man I don't know stands on my porch, extending a glossy half-sheet appearing to be some kind of voter pamphlet. I can just make out a smiling photograph of Odell Graham on the front of it—the city councilman friend of Russ Emory.

When I don't reach to accept the flier, the man cocks his head. "It's getting to be that time of year again. A couple of your city council members are up for reelection, and we'd like to ask you to vote for Odell Graham."

"Nope." I shake my head with unmistakable edict. "Can't do it."

His brow twists as he confers with his clipboard. "Hmm, I've got you down as a supporter in past elections. Is that not correct?"

"Yes, it's correct."

"You know, Odell has done a great deal for the city and--"

I hold up a hand to cut short his spiel. "Look, I not only voted for Graham every time he's run, but I was on the police officers' political action committee that endorsed him his very first time in office. I even walked precincts for the guy on my day off."

"Mind if I ask what happened? Why the change of heart?"

I take a breath, half wondering why I should even bother telling this guy how I feel. I'm almost too disheartened and too tired to talk about it anymore. Almost.

"Simply put, I lost respect for Mr. Graham when I saw how he handled the recent scandal involving the city's police chief."

"These are difficult issues," he says.

I hold up my hand again. "Look, I know all about how difficult these issues can be. But Graham folded up like the rest of those puppets, and he chose to listen to the municipal administrator's bullshit. He could have . . . no, he should have forced the issue and demanded to see the memo. You have the word of six highly respected and ethical police administrators who typed out seven goddamn single-spaced pages of facts outlining the gross misconduct of a public servant, and your so-called elected official, the one that I've supported for years, immediately comes out in the paper saying, 'I stand behind the chief. I think he's done some tremendous things for the city'?"

To this guy's credit, I see he's scribbling notes onto his clipboard. I'm certain that between the intensity of my words and the specifics of my facts, he's managed to figure out who I am.

He thanks me for providing the feedback and promises to relay what I said to Odell.

Working each day feels like I'm walking around in a thick fog. I pass employees who I used to slap on the back and joke with, but now I'm not sure whose side they're on or what they're thinking about me. People around here are falling into one of two camps:

Camp 1: Yeah, sure, everybody knew the chief was a piece of shit, but the six commanders shouldn't have gone public with their misconduct allegations.

Camp 2: The chief was a piece of shit, he let us all down and he deserved what he got.

Literally no one, even the chief's closest buddies, make any effort to refute the allegations against him. Regardless, tension oozes from every corner of the building, and I can see it on the employees' faces—the feeling that we're riding into a storm on a ship without a rudder, or a captain, and no crew. We're just a bunch of confused passengers, bobbing along, waiting for the next rogue wave to hit.

I exercise with Gale early every morning before work, before our girls get up for school. It's still dark when we leave the house and run our three-mile course around the university. I talk excessively during the entire route, barely catching my breath before the next expletive-filled complaint spews from my mouth. *Hector Lara this, Carl Bradford that, and Evan Casey, that son-of-a-bitch. Not to mention those spineless, goddamn city council jerkoffs!*

Meanwhile, our attorney continues to pummel the MA's office and the city attorney with letters outlining all the reasons the memorandum should be disclosed. He's pointing out to the city council how duplicitous Hector Lara has been in both his dealings with them as well as with us.

The mayor, having hitched herself so tightly to the municipal administrator, is now too enmeshed with him to break free. Not only does she look like a fool for having stood by Lara when he wouldn't show the council our complaint, but she has now reversed course and wants to see the memo—though treading very lightly so as not to appear critical of Lara.

According to the most recent news article about the ongoing police soap opera however, Lara still refuses to produce it—even to her, his biggest ally.

It also comes to light that none of the councilmembers, including Mayor Behrman, had initially been told that a memo even existed—hence the reason Lara ordered us to destroy all copies of it. Apparently Lara believed we had. Now some members of the council are saying that they were blindsided by the newspaper's disclosure of our complaints, and they're beginning to hint at their displeasure with Lara about leaving them in the dark.

The lack of clout demonstrated by the Mayor, along with her flip-flopping position about wanting to see the memorandum, is creating a serious image problem for her and the rest of the city leaders. A group of business owners and community members, who until now have been a silent minority, are beginning to voice their displeasure, and talk of a mayoral recall has surfaced. I'm now wondering if this thing might actually cost Behrman her job.

It seems as though only a day or two go by before there's another front-page photo of the sad-faced chief, and a story with barely more information than the last one. In between those days, a letter or two to the newspaper editor gets published. The latest one suggests that Lara is complicit in Bradford's misconduct, and blasts the MA for not paying attention during the years the chief neglected his job. Days like that leave me with a glimmer of hope.

Thus far, however, only one councilmember has completely broken ranks and publicly challenged Lara's handling of the affair. Odell Graham, the friend of Russ Emory, is suddenly on our side. I'm thinking that my emotional diatribe to Graham's campaign aide got back to him, and that the councilman finally caught a case of conscience.

Meanwhile, in addition to juggling the council's political balls, Lara is feverishly working to get *his man* in here as interim chief by the time Jenner actually leaves. It would kill the MA to have to hand me the police department's reins—even for a few days. At the same time, he's got yet another ball in the air—this mystery firm he's trying to find . . . The one that will conduct an *objective and independent* investigation into our complaints against Bradford.

* * *

"The chief is officially gone." Hector Lara stands at the podium in front of a packed house. "I've decided that in order to move forward, it's best to permanently separate Chief Bradford from the police department—so yes, he's definitely gone."

It sounds final enough, but I can't help wondering why he hung on to the guy as long as he did. Seems as if Lara could have cut his losses a while ago, and saved his own skin from the very beginning. I don't see the MA as a particularly loyal guy, so I can only come up with a couple of reasons he loitered so long on the deck of the fast sinking SS Bradford. One possibility is that the chief has something on Lara, and the fear of disclosure has kept Lara working so hard to give Bradford an undeservedly soft retirement. The other possibility is sheer male ego. Lara may be so pissed off about us forcing his hand, that his efforts to save the chief, even at Lara's own demise, outweigh logic and sound judgment. I tend to go with the latter, since cutting the chief loose, as he appears to be announcing today, would be an argument against the former scenario.

At any rate, we're moving forward without Bradford on the payroll. And according to the second part of Hector Lara's speech to the department, he's now bringing in an "interim" police chief.

Lara meets privately with the command staff immediately after the departmental meeting, to provide additional information. The guy he's bringing in is a retired chief from a police department across the bay. I don't know the guy—never heard of him—but I'm sure that as long as he shows up for work and can make a decision once in a while, we'll get along just fine.

And even though Lara tries to frame the hiring as a positive step forward, some feel that his decision to go outside the department for leadership is retaliatory. Another article appears in the newspaper claiming that the rank and file, represented by the PBA attorney, is insisting on a promotion from in-house. But the administrator and his council stooges stand firm in opposition of it.

I'm invited to an early morning "strategy meeting" with Russ Emory. This time we meet without the departing deputy chief, at Emory's office in the industrial section of the city. I don't know if the urgency of the meeting has to do with some new information or simply that Emory wants to hear my thoughts about the latest newspaper article. But as soon as I sit down, he jumps right to it.

"Hector Lara and the city council are coming after you," he says.

I feel my morning coffee refluxing in my esophagus. "How do you know?"

"Because Lara actually said it to the council," says Emory. "He told them that your career is dead, and that he's bringing in the new chief to get rid of you."

"He said me? Personally? By name?"

Emory nods.

"Why would he want to get rid of me?"

"Lara figures you for the head of the spear," he says. "He already got his pound of flesh from Jenner—he's retiring. But you're the one he really wants."

"And you know this for sure?"

"Heard it straight from one of the councilmembers."

I feel my hand unconsciously rubbing an aching spot in the center of my chest. "The city council is okay with that? They support him coming after me?"

Emory shrugs. "They support Hector Lara, and he's got them convinced that you are the one causing all of the trouble down at the police department. That it was you who masterminded this whole thing."

"But there are, or were, six of us. The memorandum was signed by the entire command staff."

"The deputy chief is on his way out, and it's no secret that Bradford treated him like shit. So Lara convinced the council that that was Jenner's motive. The two lieutenants; they were just following their bosses' orders, so there's their motivation. Everybody knows that Zavala is a short-timer, and Lara's got the council believing that he also just went along with whatever you and Jenner told him. So that leaves Claire Melville, who did whatever you told her to do because you two are having an affair."

"Whoa, back up!" I nearly come out of my chair. "Claire and me are what?"

Emory grins. "Yep. You can thank Bradford and his cohort, Evan Casey, for circulating that rumor."

"Casey." *So the snake finally crawls out from under his rock.*

"Nevertheless, Lara has pretty much laid this whole mutiny on you. And now he's bringing in an interim chief to pressure you out."

After finding out that I'm now public enemy number one in the city council's eyes, I schlep into my office to start the day. My desk phone rings and I don't even want to answer it.

"Hello," I exhale a gust of angst.

"It's me, Shanti Patel."

The light Indian accent combined with the name harkens me back to the sari store on Mission Street. "Oh yeah, hi."

"Hi."

With my head pressed to the earpiece, I'm waiting to hear the reason why she called. "So," I finally say. "Any more vandalisms to your store window?"

"Yes, again it happened. Another broken window last night." She lets out a strange little giggle. "I know it's only a window, nothing more than that. But still, it costs quite a lot to fix. Not that I'm about the almighty dollar."

Her choice of the cliché American phrase doesn't really fit. It almost makes me laugh, but I'm just barely holding it together these days. Anyway, I wish she'd get to the point.

"You should come by the shop to see it sometime," Shanti says. "The window. And I will make some tea for us."

"Thank you. Yeah, maybe when I'm down that way I'll try to drop by." I half-cover the mouthpiece and tell an imaginary person that I'll be right there.

She hears it and ends the conversation. Strange call.

* * *

The new chief starts just about the same time that Danny Jenner leaves. There's no promotion to fill Jenner's empty spot, and Lara is quick to permanently eliminate the entire deputy chief's position under the pretense of budget cuts. Not only does the move make good on his promise to kill any upward mobility in my career, but he also directs the new chief to dump all of Jenner's responsibilities and duties on me—in addition to everything I'm already accountable for in Patrol. It doubles my workload and increases my span of responsibility to two entire divisions instead of one. So in addition to all uniformed patrol squads, I now manage the traffic bureau, crime prevention units, downtown foot patrols, Southgate Mall officers, East Bay Community College security officers, special duty enforcement units, the street narcotics unit, the undercover narcotics and vice units, the police reserve officer program, the police explorer program and lastly, the city's animal shelter. *What else is left?*

The added workload swells my personnel responsibilities to over five times that of the other two commanders. Lara then begins scrutinizing all of my monthly patrol statistics—an unprecedented level of involvement by any municipal administrator in the city's history. When he can't find anything amiss there, he looks elsewhere in my distended span of command.

I find out from one of the animal shelter supervisors that Lara has scheduled a series of meetings with the employees there, to assess "management problems." I'm neither told by Lara about the meetings, nor invited to attend them. The shelter is my Achilles heel, and the administrator knows it. The place has been plagued with problems for years, which is why it's been passed around the police department like a case of smallpox. That's also why Lara wants me to oversee it, and it's why he's looking for trouble there. Even the old blind dogs can smell the years of neglect at the place. But rather than take responsibility for years of budget cuts and a substandard, decaying facility, Lara is going to parlay it into open season on me. He'll convince the council that the operation fell apart on my watch—never mentioning that he only dumped it on me a few weeks ago.

I'm just getting to know Patrick Vincent, the interim chief. And although he seems like a fair guy, he hasn't been around long enough for me to fully trust what he says—especially after hearing that the main reason Lara brought him in was to sack me.

"Sit down and tell me about the animal shelter," Vincent says to me one day, more or less out of thin air.

I take a seat and give him some of the history as to why it's even under the administration of the police department.

"Why is the MA suddenly so interested in it?" he asks.

"Well . . ." I have to think about how to word my answer. I'm not sure that I'm ready to show any of those cards to Chief Vincent yet. "It's an off-site operation," I tell him, "The building is a few miles away, so they're somewhat autonomous. And the treatment of animals gets a great deal of attention in this town. A kid can lose his life in a drive-by shooting, and maybe it will make the back page of the newspaper, but anything involving animals is going to be front-page news. It will get the community going, and the political fallout will get city hall going. Besides being under the public's microscope, the shelter is generally underfunded and has a history of being ignored. They have a huge volunteer base, and some of them are well connected at city hall. So when the volunteers are upset with something, it rolls downhill fast."

Chief Vincent nods. "It was the same way in the city that I came from. Anything else I should know?"

"Yeah, the civilian manager running the place is kind of a screw-up. He's a nice guy, but doesn't always make the best decisions. And we've had a couple of personnel complaints against him; nothing too serious, just dumb comments that have upset the employees."

He nods again. "Well, Lara wants to meet with me down there. Do you have time to drive me over?"

I quickly accept. But it's unclear if the MA wants me to be there or if he even knows I'm coming. Either way, Lara's been nosing around the shelter for weeks and it's about time I find out why.

As soon as we walk in I can tell that Lara is pissed off that I've joined them. I'm only there a couple of minutes when he tells Chief Vincent, "I forgot to bring my copy of the shelter's annual report and budget." Then Lara turns to me, and with the most condescending flick of his hand, he says, "Go back to the police station and print me a copy."

I feel my teeth clench and the hair on my neck rise up like a porcupine's. I'm sure my jaw muscles are undulating, as I grind my molars down to nubs.

"Sure, no problem." I say it with a forced smile, as if I'm not offended by the slight, and I've got nothing better to do than print out a budget document that I know he doesn't need.

186

Unsatisfied with my lack of reaction, Lara adds, "And hurry it up, I don't have all day."

I know that Lara wants me to react in front of Vincent, but I won't fall for it. I also suspect that he's trying to get me out of there so he can talk to Vincent alone, point out all of the shelter's shortcomings and badmouth my administration of it. It's what he was going to do anyway, before I showed up. But there's not much I can do about it either way. So, I take my time driving back to the station.

While Carmen prints out the budget report for me, I pour a cup of coffee and return a couple of phone messages. It does nothing to prevent the invective being heaped upon me behind my back by the MA, but it makes me feel better to take my sweet time, knowing that he's expecting me to hop to it like one of his lackeys.

When Carmen lays the thick report on my desk, I use it as a coaster for my mug. Then I tear out the staple and replace it with a funky paperclip, too small to secure all the pages.

Lara and Vincent are sitting in the shelter manager's office when I get back there. Lara sneers at me and glances at his watch. I hand him the coffee-stained cluster of papers, and a couple of pages come loose as I hand it to him. He frowns and dismissively tosses the whole thing aside. He never needed them in the first place.

That's when he starts riding me about the clod that we've got managing the shelter. "What are you doing about him?" Lara asks, his arms crisscrossed and his eyes locked and loaded, like little black bullets. "Or are you just ignoring all of the problems and issues down here."

For a second I actually visualize myself diving over the table, past my new boss, and beating the dogshit out of the municipal administrator. And then I realize he's actually baiting me to do something—although probably not a physical assault. But I'm sure he hopes I'll lose my cool and cuss him out in front of the new chief. Instead, I tossed my head back and offer a carefree laugh.

"Oh him?" I say, flicking my hand as equally dismissive as he had done to me. "He's like my second job. But rest assured, I'll get to him when I can."

Lara leans forward in his seat, narrowing his eyes and glaring at me with as much challenge as one can do without words. I smile back, and then try to force a yawn.

On the drive back to the station I can see in my periphery, Vincent looking me over. Finally he asks, "What's going on between you two?"

I act like I'm not sure what he means. But I think Vincent either suspects or knows more than he's letting on. And although he allowed Lara to treat me like shit, and he never said a word in my defense, Vincent doesn't get on my case for taking so long to get the budget report, or for my cavalier responses to Lara's questioning.

That night I'm still boiling inside. I tell Gale about the meeting, and how angry Lara made me. She's nodding as if I've already told her the story, and then I realize that her expression isn't because she knows the story, it's because she knows something else.

"What?" I ask her. "There's something."

She admits there is . . . that she was going to tell me, but was waiting for the right time. "Brian, the attorney I work for . . . you know, he's pretty well connected, plugged into the local political scene."

"Yeah, and?"

Gale gives me a pained look. "He also heard that the municipal administrator is after you, going to find a way to get rid of you. Brian said someone on the council told him."

Not surprising to me, Gale's information is more confirmation of what I pretty much already know.

A few days later Carmen comes in with a stack of messages for me, the most compelling from the secretive businessman, Russ Emory. I use a phone downstairs to call him back.

"Some firm from southern cal," he says, as if we're already in the middle of a conversation.

"The city's investigation?"

"Yeah." Emory moves his mouth so close to the phone that I hear the stubble of his beard bristling against the speaker. "I got it from my source on the council—Lara just told them that he's hired an 'objective body' to do the investigation, and he's going to announce it to the press later in the week."

"I assume this group he's hired will want to interview me."

"Probably," Emory says. "At least they'll go through the motions of an interview." Then he laughs.

I feel as sluggish as a guy emerging from a coma. "This whole thing is starting to move pretty fast," I say.

Emory agrees. "I don't know anything about this firm the MA has hired, but if Lara picked them, then he's paying them to say what he wants them to say. So strap yourself in, it's going to be a bumpy ride."

188

This "objective investigative body" has got bullshit written all over it. *A Los Angeles law firm? Are you kidding me?*

I continue to be amazed that no one even thinks to question why with over 160,000 lawyers in the state, Hector Lara had to go 350 miles outside the Bay Area to find one to conduct the investigation. Not the council, not the press, and not the community—not one person seems to find that little maneuver even the slightest bit suspicious.

But what can I say at this point? How can I protest? I've already shot my wad with the memo that took out the chief. If I complain about this now, I play into his hand. I look like the consummate problem-starter. So I gather my evidence, my three binders of documentation, and wait to be summoned.

From an investigative standpoint, this firm does everything backwards. Normally, in any case, you would want to talk to all the complainants and witnesses first. Learning the facts that support the accusations against the subject of the investigation is a basic first step—otherwise how could you know what questions to ask the subject? It's Basic Investigations 101. That's if you really want to know what the person did. If not, you'd do what this L.A. firm does. They call Bradford in first. Then, having seen none of the evidence against him, they take his statement and then send him on his way.

Now, after hearing Bradford's side of it, they start *questioning* us—the Six Horseman of the Apocalypse, the Judases that turned against their boss. Right from the beginning, they treat us as if *we* are suspect. *Objective investigation? Not even close!*

They ask Claire how much time off she took when her father died of cancer two years ago, and wasn't it Chief Bradford that had been good enough to grant that leave?

They ask Bobby if Bradford had lost confidence in him, all but accusing him of initiating the chief's *Bradford's Ghost* moniker and coming up with Evan Casey's nickname, *The RC*.

Me? My three binders of information are never touched. They don't even look at them; the cell phone bills, the payroll records, the email printouts—none of it. They're not interested. Instead, they question me about my loyalty to the police department. They asked me if I ever sent anonymous letters to the municipal administrator, complaining that Chief Bradford was disengaged and absent. Their line of questioning focuses on my role within the commanders, as if they are more interested in identifying who in the group merely went along and who was the driving force behind the memo.

To me, it's clear that they have been coached and guided by Lara and they are reporting back to him—probably daily.

Regardless, all six commanders speak to them with one voice—having been insiders to the most dishonest and disappointing abuse of authority that any of us had ever experienced. Each of us tells of similar occasions where important calls had not been returned; meetings had been cancelled at the last minute, leaving dozens of people waiting; long stretches of absenteeism and falsified payroll records. To all of this, the *independent and objective* investigators from L.A. respond with denouncing expressions and yawning disinterest.

I feel in my heart that this investigation isn't going to end well. I know that Hector Lara will somehow find a way to turn the tables on us. On me.

The actual interviews take no more than a couple of weeks, yet announcement of the results drag on forever. In my mind, the delay is more evidence of Lara's manipulation of the investigators, and probably his efforts to *wordsmith* the final report. There is no way that he would actually leave something like this to chance.

On Friday, March 19, 2004, more than eight months after our misconduct allegations were first brought to light, the results of the city's $50,000 investigation are finally released. My head pounds as I read the headline: FORMER POLICE CHIEF CLEARED – INTERNAL AFFAIRS FINDS NO MISCONDUCT.

If you were to read the article, which I'm assuming most people won't, you'd see that the headline is a gross misstatement of fact. The police chief was not, in fact, cleared. The law firm actually found Bradford guilty of several of our accusations—yet none were deemed to be violations of criminal laws.

I'm working hard to find some solace in the fact that even the great and powerful Lara wasn't able to get Bradford cleared of everything. But there is no silver lining on this one. The only thing folks will remember is the photo of the beleaguered chief and the accompanying headline, stating in effect, that poor Bradford did nothing wrong.

I feel like barfing up my English muffin.

This day rates as one of the worst ever, and I don't even want to leave the house. My shower drags endlessly, and I finally dress for work. I'm driving in wide circles around the city, trying to calm myself, trying to gain some strength. I'm struggling to look at this from a better perspective, find a positive, but I can't.

Eventually my orbit around the police building tightens until I'm actually driving around and around the block. I finally conclude that I don't have the luxury of avoidance. Besides, this isn't about me; it's about the police department and the employees who work here. And I know that amid the chaos and political upheaval that has come our way this year, they deserve competent leadership. So, I force myself to drop the partisanship and self-pity, and I walk into the building with as much confidence as I can muster.

Reading reports and working on the day-to-day issues actually helps me feel better; it refreshes me and is lightening my mood. I pour myself a second cup of coffee and head over to the Xerox machine. I'm standing there waiting for my copies to fall into the tray when the morning newspaper is slapped down in front of my face. One of the inspectors, a guy whom I thought was a friend, digs his finger into the lead story. "Hey Captain, what does this say? Huh?"

I slowly lift my gaze until my eyes are burning into his. "Yeah, I saw it." My words are devoid of tone, but my face feels like it's on fire.

He doesn't take the clue. "Police Chief Cleared," he reads the words to me slowly, articulating each one. "Huh, imagine that. What does that mean about you guys?"

I'm actually afraid that I'm just going to lose it and go at the dumb fucker right there in front of the whole investigations bureau. So I do my best to nod, as if I've got more important things on my mind—which I don't—and I take my copies back to my office. People seem to be avoiding me, probably out of embarrassment about how badly the article made us look. I sit in my office with my head buried in my work for a few more hours, but I'm not really reading any of it. All I see is that inspector's finger pointing at the headlines. *What does that mean about you guys?*

It was actually a fair question. But as much as I'd like to marshal some dogged strength from somewhere in the depths of my psyche, I can't. It feels like I have no more left to give—as if this thing has finally broken me.

I grab my car keys and leave work. I drive home in a sort of haze, and then, without even changing out of my slacks and dress shirt, I take a sledgehammer and attack my backyard deck as if it were Hector Lara, himself. I swing wildly, pounding away for hours, until there is nothing left but a huge pile of splintered wood and a six-foot deep crater off of the family room. It's an ugly mess, and all I can do is collapse into the shaded pit of dirt.

Thankfully Gale is still at work and the girls are in school, so nobody had to witness my psychotic episode, but maybe a nosy neighbor. I'm no less angry than when I first started though, and when I see a missed call from Bobby Roselli on my cell phone, I know my mood is only going to get worse. I clench my jaw and listen to his message.

"I was just in a meeting with Chief Vincent and he accidentally let something slip." Bobby pauses, just as he would do in a real conversation. It drives me nuts when he does that, and I feel my teeth grinding as I wait with the phone pressed into my sweaty face. "Lara didn't show the investigation's findings to the newspaper; he only summarized them to the reporter. So he was able to put his spin on that whole thing, too. Or maybe he completely lied, who knows? But it gets worse." Another pause. "He's not going to release that document to the city council, either. Says it's confidential. Anyway, just thought you'd want to know." His message ends and I find myself just standing—frozen with the phone against my ear.

"If you want to erase this message, press seven."

I'm blind with rage, and I feel a sea of molten lava pumping through my body and into my head. The administrator has even found a way to control this!

Then something strikes me like a sledgehammer: Lara had controlled the law firm's findings, yet they still had to admit that some of our accusations were sustained. That wouldn't have happened unless the *real findings* were much more damaging than that. Otherwise, why would the MA even keep that report from going public? Just like our original memo, the sheep on the council are content only to hear Lara's twist on it. *What in the name of God is wrong with these people?*

I have tried so hard and for so long to do the right thing, but I can't swallow any more of this. I can't do it. And I can't be anywhere in this city right now. I have to get out!

I'm in a haze as I drive myself down to the transit station and then take a train over to San Francisco. The first place I come to is a Bavarian tavern just off the Embarcadero—a dimly lit place with a long oak bar extending down the entire wall of the restaurant. I screw myself into a stool and order the first of many drinks. Sometime during the evening, the electricity goes out and the whole building is plunged into darkness. A candle is lit, and some food is brought out from the kitchen—laid out on the bar before it goes bad. But I'm not interested in the food.

Another drink comes. My third or fourth, I've lost count. I hover over it, frowning at the candle in front of me, watching it flicker to and fro like little fingers flipping me off. "Fuck you," I hear myself say in a low, gravely voice that sounds like it's out of the *Exorcist* movie. "Fuck you all."

Besides a pounding headache that wakes me up in the middle of the night, I feel like my blood pressure is going to blow the top of my head off. I'm angry that I've allowed the pipsqueak MA to get away with this, and now I can't even sleep. I'm staring up at the ceiling and thinking, just like I've done my whole career. Just like I've done when saddled with a federal grant application, or when I've had to investigate a particularly tough criminal case. Or when the planning for a tactical or undercover operation has dominated my thoughts. Only this time it's different. It's more personal. It's unpleasant and sour, like the whiff of something rotting, its odor stuck inside my nostrils long after I get away from it.

"What's on your mind tonight?" Gale turns to face me in the darkness of our bed.

"The municipal administrator."

"Of course," she mumbles. "What else?" There's a sarcastic note in her words, and I'm unclear if she's just tired of the subject, mad about the pulverized deck, or pissed off that I came home from San Francisco drunk. Probably all of the above.

"I'm not the bad guy here," I tell her. "We all did what we were supposed to do, and we got screwed for it."

"Okay . . ." She leaves it hanging there as if what I had just said didn't justify anything.

I lean up. "Hector Lara! He's lied to everyone and gotten away with it. Even the mayor and the council, they're nothing but a bunch of bums. They just believe every lie he feeds them. Nobody is ever going to challenge Lara. Nobody is ever going to stand up to him. I hate that son-of-a-bitch!"

She doesn't say anything for a couple of minutes, but I can tell by her breathing that she's still awake, thinking. Then, finally, "Do you want to know who you're really pissed off at? Yourself."

"What?" My boozed breath fills the space between us. "I've given my life's blood to this job! I've trusted those people, believed that we all shared the same values and integrity. Trusted that the people running the city actually gave a shit about something more than keeping their jobs."

"Exactly," she says. "That's why you're angry with yourself. You trusted people and they let you down."

"Are you saying I shouldn't have done what I did?"

"No," she says. "But you've allowed this thing to get inside you, and now it's eating you alive. It's consumed your life. It's consumed our lives. It's all you think about and it's all you talk about."

"Yeah, well I can't just walk away from it."

"No, but who wins when you're so pissed off that you can't even sleep at night? Who wins when you can't even enjoy your days off or time with your family? You think you're getting even with Lara and the council by drinking yourself blind over in San Francisco? So, how's that working out for ya?"

I hate Gale's way of putting me in my place with a series of snappy questions. And her use of "*ya*" at the end just irritates me even more. I take a breath. "All along I've been thinking that I could overcome this thing by playing by the rules," I tell her. "I think I just believed that the MA and the council would eventually come to their senses, and they would see that we did nothing wrong by bringing Bradford's misconduct to their attention."

"And since then you've been straddling that line, like a damn Boy Scout who's mad at his troupe leader but is afraid to push back too hard. You won't cross the line, afraid of violating some sacred oath, all out of a misguided sense of honor. Honor to who, them? You've been trying to stay on everybody's good side, playing by their rules and hoping they will ultimately see it your way. Face facts; it's not going to happen. They don't even play by their own rules. They don't like you anymore and they never will again."

I ease back into my pillow feeling the warmth of truth in her words, like turning a picture on its side and seeing a completely different image. "You're right."

"This isn't like you," she says. "When you get mad, your anger usually turns to action. What about that attorney you guys hired? Why don't you use the guy to sue the hell out of them? It's pretty obvious that Lara and the council are retaliating against you."

"That would mean filing a law suit against the city."

"Yeah? So?"

I think for a second. "I couldn't sue the city. It would feel like I was suing myself." I sigh. "What I'd really like to do is go after Hector Lara, just like I would any other piece of shit who was trying to destroy me."

After a lazy stretch of her arms, Gale turns on her other side. "Then why don't you?"

"What do you mean?"

"I mean, I think you need to let him know who he's messing with." She yawns. "But do it tomorrow, I need to get some sleep."

She's out in less than a minute, but the dialogue inside my head continues. *That cunning little asshole of a municipal administrator thinks that he's smarter than everyone else; that he's some kind of shrewd strategist who can think and plan several steps ahead of the rest of us. Lara wants to take me down, but I'm suddenly freed by the reality that my career was over the day I signed that memo. With my destiny no longer in question, my options are many and I have nothing to lose. It will confuse Lara because he'll hold nothing that I want, nothing with which he can control me. I'll be an enigma, an adversary he'll never figure out or be able to predict. I'll study Lara and use his own tactics against him.*

It's taken me a long time, probably too long. But finally, I smile into the night. "The gloves come off today. Lara should never have taken me on. Now I'm going to be that man's worst nightmare."

LESSON 19

"Dangerous consequences will follow when politicians and rulers forget moral principles. Whether we believe in God or karma, ethics is the foundation of every religion."

~*Dalai Lama XIV*

March 22, 2004 (Monday)

Claire finds me sitting in her office when she gets to work on Monday morning. I'm on my third cup of coffee and wound pretty tight. She lays her bulging purse on the desk and just looks at me, trying to read my face.

"You look pissed. I'm gonna get some coffee." She walks to the conference room and returns several minutes later with a cup that's wearing half of her lipstick. "Why don't the men around here ever make a new pot when they drink the last of it?"

I ignore the jab. "I need to talk to Pam over in city payroll." I toe her office door closed. "She has some information that I need about Bradford's vacation usage. But I don't really know her well enough to just walk in there and ask to see it. What do you think? Would Pam open up to me?"

Claire takes in a slow sip from her cup. "Not sure. But you know who knows her pretty well? Your SWAT guy, Longmeyer."

My frown prompts her to explain what seems like the oddest association of any two people in the city.

"He dealt with her quite a bit last year when he was put on administrative leave after his shooting. The city screwed up his paychecks and Pam helped him straighten it all out." Claire eases back into her chair.

I wonder how Claire always seems to know this sort of stuff.

"So, are you going to tell me what you're up to?" she asks.

"I'm not sure yet." I thank Claire for the information and walk across the hall to my office, realizing that I don't have an answer to her question; I'm not really sure what I'm up to. But since strategy and planning is what I do, I figure I had better organize my thoughts into something more concrete than just wanting to make Lara's life a nightmare. *It sounded so good the other night.*

I scroll through a mental register of all the people in the police department, trying to zero in on those I trust most. It strikes me that some won't have the huevos to carry off what I have in mind, and others will talk too much. My needs will require both guts and discretion. I simmer the names until my list congeals to only three: Paul Longmeyer, the SWAT sniper that Claire had just mentioned, is one of them. John Flores and Chase Klemer are the other two—both from my old street crimes task force. But since Klemer is going through a tough divorce, I remove him from my list.

I decide right away that an important feature of this little group will be *plausible deniability*—the ability to swear under oath that we never talked and that they didn't get their orders from me. It's a means of keeping their jobs safe if things go bad. I'm also hoping to accomplish all of this without ever meeting as a group, and without even meeting one-on-one. In fact, I'd rather they don't even know the identities of the others involved.

It takes me a couple of weeks for the whole idea to come together. I've worked patiently to put a few things in place first; one of them is how I can communicate with each guy individually, without face-to-face contact. An idea comes to me while I'm sitting at my desk one day, and I take the stairs down to the hallway near youth services—the same area where Bosworth committed his nasty little deed on Darnell Wallace.

The back door to the jail is here, and a set of rarely used gun lockers. No guns are allowed inside the jail, so by policy we lock them safely in the lockers before entering. Anyway, there are six small lockers near this door.

So I take the key out of locker #6 and drive to a locksmith friend of mine downtown. He makes three duplicates for me, and I pay in cash. This is how I will communicate assignments and retrieve information to and from my little band of . . . well, some might call them mercenaries. I call them patriots.

I use a computer downstairs to write and print my first of many cryptic messages:

I need your help with a confidential mission. All information between us will be exchanged in Youth Services jail entrance – gun locker #6.

I place the note and the key into an envelope and leave it in Longmeyer's mailbox. I then leave his assignment inside the gun locker:

> Contact Pam Ackers (city payroll) regarding excessive vacation accrual by Chief Bradford – and anything else you can find out about his retirement/leave payout. Place the information back in this locker.

Longmeyer will guess from the subject that the note came from me. He probably won't be at all surprised. We've both worked undercover, and we've both been on covert intelligence-gathering and enforcement operations together. So the guy not only knows the way that I operate, but I know how he operates.

Now, someone outside this profession might wonder why Longmeyer would ever do this, and how I could be so certain that he would. The answer is a little difficult to explain, except to say that it has something to do with trust and faith; his trust that I wouldn't ask this of him unless absolutely necessary, and my faith in that trust. These relationships have been cemented in a history of getting through situations together—some, dicey in-house mine fields, and some life-and-death events on the street. In other words, this isn't the first test of loyalty for either of us . . . John Flores, either. In any case, not everyone who has worked for me would do this—which is why I've made my selections so carefully.

Longmeyer has been away at a training class for the past week, which has been another test of patience for me. It's Wednesday, April 7th, when I finally hear back from him. I've wandered downstairs, making sure it's late enough that most of the youth services staff is gone. I slide my key into gun locker #6 and pull it open. A plain white envelope sits squarely inside, with a handwritten message penned on the front of it. It reads: *You're not going to believe this one.*

Twenty minutes later I've gathered the commanders and we're standing on the tar and gravel roof just outside the *penthouse*—a euphemistic reference to the police department's third floor attic. It's a creepy space, full of emergency rations, military gas masks, outdated radio equipment, and mice. And since employees rarely have a need to go up there, it's the perfect place for a covert meeting with what's left of our group. By this time, Miguel Zavala has also put in his retirement papers and is enjoying what's left of his unspent leave.

198

I'm standing in the long shadows of dusk, holding Longmeyer's envelope up like a beacon before Claire, Gary, and Bobby. My voice is barely audible over the wind as it whips through the rooftop antennas and slaps the cabling against the building.

"What?" says Bobby Roselli. "What now?"

"I had someone check Bradford's payroll records to see what kind of sweet deal the administrator cut him." I flip the envelope like a fan in front of my face. "Since the guy had taken more time off than anyone else, yet somehow managed to retain such a huge cache of vacation time on the books . . ."

"Does it even matter anymore?" Gary asks. "I mean, seeing as how Bradford retired nearly four months ago?"

I look back at my friends, too disgusted to even form the words.

"How much?" asks Bobby. "How much did Lara pay Bradford?"

I shake my head again. "Nothing. He hasn't given Bradford a final payout."

Claire's eyes squint. "What do you mean, no payout? He got nothing when he left?"

"Bradford never left." I open the envelope and pull out a copy of Carl Bradford's personnel action. "He's still on the fucking payroll."

I'm staring back at three sets of vacant eyes. Finally Claire gains control of her slack jaw. "Impossible. Pat Vincent is on record in the chief's position—his name is listed in the position control number now. Besides, we get monthly copies of all of the payroll records in our divisions. Bradford's name isn't on any of them."

I hand Claire the paper. "That's because he's no longer being paid out of the police budget. Lara hid him under his own budget—out of the MA's office—and, get this, he's paying him as a *sixth-step* police officer."

"There is no 'sixth step,'" Gary and Bobby say at the same time.

Claire shakes her head as she gazes down at the personnel action. "Lara created it, made it up so he could keep paying Bradford his police chief's salary."

"Wait a minute," says Gary. "Bradford walked out of here on August 1st, that's eight months ago. You mean to tell me that he's been paid for working all this time?"

I nod.

Bobby says, "That means he's still getting full medical benefits, and all this added time will be calculated toward his retirement."

"And . . ." I have just a bit more salt to pour. "He's still receiving a monthly vehicle allowance, unlimited city cell phone use, and he's even accruing sick leave and vacation time!"

"Fuck this." Bobby flips off the building that looms behind us in the last apathetic light of the day. "Lara's still taking care of that useless piece of shit, meanwhile we've spent over twenty thousand dollars of our own money to defend ourselves."

He's right. We hired the attorney on advice of the MA, and have been paying for him out-of-pocket. Our group decides that since we took these actions as part of our employment with the city, it is the city, not us, who should pay the cost of our defense.

Claire hasn't said much, but I can tell she's livid. "How can Lara get away with hiding Bradford under a non-existent position? That's just so wrong. And he looked us all in the eye and said he was gone."

Gary's face is red. "If only the community knew about this--"

I cut him off, mid-sentence. "Oh, don't worry. I can promise you, they're going to know about it."

April 10th, 2004 (Saturday):

BRADFORD STILL A CITY EMPLOYEE. The newspaper's subheading announces that despite the former chief's resignation, he has been allowed to stay on in a sworn position. I read through the article, so delighted with myself that I'm afraid I'll spill my morning coffee all over the paper. I notice that the municipal administrator has managed to avoid the obvious question, and refuses to comment on why the accused chief has retained his employee status. This is a good thing for me, because the only time Hector Lara doesn't comment on something is when he's been caught unprepared. Former Chief Bradford still refuses to answer his phone or return press calls, and the mayor cannot be reached for comment. All good stuff as far as I'm concerned.

It quickly occurs to me that the MA won't sit quietly for long. Soon there will be a follow-up article, and by then he'll have gathered his wits and had ample time to spin it to the council. He'll find some way to flimflam the press, and he'll be trying to turn this thing back in his favor. The next article comes out one week later.

April 17, 2004 (Saturday):

EX-CHIEF'S STATUS ANGERS OFFICERS. The subheading that follows says that police feel deceived that the chief remains on the payroll. The article itself contains quotes from the PBA's attorney, calling the municipal administrator dishonest and accusing him of a cover-up. And while I love the labels he's laid on Lara, there is something fishy about the way the story is written. It smells of more manipulation by the MA.

The article's placement is in the local section instead of the front page, and it's all the way on the back of page six. I flip back to the front of the paper and I'm underwhelmed. Seems like this story could have competed with the *big* news: The Transbay Tube may not withstand a major earthquake, and the war in Iraq is another Vietnam. *Shocker!*

I return to *my* article and the first problem is right there in the headline, the word choice: *Ex-chief's status?* If you missed the first story last week you'd never understand what this is all about. And the article never really does address his *status.* How can he be the "ex" chief if he's still getting chief's pay?

Maybe Lara was able to influence the newspaper editor or maybe not. But the change in the tone of the article just doesn't sit well with me. The only highlights are the quotes from Lara. I thought a week would have given him plenty of time to come up with something better. Instead of standing tall and defending his actions, he wants to dicker over wording, claiming to have told employees that Bradford had resigned as *"police chief,"* without actually addressing his employee status. Lara also declines to respond to allegations that he's been deceitful, saying, "I'm not interested in rehashing the past."

His attempt at finding grammatical loopholes sounds pathetic, and the only thing worse is the mayor's response. Without having seen any supporting information, she says, "It's difficult to explain, but Chief Bradford is getting no more or no less than he deserves."

My only hope is that the public sees her as the fool that I do.

I call my dad, thankful that he's an early riser. He's already seen the article and he's as pissed off as I am. Maybe even more.

"*Angers officers!*' he barks into the phone, quoting from the headline. "Why isn't the damn newspaper angered? They were duped as much as everybody else. They ought to be outraged!"

I'm nodding at the other end of the line, as if he can see me. Not one news report since Bradford's "departure" has ever contained a quote from him, yet this article has an air of defending the guy—explaining to the public that delayed retirements are common in worker's compensation cases.

"And those idiots on the council let Lara get away with this?" he asks.

"Apparently so. But this is only our first shot. We've caught Lara off-guard, and he doesn't like that. He's embarrassed now and we've forced him to be on the defensive."

"What's next?" my dad asks.

"I'm going to put a surveillance on the son-of-a-bitch."

By now I've read the original and follow-up articles exposing Bradford's continued chief's pay several times. Hector Lara never really defends keeping the former chief on the payroll, and instead focuses on lesser details: "The chief never received a vehicle allowance . . . that I'm aware of." *It's another verbal loophole.*

Since I know that isn't true, I send Longmeyer back to Pam Ackers at City Hall to get copies of all Bradford's payroll records—including the car allowance records and copies of his city cell phone bills. But we've moved too slowly, and someone's gotten there first. Pam Ackers has been abruptly transferred out of payroll to another city department. Longmeyer finds her at her new position in another section of city hall.

"I got to work early in the morning and found the lights on in the file room," she tells Longmeyer. "One of the file cabinets had been gone through—the one with Carl Bradford's payroll records in it. All of his records were missing. Someone had purged them."

Longmeyer leaves me a handwritten note explaining the rest of the conversation. It says that Pam reported the incident to her supervisor and was told, "Keep quiet about it if you know what's good for you." Pam was transferred the next day.

Lesson learned for me.

The whole subject of personnel files gets me thinking, trying to wrap my head around the concept of an administrator who would get his hands that dirty. So I go to a guy I trust, Hank Barone, a former attorney for the city. I run the scenario by him, explaining the story in hypothetical phrasing. Half way through, he leans back in his chair and smiles.

"Let me tell you a little story," he says. "When I worked in the attorney's office at city hall, I was assigned to look into a sexual harassment complaint filed by a female employee. The alleged perpetrator was Hector Lara, who was the assistant MA at the time."

I glance around to make sure nobody can hear us. I'm already shaking my head as I sit down in a chair across from Hank.

"So, Lara comes into my office a few days later and wants me to drop the investigation. When I tell him that we're obligated by law to look into it, he gets angry, orders me to stop investigating the woman's complaint. Lara storms back out, and then a few days later I get a written notice of disciplinary action against me. It had apparently, and quite suddenly, come to the city's attention that I'd been receiving pay for work outside the city—without the required *outside employment* authorization."

"They were going to investigate *you* now?"

He nods. "Worse. They were after my job—they were going to fire me. Only I'm not stupid, I'd filled out the paperwork and it had been approved several months prior. Yet when I looked through my personnel records at city hall, the signed form was gone. Someone had taken it out of the file. But you know me; I had retained a copy of it in my own records. So, I went home and searched through all my personal stuff until I found the copy of the approved request form."

I'm dumbfounded, but I don't know why. There's no level too deep for Lara to sink in order to control things for his own benefit. *Good to know.*

"So yeah," Barone says, "I wouldn't put it past him to purge payroll files, especially if they would expose him as a liar. Oh, and one more thing you should know."

I've started to get up, but now I sit back down.

"The deal that Lara cut with Bradford? It also included a legal settlement releasing the chief of any and all damages and liabilities relating to his employment with the city."

"How do you know that?"

"I used to work in the city attorney's office," he says. "I know. So even if Lara's so-called independent investigation had turned up theft, embezzlement, fraud, or anything else on Bradford, the administrator had already given him a free pass."

As soon as I leave his office I have Carmen pull my personnel file and copy everything in it. After my talk with Hank Barone, I'm thinking it would be wise to keep my own set of records— somewhere off-site, where Lara can't get his hands on them.

While that's getting done I leave a gun locker key and a message in John Flores' mailbox. He's another one of my trusted comrades who wouldn't blink at a request to set up surveillance on the municipal administrator. A few days later I meet up with John after work. We're in separate cars outside the city hall parking garage, each with a photo and the license number of Lara's car. We have a pair of non-police issue, handheld radios through which to communicate. And as an added precaution and a nod to my old undercover days, I'm wearing dark glasses and a full beard, glued in place with spirit gum.

We're posted there for a couple of hours, but no sign of the MA. Suddenly a black Volkswagen rolls slowly through the parking garage and out onto the street next to city hall.

"We got a rat in the house," says Flores.

"Is that Casey's car?"

"It's one of them," he says. "I'm guessing he's here to meet Cheesecakes."

Evan Casey's large-bottomed former secretary transferred out of the police department to a job at city hall a while after Casey retired. Since then, the two have been spotted several times slinking around the dark recesses of the city parking garage.

"Do we want to follow him?" asks Flores.

"A bird in the hand." And though I'd rather have Lara in my crosshairs, the weasel, Casey, is a strong second—too attractive for me to pass up.

We watch him circle the block a couple of times before parking under a tree on a side street. He's sporting dark glasses and a baseball cap worn low over his brow, like a celebrity ducking the paparazzi. Then, as if part of their daily routine, a maintenance door opens on the north side of the city hall building and out runs Cheesecakes. The two spirit off together in his little VW—John Flores and me following in a loose, two-car surveillance.

They park in a narrow alleyway behind a small restaurant/bar downtown. And though they're glancing around as if their spouses might show up at any given moment, they can't restrain themselves from holding hands like a couple of high school kids.

By this time I've grabbed my 35mm camera and telephoto lens from the backseat, and I'm holding it at the ready. I bag a half-dozen decent photos of the two of them on their way inside. Now that I've got their routine and at least one of their secret meeting spots, I'll plan on putting a nice file together on him as well.

But afternoon traffic is getting thick and I've got dinner plans with Gale tonight, so we call it quits for the day. I radio my thanks to John, and we both head our separate ways.

During my dinner that evening I'm struck by lightening for the second time in one day—but in a good way. Unbeknownst to me, the restaurant where Gale and I have chosen to eat happens to be a favorite of the municipal administrator. I'm in a corner booth, facing the front door but with my back to the bar.

"Hey, Phil." Gale says, staring straight down at her plate. "Don't turn around, but I think I see your buddy at the bar."

"Who?" I fight the urge to look.

"Hector Lara." Gale glimpses a quick peek before continuing. "He's tucked back in the dark, at the far end." And then she asks, "Does his wife happen to be a cute blond?"

I feel an uncontrollable grin spread across my face. "Nope, she's a fat Mexican."

After a minute or so I venture a furtive glance. Sure enough, there's the administrator, cozied up in the corner with some little tart. I recognize her as a businesswoman who works and lives in the city, and is also married. I think her name is Joy Talbot.

Five minutes later we've paid our bill and have slipped out of the place without Lara spotting us. I move the car around to the front of the building, into a position with a clear view of the doorway. Thankfully, my camera is still sitting in the backseat.

I'm scanning the street and parking lot for Lara's roadster, so I can get a better shot of him. But it's dark and I don't see his car anywhere. Finally it dawns on me that he probably wouldn't take his own car to meet a woman in town. He's got personalized license plates and a lot of people know his car. This is when I spot Mrs. Lara's mini-van parked behind me.

Our seats are reclined all the way back, allowing Gale and me to sink down low. I'm afraid that Lara and the woman will have to pass right by my car on their way to the mini-van. But the lot is crowded and I'm not sure I could find another spot with as good a view.

Suddenly a patrol car turns off of the main thoroughfare and pulls into the parking lot. Gale and I scrunch down farther. I don't know which would be worse, being seen by Lara or by one of the cops who work for me.

My answer comes in the form of an authoritative tap on my driver's window—*worse to be seen by the cop.*

"Good evening, Captain."

"Hey, yeah, how's it going?" I straighten up in my seat and Gale does the same. Luckily it's Paul Vega, a sergeant who was assigned as my assistant when I was a lieutenant. We're good friends, but I'm not sure any explanation would cool his red-faced grin.

He shines his flashlight over at Gale, then back at me. "Aren't you two a little old to be doing this kind of thing in a car?" He cracks himself up with that one. But then his eye catches my camera, out of its case now and set within reach on the backseat. He momentarily frowns and then scratches his head.

Just then I see Lara and the blond emerge from the restaurant across the street. The sergeant follows my line of sight, and of course, immediately recognizes the municipal administrator. He quickly connects the dots—us hiding in the car, the camera on the back seat, and the MA in the restaurant. His flashlight suddenly goes dark.

"Quick, get out of here," he says.

In my rearview mirror I see the sergeant turn back towards Lara and strike up a conversation with him and the woman. He blocks their view, and I know he's doing it so I can slip out of the lot without Lara seeing me. Gale and I make a clean getaway, and I've been given the gift of knowing another potential weakness: The MA's got a girlfriend. I leave myself a message on my work phone to get back in touch with Russ Emory.

I'm back at work early on Monday, ready to gather some more information about Lara's personal life. But as I'm leaving a message for my businessman informant, Chief Vincent comes into my office and closes the door. I immediately suspect the worst—perhaps someone saw me stalking the MA, or the sergeant himself ratted me out. But I'm relieved when he takes a seat and starts up a casual conversation: *How was your weekend? Any updates on the gang shooting? My wife and I had a pizza on Saturday and split a bottle of wine.* It's the kind of friendly, affable chat that would never have been possible with the former chief.

Then Vincent gets a more serious look. "I had a run in with Carl on Friday."

"Bradford?" I'm trying to figure out how the two would even meet. "Face to face?"

Vincent nods. "I've been telling the administrator that some of Bradford's clothes are still in my office closet, and he's got some things in the safe. I can't get into it or reset the combination until he opens it. So I guess Lara finally got Bradford to come down and take his belongings."

"Bradford came here, into the police department?"

Vincent nods again. "Showed up late on Friday, through the back door after everyone was gone. I just happened to be working late when he came in. He even brought a buddy with him, I guess for backup." Vincent chuckles. "Anyway, wow, what an asshole. I tried to put Bradford at ease, you know, show him some respect, but he couldn't find a belt or a tie he had left in the closet, and he actually accused me of hiding them from him."

I roll my eyes. "Lucky he didn't do worse."

"Yeah," he says. "I thought about calling a couple of uniforms upstairs to escort him out of the building. Was this the kind of belligerent behavior you guys had to put up with?"

"Mostly Danny Jenner, the deputy chief. Bradford took a lot of his anger out on him. But yeah, he was never wrapped very tight. Always unstable and quick to blow."

"Hmm," he says, as if that helped him understand. "I'll tell you something else I haven't mentioned to anyone. I found some weird shit on Bradford's computer."

As much as I want to ask exactly what he had found, I resist.

"I'm sending it out to a computer forensics team in San Jose. I'll have them sweep the hard drive and copy everything for me."

"Are you going to tell the MA about it?"

He squints upwards. "Not sure. As long as they don't find anything criminal I may just keep it to myself—hang on to it as an insurance policy in case Bradford ever tries to get in my face again."

I still don't ask what it was he found.

"What do you make of the guy?" Vincent asks. "Was he a perv?"

The question tips me off as to what Bradford left on his hard drive—pornography, or perhaps some kinky thing related to his dating profile.

"I think Carl Bradford was depressed," I say. "The guy had very few real friends, and he depended heavily on Evan Casey. And that is what really cost him. Relying on that self-serving opportunist meant that the chief had no one to keep him grounded or talk him out of his worst instincts. In my opinion he was a very weak man. But a pervert? No. I never saw that."

Bradford is gone and other than having gotten rid of him, I'm not out to badmouth the guy or make his life any worse than it already is. But Hector Lara is another story. I decide not to confide anything to Chief Vincent yet, but I am comforted that he feels close enough to share as much as he did.

"Oh, and one more thing," he says before leaving my office. "I'm scheduled to attend a police chief's symposium next week. Will you be around?"

I tell Vincent that I have no plans.

"Great," he says. "I'd like you to be the acting police chief while I'm gone."

He leaves me sitting at my desk, wondering if he has any idea how much the municipal administrator hates me. Or maybe Vincent doesn't care. Then a thought momentarily flashes through my mind: What if Lara and Vincent are working together, colluding to make me look bad? This acting chief thing could actually be some kind of setup.

But I'm usually a pretty good judge of people, and I see Chief Vincent as more of a cop's cop. I believe the guy actually likes me and appreciates the way I work. And I really enjoy working for him.

When Russ Emory calls me back later in the day, he makes it clear that he's been keeping up on developments—mainly the article I leaked about the MA hiding Bradford on the payroll. And he's eager to talk with me about it.

"My man on the city council is pissed off," Emory says. "And even more now that Lara is also withholding the Bradford report from them."

It's good news—a fractured council will erode Lara's power. I'm careful not to say too much over the phone, but I let Russ know that I've finally decided to push back. I'm playing hardball now—done keeping tabs on Bradford, and now I've focused all my efforts into putting a file together on Lara. The rest of what I've got to say, I figure I can tell Russ Emory in person.

After a long pause he says, "There's someone I think you should meet. Can you come by my office early tomorrow morning?"

We make the date.

I have no idea who Emory wants me to meet or why, but at this point it doesn't matter. I'm pulling out all the stops.

Why not?

LESSON 20

"There is no such thing as a fair fight.
All vulnerabilities must be exploited."
~Cary Caffery

Russ Emory has to reschedule our meeting—says the guy he wanted me to meet had some sort of conflict. It's probably just as well; I'm the acting police chief this week, and something feels wrong about doing this subversive stuff when I'm supposed to be running the entire department. The last thing I want is to become what Bradford was. My guilt extends only to the police employees and the residents who live here, however, not to anything I owe Hector Lara or the council. So I stay put and keep focused on my job.

The week jumps into high gear quickly. Desmond MacLeod, the newly appointed captain who oversees the school resource officers, comes into my office with an apologetic expression.

"What's up, Mac?" I set down the budget report I'm working on.

"A couple of my cops working at Mt. Vernon high school picked up some scuttlebutt about a gang war," he says. "Apparently some shit went down at a party over the weekend, and some gangbangers from Oakland have threatened to come by and shoot up the school."

Desmond is a friend who has worked for me several times as we both moved up the chain. He's not an alarmist, and he knows the terrain pretty well. In fact, he used to attend Mt. Vernon, and his family lived only a few blocks from the campus.

"Do the threats sound legit?"

"We're still running down leads," he says, more serious than his signature lighthearted manner. "So far we've confirmed that a fight occurred at a party over the weekend. One guy was stabbed and the windows were bashed out of someone's car. Sounds like it started over a girl, but it quickly turned into a gang thing."

"Any guns?"

"Nobody was hit," says Mac. "But shots were fired from a car as one group left the party. And even if the drive-by threats aren't serious, you know these campus rumors. The kids will get caught up in the hype, call their non-student buddies for backup, and then pack their guns to school. It'll take on a life of its own."

"Okay, stay on it," I say. "And get me the name and number of the principal, and we'll meet again in twenty minutes. Have Bobby and Claire come, too."

I always tend to be overprepared than under—it's sort of a SWAT motto: *failure to prepare is to prepare for failure*. I'm also more than familiar with recent campus shootings around the country, mainly from the perspective of organizing a tactical response. In any case, I'm not about to let something like that happen here. In truth, regardless of what comes of my conversation with the school principal, I know how I am going to handle this before Mac even leaves my office.

It doesn't take long before the high school is coming undone. Word has spread and parents have begun pulling their kids. Thankfully, the principal is an even-tempered guy who is a good balance between district politics and reality. After talking with him, I have a sense that he agrees that this is not a situation for subtle discretion; it's best handled with decisive visibility. But he wants it to be my call, not his. Apparently the district, not unlike the city, finds a strong police presence distasteful and crude, particularly around kids in an academic setting—regardless of the fact that the place could easily become a bloodbath without it.

We meet twenty minutes later in the chief's conference room, Mac, Bobby, Claire, and me. The plan is simple: we bring in a half-dozen reserve officers to provide extra security in the school parking lot and surrounding neighborhood, and then reassign other school resource officers to augment presence on the Mt. Vernon campus.

In the meantime we put the gang unit and a couple of inspectors on the trail of these rumors, the objective being to verify their validity and to locate and arrest those responsible for the stabbing and gunfire at the party. In my experience, the combination of a visible presence and aggressive enforcement is a huge deterrent—quickly taking the motivation out of hastily conceived gang threats. I once used this method after a couple of our street team officers gunned down a gang member who had tried to run them over. When the gang made threats to take out a cop in retaliation, we pushed back with double units around the clock and a flurry of heavy enforcement—searches and arrests.

210

Not only are the four of us in agreement, but we also share ideas and resources without being territorial. It feels good to work in a group with such a cooperative spirit, and it translates to an image of solid leadership to the cops and civilian employees, and to the school administration as well.

After a few days of our enforcement plan, everyone has gotten the message. Gang activity ceases, the principal is happy, students and parents feel safe, and the rumors have died a slow death. Both the campus and our police patrols return to normal.

By now it's mid-week and I'm in my office, shining my uniform shoes for a neighborhood meeting later in the evening. Carmen steps in to tell me that the administrator is on hold for me.

"Hello, Mr. Lara." I figure he's calling about the community meeting tonight.

He wastes no time dropping the hammer. "I understand that you reassigned a significant number of personnel to the Mt. Vernon campus this week."

Although he hasn't said the words, his tone is a strong indicator that this is going to be a criticism. But if he thinks I'm going to scramble to make an excuse, I'm not. "Yes, sir. That's right."

"Well," he finally mutters. "Nothing even happened there."

"That's right."

"I understand that there were upwards of a dozen officers on campus," he says. "And the gang units and others were also seen."

His facts are a little murky, but to correct him could come off as defensive. Besides, he didn't ask me a question. "Hmm," I respond. Not great, but not terrible. At least I don't sound afraid of him, and I'm certainly not tipping my hand to the fact that I'm getting more pissed off with each word he speaks.

Finally he makes a last push to get me to take the bait. "Sounds to me like an excessive use of departmental resources. You wasted a great deal of personnel, not to mention salary and overtime expenses, and all for what? For nothing. Seems like your little plan was an irresponsible use of the city's budget."

I cover the phone with my hand as I take in a long breath and let it out. Besides being wrong about using any overtime, I really want to remind him about the hundred grand he wasted keeping Bradford on the payroll, or the fifty thousand he just spent on the farce investigation into Bradford's misconduct. But I don't.

Keep focused, I remind myself.

"It's difficult to quantify something that *didn't* happen," I finally tell him.

211

"What does that mean?"

"It means that we'll never know how things might have gone if this situation had been handled differently. For instance, if we had taken a casual approach and the Mt. Vernon campus had been shot to hell, I'm guessing you and I would be having a very different conversation right now."

"Hmmm," he says with a smirking tone—almost as if he sees what I did as a typical enforcement-minded overreaction.

I debate for a second before deciding to continue. Not in a disrespectful way, but with just the lightest touch of condescension I tell Lara, "My training is in the public's safety and in how best to prevent things like campus shootings and gang wars in schools. I make my decisions based only on those things, not on budgetary impacts." I stop just short of reminding Lara that that's why I'm where I am and he's where he is.

He's silent on the other end of the line. Bristling, no doubt.

"Was there anything else, sir?"

"Yeah," he says with a haughty air of superiority. "The request for reimbursement for the commanders' attorney fees is denied." He mumbles a guttural conclusion to the conversation and then hangs up. I know he's going to rip Chief Vincent's ass when he gets back, for ever leaving me in charge in the first place.

The conversation leaves me pissed off all over again. And it's also a clear insight into how Lara's going to handle me from here on out: scrutinize everything I do, criticize every decision I make, and try to bait me into getting angry. I'm sure he's also painting all this for the council, in hues that are the least complementary to me: *Ribera turned the Mt. Vernon campus into an occupied war zone.*

"To hell with the municipal administrator," I say to myself after hanging up the phone. Acting chief or not, I'm done waiting. I dial Emory's number.

"Russ, we need to talk."

We set up a meeting for the end of the week at his company's headquarters.

On Thursday morning I go directly to city hall for a meeting with one of the fire department's battalion chiefs. Since I'm the police department's representative to the county's office of emergency services and the city's emergency preparedness committee, I'm obligated to attend these monthly meetings. And unfortunately the fire department's management is housed in the city hall building.

I suffer venomously through the meeting and then leave, grateful to have avoided the fourth floor political crowd. I feel like an infected wound needing fresh air as I pull my car out of the underground parking garage. Suddenly I hit the brakes.

There, right across the street from me, is Hector Lara—strolling in arrogant nonchalance up the south sidewalk of J Street. It's a quarter past ten in the morning, and he's sauntering along past the empty storefronts, dive bars and boutique coffee shops, as inconspicuous as a paperboy on a Sunday morning. But, the MA doesn't seem to be interested in stopping for coffee or chitchatting with the merchants. No, he's just moseying along, shuffling up the street with his hands tucked into the pockets of his khaki Dockers— *Aw shucks Aunt Bea, that was some mighty fine apple pie.*

No way. I'm not buying it—he's trying too hard to look ordinary. The big question in my mind is why?

The street he's walking up is one-way, and I'm on the wrong end to follow in my car. Instead, I park and quickly get out on foot. This isn't the best way to tail someone; in fact, it's probably the worst. If he turns around, I'm screwed.

Lara pauses, glancing back over his shoulder, and I duck into the doorway of a pawnshop at the corner. This isn't going to work. I jump back into my car and haul ass around the corner and up the parallel street. I come back to J Street a block ahead of the MA and wait in a bank parking lot for him to pass. But after a couple of minutes, he still hasn't come by. I edge my car out onto the street and he's gone. Disappeared.

I know he didn't make it this far up the block, so I'm thinking that he's got to have ducked into one of the businesses. Banking on the fact that he didn't cross the street, I concentrate on this side of the block. It's more likely and will narrow the possibilities.

I drive slowly down the street to where I last saw him, checking stairways and shop windows as I go. No sign of the little weasel, whatsoever. Parking at the opposite curb, I wait. But after thirty minutes he still hasn't come out. I'm studying the buildings, writing down all of the possible addresses. There are only a handful of businesses: the pawnshop, a dance studio, a guitar store, a nail salon, a bakery, a beer bar, and the bank where I initially stopped.

Glancing above them, I notice a row of windows on the second floor of the brick building housing a few of the businesses. Strangely, in all of my years on the street I never knew there were offices up there.

As I look closer, I see that sandwiched between the bakery and the dance studio is a tiny recessed doorway covered by a security door. I glance up again, and now I notice subtle differences in the windows and the interiors—indicators that they are not business offices at all; a pair of Levis hanging behind a curtain, a box fan in another, and so on.

These are residential apartments.

I circle the block and cut behind the bank to the back of the same brick building. Sure enough, a small parking lot is tucked back there, along with another security door. Four more apartments face out over the lot—all on the building's second floor.

He's in there. I can feel it deep in my gut. The questions burn in my mind: Who is he with, and why?

My meeting with Russ Emory falls on Friday, the last day of my stint as the acting police chief. It's early morning, before the start of my normal workday. Emory apologizes again for the friend who was unable to make it, but promises that the guy will have some "good info" for me when we finally meet. But since I don't know anything about this mystery guy, and have no idea what his motivation is for wanting to talk with me, I'm naturally suspicious. The fact that he already flaked twice doesn't make me feel warm and fuzzy about this, either.

For those reasons, I decide to hold off on telling Emory about my observations yesterday, or even the fact that I've taken up following Lara around town—just in case he would share it with this *untested* friend of his.

Emory kicks it off by telling me that Odell Graham, his buddy on the city council, is angry and distrustful of the MA, and is now firmly on our side of this thing. The fact that Hector Lara has refused to let the council see both our memo and the results of the Bradford investigation has pushed Graham to the point that he's now hiring an attorney to force Lara's hand.

"That's nuts," I tell him. "Hector Lara isn't elected, he works for the council. If Graham can build enough support among them, they can fire Lara."

"Hey, you're preaching to the choir," he says. "And Odell knows it too. He says Lara is the tail wagging the fucking dog in this city. But like I've said before, as long as the MA has got the council majority behind him . . . And the rest of the council, even if they agreed with Odell, are too weak to take Lara on."

It's all good news for me, though. I'm a novice when it comes to politics, but even I recognize that a legal action initiated by a councilmember will further divide them and erode Lara's power. He'll try to head off this lawsuit, and the rest of the council will want to hide it from the public.

The guy is beginning to look like a juggler who's losing his grip. My hope is that when one ball falls, they will all fall. Now is the time to ramp it up even more—go after him with everything I've got.

"The press needs to know about Odell Graham's lawsuit," I tell Emory. "Do you have any connections at the paper? Someone you can leak it to?"

He shrugs. "Not really, but I might be able to get my hands on the legal paperwork regarding the suit. The press likes those kinds of facts. Puts them at ease."

It suddenly occurs to me that I should have developed my own media connection. I make a mental note to call a reporter I've talked with a couple of times, and invite him to lunch.

Emory's secretary comes in, brings us each a cup of coffee. She's a beefy lady who looks comfortable in her skin. Probably been there for years, loyal as a St. Bernard. Makes me think of the chief's secretary, hiding Bradford's misdeeds and shredding all those documents for him. I thank the woman for the coffee.

When she leaves I have a moment of regret for being so angry with the chief's secretary. She's not a cop, probably has a completely different sense of honor and integrity. Poor woman was only doing the best she knew how in order to support her old boss.

"So what's Lara like outside of work," I ask Emory. "Does he have hobbies, spend time with his wife and kids?"

Emory shrugs. "Not really sure. Mostly what I know of him is by reputation, things I hear from other business owners and people in the chamber of commerce."

"And what's the reputation?"

Emory stares off, thinking. "He likes to be involved at the micro level, especially with developers. I don't know . . . he jogs. Oh, and he definitely likes the ladies."

"The ladies." I tamp down any reaction, having withheld the information about seeing Lara at the bar. "Any lady in particular?"

"Not that I know of, but he'd probably take any woman he could get his hands on." By this time Emory has figured out where I'm going with this. "If you want to set him up," says Emory, "using a female would be a good way to do it."

I smile, and I can tell that Emory knows I've decided to step up my game. He nods, recognizing that I've turned the corner with my tactics.

"In fact . . ." Emory touches his fingertips together and eases back in his padded chair. "I once heard that he had a secret little hideaway downtown—a place to take his girlfriends."

"Is that so?" I struggle to form an expression of mild surprise. "Any idea where downtown?"

"No, but it would have to be a place close to city hall."

I nod. "Makes sense."

We both sit for a minute without talking, and I get the feeling there's something more that Emory wants to say.

"Anything else?" I ask, like we're wrapping up the conversation. But I don't make a move to stand up yet.

He takes another few seconds to weigh it in his head, like he's wondering how much information he can trust me with.

"Possible payoffs from developers," Emory finally says. "That's why I want to get you together with my friend. Another business person, like me, but with some firsthand knowledge."

This time I don't have to struggle to appear surprised. "Does Graham know about the payoffs?" I ask.

"Suspects it," says Emory. "He's convinced that the FBI is going to show up one of these days and take Lara out of his office in handcuffs. But Odell has really got to walk lightly around that shit, at least until he comes up with something concrete."

We conclude the meeting and I drive back to the station.

First thing I do when I get into the police building is head back to youth services and slip a note for Longmeyer into gun locker #6. It simply says:

963 J Street – Find out whatever you can.

Now I'm itching to set up this meeting with Russ Emory's friend, and I still have to arrange a lunch date with the reporter. I hustle upstairs to my office with giddy anticipation.

"Captain?"

I turn. "Oh, hey Carmen." Then I rush past her.

She calls out, "There's a woman waiting for you in your office."

Carmen sees my arching eyebrows as I stop and turn around. Her shoulders go up apologetically. "The woman said you wouldn't mind if she sat in there until you got in."

Turning the corner into my office I see a woman sitting with her back to the door, facing my empty desk as if someone were sitting behind it. She's wearing a scarf around her head and big dark glasses, like an Indian version of Jackie Onassis.

"Mrs. Patel?" I say, stepping around to fully view the woman who owns the Indian clothing store on Mission Street. Although we've been acquainted for several years, and she's called several times, I suddenly can't remember the woman's first name.

She turns slightly and smiles, but doesn't remove the dark glasses. It goes through my mind that she's been beat up in some sort of domestic mess and has come seeking my advice.

"How are you?" I ask. And just as she starts to speak, her name comes to me. "Shanti," I blurt, a little too suddenly to sound smooth or sincere.

Wait a minute! Something suddenly occurs to me. She's got to be the business owner—the friend of Russ Emory. Why else would she be here? Did Russ ever indicate the gender?

Shanti's head isn't moving, but she appears to be staring at me through her dark shades. "You know why I'm here?"

"I . . . I think so." Easing behind my desk and into my chair. "You know something about the municipal administrator?"

No reaction. Then after a few seconds, "Mr. Lara? I've met him."

I want to rub my hands together like a kid who can't wait to open a gift. "And you were told to come talk with me, right?"

Shanti nods. "I told my mother what I was about to do. She said that if I really feel that strongly in my heart, I owe it to myself to say something . . . To tell you about it."

"And you feel pretty strongly?"

Shanti nods again. "Yes."

I don't want to scare her, but I have to ask. "Strongly enough to testify, if it comes to that?"

She looks confused and I want to kick myself for pushing too hard too fast. I was going to mention wearing a wire, too, but now I'm glad I didn't.

"I only tell my mother," she says. "Yes, I think I testify to her?"

What? I've probably gotten ahead of myself, miscommunicated everything. "Let's go back and start at the beginning," I say to her. "Russ Emory told me that you have firsthand knowledge about the administrator."

Now she's even more confused. "I . . . I'm sorry. I don't know this person, Russ Emory."

"You don't? He didn't tell you to come talk to me?"

Shanti shakes her scarf-covered head. "I come here on my own."

"Wait a minute." My eyes stare blankly as I try to reassess this situation. "Came here on your own . . . for what? Why *are* you here?"

She reaches up to remove her sunglasses, and I can tell she's been crying. "I came to say that I'm in love with you."

I'm staring back at Shanti Patel, waiting for my brain to process what she just said. Waiting for words to form in my open mouth. Waiting for Allen Funt and the Candid Camera crew to jump out of my closet.

"You have always been so nice and helpful to me," she says. "Even when my husband was going to be deported, you helped us then, too. Remember?"

"Uh, yes," I answer weakly. "How *is* your husband, by the way?"

"We're divorced. He lives in Fiji."

I nod, realizing that this woman is serious. I think back to what I may have done to give her a wrong impression. I go over it all in my mind—back to when we first met, when I was a young patrol sergeant working the street. A heroin addict had overdosed in an apartment across the hall from hers, and I contacted her as a possible witness. It was a hot day and she offered me a coke. Since then we've just run into one another on a few occasions during community events or business functions—not that many times, really. And then there were the phone calls recently, about her store window being shattered.

"I'm by myself." Her words shake me back to the present. "And I'm very lonely."

"Well, you've got your mother," I say it with a playful lilt, but it comes off sounding stupid. Then I add, "You should know that I'm married. Happily married. And I have two daughters, too."

"Yes, I know. That makes you even more attractive." Shanti waits a beat and then, "You don't have to leave your wife. Just come to my apartment whenever you--"

"Whoa," I unconsciously thrust up my hand like I'm stopping traffic. But Shanti talks over it.

"Even for one or two hours a week, we can be together."

Just then a tap on the door stops her from bettering her last offer. The door is cracked open an inch, but Claire pushes it open the rest of the way and steps inside.

"Here's that tape recording you wanted of the vehicle pursuit last night." Claire's eyes are glued to the woman who's quickly putting her glasses back on. Claire fumbles the cassette onto my desk, still watching Shanti.

Claire glances at me, then to Shanti, and then back to me. "Yeah, okay, right . . ." She turns and walks out of my office.

I make short work of my unexpected suitor, who seems to have an uncanny knack for calling or showing up at the very worst times. I tell her that I'm touched and humbled. *Humbled? Seriously?* But it's all I can think of, especially since this a first for me. As I escort her to the elevator, I end by making it perfectly clear: "I'm sorry, but no. Never going to happen."

As the elevator doors close on what will undoubtedly be the topic of many a musings, I exhale a hugely palliative breath.

"Who the hell was that?" Claire is leaning against the half wall of the secretaries' cubicle when I turn back toward my office.

I'm not sure of any other way to tell it, so I just say that Shanti is a local businesswoman who apparently fell in love with me.

Claire coughs a single raspy laugh that sounds almost like a bark. "You better watch it," she says. "That chick looked like she was about to go out to the parking lot and light herself on fire over you."

"Wouldn't be the first time," I say, now that the crisis has passed and my male ego is starting to kick in.

"Yeah!" Claire smirks. "Gale would have your ass!"

That quiets me down, quickly.

I get a couple of calls from the watch commanders and the other captains during the weekend, but nothing of any significance. By Monday morning Chief Vincent is back in the driver's seat and I'm feeling pretty good about myself. And when I go downstairs and check gun locker #6, I feel even better.

Longmeyer has left me a listing of all the J Street building's tenants, their PG&E utility records, a handwritten diagram of the second floor layout, and a set of keys to the building's front and rear security doors. How he managed to get those, I'm not even going to guess. The diagram shows a total of eight small apartments, and I mean small—maybe enough room for a double bed and a dresser. They each appear to have a bathroom and barely enough room for a hotplate, probably no more than 160 square feet in all.

But when I scan through the names listed on the rental and utility records, Hector Lara isn't one of them. I'm not sure what I expected—the guy would have to be a complete idiot to use his own name. I'm guessing he's paid someone else to rent the place, or possibly he's using an alias. I wouldn't put it past the guy to have a phony ID, either. Whatever the case, it's going to take me more time to research each of the tenants, one-by-one.

As eager as I am to jump into it, I've got to brief the chief on last week's events. He and I sit down and I give him a one-page document with a dozen or so bullet pointed subjects—each of them advising him of the issue or incident and what action was taken. Most are for his own edification, such as the action at Mt. Vernon High School. I also provide him with the verbal addendum: "I don't think the MA was in agreement about how it was handled."

Chief Vincent smiles. "Too bad. It was your call to make, not his. And for the record, I agree with you one hundred percent."

I'm really starting to like this guy.

Later in the week things are heating up on the council. Rumors are flying around the city about Odell Graham's suit against the MA, and the rest of the council has distanced themselves from the drama, treating Graham like an Ebola victim. Mayor Behrman is openly hostile to him during council meetings, and there is now talk of a legitimate recall effort to get her out.

Since she's Hector Lara's biggest fan, it's got to worry him. And my hope is that the other council members will start to realize, even privately, that Lara is piloting their city toward disaster. They're all going to go down like the Hindenburg.

In an effort to help fan the flames, I take the newspaper reporter to lunch. We talk casually, and all the while I'm trying to size him up. He's a chic, ex-New Yorker, who likes cops and doesn't mind going against the grain. We transition to the topic of city politics, and I can see that he knew all along that I was headed there. He slides out his notepad and begins writing as I fill him in on the most recent developments—Lara's secret agreement protecting Bradford from legal action, the fact that Lara has hidden the Bradford internal affairs report from the council, and about the suit by Graham compelling the MA to cough it up.

A few days later: CITY RECALL CAMPAIGN TAKING OFF.

The story focuses on the mayoral recall effort, now broadening to include a vote to replace all seven council members. And the impetus behind it? The council and administrator's handling of the police chief's departure. There's much criticism of Lara's payroll deception, and about the no-fault agreement, and of Lara's hiding of pertinent reports and investigations from the council and the public. There is even a quote about Bradford from the woman who heads the city's Neighborhood Alert program—probably the most loyal and involved resident in the entire city.

She says she feels for the former chief, "but he just wasn't doing his job. Anyone who worked in the police department knew he wasn't there," she said.

Another accompanying article the same day discloses the terms of Bradford's sweet retirement deal, drafted by the administrator, endorsed by the city attorney, and approved by the city council. He's been placed on paid medical leave, but the city has maintained his top step chief's salary, as well as continuing 7.5% educational incentive pay. And any internal investigation conducted by the city relating to the matter must be sealed and *not* placed in Bradford's personnel file.

As if all that negative press isn't enough, a stinging letter to the editor appears in the morning paper—ripping Lara for allowing the Bradford debacle, and the council for turning a blind eye to Lara's shenanigans. Curiously, the letter is written by one of my dad's best friends. More than likely, it was written by Dad and signed by his buddy. His heart is in the right place though, and I would probably do the same for either of my daughters.

By the end of the week I'm finally able to get back in touch with Russ Emory. He sets up yet another meeting between his mystery informant and me, this being our third try. Only this meeting Emory won't be able to attend.

"That's fine," I tell him. "Just give me the name of the guy, and I'll introduce myself."

"You already know him," Emory says. "Or at least he says he knows you. And he knows your wife, too."

LESSON 21

*"We must always take sides. Neutrality helps the
oppressor, never the victim. Silence encourages
the tormentor, never the tormented."*
~Elie Wiesel

"So, we're finally able to meet." I lean across the small table to shake
Z's hand. "Can I buy you a coffee?"

He's sort of smiling and looking around, like he's either nervous,
or he's excited to be involved in this thing—whatever *this thing* is.
I don't even know what Emory has told him.

I return with two coffees and take a corner seat across from him
at Starbucks.

Turns out we've met a couple of times, and have a few mutual
friends. He's part of a prominent family in town—responsible for
developing some of the largest projects in the city. Z is also the
property manager for the building that houses the law firm where
my wife works. Apparently that's how he knows her.

As we begin talking casually about Emory and some of the other
people we know in common, I can tell that the guy is getting into it.
And when the conversation transitions to Hector Lara and his
antics, there is an adventurous thrill in Z's voice. I get the feeling
that his life as a property manager is fairly routine, and to him this is
like doing espionage for the CIA.

But it seems after all the buildup, his firsthand knowledge
amounts to only a single questionable incident. "I was at a meeting
between Hector Lara and another developer," Z says. "They were
negotiating the sale of the abandoned city building on Washington
Street."

So far, this part makes sense. The eyesore structure has been the
topic of public criticism for years, and the city has been trying to
dump it off to a buyer who could turn it into something decent.
"Who was the developer?" I ask.

"A guy named Peter Tang, with BMX Property Group in San Francisco."

I write down the name.

"Anyways," Z says, "Lara tells this guy, Tang, 'All these financial incentives your people are willing to pay to the city, but what about for me?'" Z holds out his upturned hand, rubbing his finger and thumb together to replicate the MA's pandering gesture. "Lara actually asked the dude, 'What do I get out of this deal?'"

I leave the meeting a little underwhelmed. A couple of things strike me as odd. First and foremost, why would Lara solicit a payoff in front of witnesses? Even as arrogant as he is, it seems like he would be at least a little more discreet than that. Second, why was this guy, Z, at the negotiation with Tang and Lara in the first place? From what I gather, Z is sort of an underling, a minor player in the family power structure. I'm suspicious that he may be trying to oversell his own importance. Although, I have no doubt that soliciting a bribe in order to move a project through the council is within Lara's skill set.

I'm not disappointed enough to give up though. I'll need to track down this Peter Tang, see if he'll talk to me, and try to verify that there even was such a meeting. And, if so, find out what was said.

To best document all of this, I have secretly tape-recorded my conversation with Z. It's actually a federal crime to do, a felony, in fact, unless it is part of the evidence gathering process by law enforcement during a legitimate criminal investigation. So, to make it official, I pull a police report number when I get back to the station. I classify it as a *public corruption investigation*, and then I leave a single page in the report jacket downstairs, stating that the confidential case file is being kept in my custody—which it actually is.

I continue following Lara as often as I can, getting a sense of his daily routines: Up early during the weekdays, a short drive to Café Francesca for his coffee and the morning paper, downtown to work at city hall, a mid-afternoon jog, and meetings at night—either official or unofficial. He seems to make a habit of driving the wife's minivan to his "unofficial" meetings.

I'm also getting to know Joy Talbot, the businesswoman we saw snuggling with Lara at the end of the bar. I make it a point to say hi at community events, and she even buys one of my donated paintings at a fundraiser. She seems nice enough, and I'm beginning to wonder if I've misjudged the context of their relationship.

I decide to bring a couple of cops with me to her open house during the National Night Out celebration. She sits casually sipping wine with her husband while we are there, mingling with neighbors. And sure enough, Hector Lara pulls into her driveway just as I'm about to leave. Seems a little awkward, with her hubby there and all. But I'm sure whatever she and Lara have going is painted as a professional friendship. And who knows? Maybe it is.

I flash Lara a great big smile and flick my fingers against my head in mock salute. I see him in my rearview mirror, sitting in his car in front of Joy's house, and I imagine him wondering how much I know about the two of them, or if it was just a coincidence that out of all the hosted neighborhood events around the city, I just happen to stop by hers.

Around this time I get a call on our home phone during dinner. It's one of the newer city council members, a frail looking guy who until now has been as mute as the rest of them, save for Odell Graham. Anyway, the councilman, a guy by the name of Teddy Rube, says he wants to come by and talk to me. I reluctantly agree, figuring it can't do any harm to hear what he's got to say.

So we hustle through dinner and clear the table to accommodate the guy's schedule. Rube comes in wearing a gray suit that hangs on him like he's jogged up the hill in it, sits down at the head of the table [my seat], and gives me a silly smile.

"I've listened to everything the administrator has had to say," he starts. "And now I'd like to hear your side of it."

First thing that strikes me is how naïve he must be. Why in the hell would I trust that Lara himself hasn't sent him over here? I'm on high alert of late, and I have trouble trusting even my own co-workers, much less some elected lackey who's shown no interest in our plight until now.

I make my response fairly generic, telling him things that by now, all of the council already know: 1) The other commanders and I reported misconduct as we have been sworn to do. 2) We have been disparaged and retaliated against for doing it. And 3) None of the council, including him, have seen any of the documentation with their own eyes—all of them being perfectly content to hear only Lara's version of it.

Rube quickly points out that he is a newcomer to the council, assuring me that as such, he is in the unique position of being able to "bridge the gap" between the commanders and the city.

But then the councilman goes into excuse mode, telling me how trustworthy the municipal administrator is. I feel myself starting to boil and I immediately cut him off. I do it politely, but definitely convey the message that I'm not interested in joining Team Lara.

"Mr. Rube, I've taken up enough of your valuable time," I say. "But thanks for stopping by."

During our weekly meeting with Chief Vincent, he asks the commanders for personnel updates. I give him the rundown from patrol operations, including significant problems with one of the recruits, Marilyn Quintel. She has struggled badly during her field training, and two of her training officers have recommended that she be let go.

Vincent agrees. "Yeah, let's get rid of her."

I remind the chief that Marilyn recently returned to the program after a long recuperation. "She was the recruit who suffered a brain aneurysm when she was in the academy," I say. "I'm wondering if there is something more we might be able to do for her. Especially after what she's gone through, and considering how much we've already invested in her."

The chief shrugs. "She's in your division, so it's your call," he says. "But in my experience, she's not going to get any better than this and we ought to dump her sooner rather than later."

Then he transitions to the subject of the upcoming city council meeting—the one where a host of speakers are planning on lambasting the council and calling for the mayor's ouster. He comes as close to warning us as he can, about our roles and about the importance of maintaining professionalism. I can see on the faces of some of the others in the meeting that they want no part of embarrassing the council. I, on the other hand, am not only planning to attend the meeting, but I've been talking it up with the PBA and the rank and file. So far it looks like there will be a pretty hearty turnout.

After our commander meeting, I return to my office and place a phone call to Marilyn's Quintel's personal physician—the doctor who actually performed the surgery on her while I sat at the hospital with her family. I introduce myself as Marilyn's boss, tell him that I'm mindful of the HIPPA laws regarding patient privacy, and promise not to speak in specifics.

He seems mildly agreeable to talk over the phone, but I can sense his apprehension.

"Let's say we have a patient who's suffered an aneurysm, similar to that which Marilyn experienced. The patient returns to work after six months and is having significant trouble with recall, mapping, remembering directions, tracking and multi-tasking." I pause to give him time to fit the pieces together, to understand that the problems Marilyn is having are going to cost her the job."

"Yes," he says dryly.

"One, could these symptoms be a result of what happened to her? And two, should we assume these are permanent conditions? Hypothetically, of course."

The doctor's response comes out almost angrily, abandoning the theoretical façade. "Listen, officer. Marilyn has suffered a serious brain injury, one that could have killed her. These things take time. The brain heals by reestablishing synapses, making new connections where old ones were damaged. It's been what, six months since her surgery? Not enough time. Not enough time. It may take a year or more for memory, cogitation and motor skills to improve. You haven't given Marilyn enough time."

The information is kind of what I thought. Only it wasn't us who pushed Marilyn to return, she pushed herself. I'm now trying to come up with a plan that is best for her in terms of safety and also for her continued recovery. Of equal importance to me is finding a solution that is reasonable and fair.

On another front, I've tracked down the BMX Property Group in San Francisco, and a private number for Peter Tang, their head of commercial acquisitions. I don't know of any other way to do this, so I just cold call the guy. I introduce myself to Tang over the phone and explain that I'm investigating a corruption allegation. Stressing that neither he nor his company are suspects, I ask if he would be willing to meet with me to talk about the case.

Tang reluctantly agrees, asking, "Can you tell me what this is all about, first?"

I pause, trying to figure out how to explain it. "Do you know Hector Lara?" I ask.

"Yes, I've met him before." A long pause follows, and I can almost hear him thinking. "Does this have anything to do with our involvement in the city-owned building on Washington Street?"

"No, not really." I'm playing it down as best I can, hoping to put him at ease. "Like I said, this has nothing really to do with BMX. It has more to do with Mr. Lara. It's about a conversation you and he had regarding the building's development, and more specifically about his compensation."

No response.

I ask, "Do you know what conversation I'm referring to?"

"Uh-huh." He's quiet. The wheels are turning and I'm afraid I'm loosing him.

"So, are you free to meet anytime tomorrow? Just to talk?"

"Uh, yeah." Tang sounds like he's writing something down; hopefully it's a note on his calendar. "I can meet you here around noon," he says.

I thank him, and hang up. He definitely knows what I'm talking about. Though I'm mildly encouraged that he's agreed to meet with me, it's doubtful that it will ever happen. I'm putting myself in his place—an up and coming manager in a large firm. He'll want to do right by the company and tell his bosses about the phone call. And they'll immediately put on the brakes. Between their financial interest in the property and the potential of negative publicity for their firm, they'll circle the wagons. They will refer me to their attorneys, and no one will remember any such conversation.

Sure enough, I get a call from Tang the next morning. "I'm sorry, I'm unable to meet with you," he says.

When I ask why, he just repeats the same words as if reading from a prepared script: "I'm sorry, I'm unable to meet with you."

I exhale my disappointment into the phone. Then, one last, pathetic, attempt at intimidation. "I had hoped to avoid a more formal investigation, thought maybe we could keep this off the record, but . . . okay, Mr. Tang, if this is the way we're going to have to proceed. Thanks for your time. You have my number if you change your mind."

Now I feel like a jerk. He's never going to call me, and the only thing that my little scare tactic will accomplish is keeping the poor kid up worrying at night. Who knows if there is even anything to it? Although I want to believe there is, this is, for all intents and purposes, a dead end.

The J Street apartment part of the investigation isn't turning out much better. Though I've been following Hector Lara around town regularly, I haven't spotted him at the apartments since that first time—and even then, I didn't actually see him go in. And worse, I'm not finding any connection between Lara and any of the utility subscribers or renters. Sure, some have Latino surnames, which could easily be aliases, or friends, or family members of his, but still, I'm not able to find the link.

My investigation is capsizing and I'm feeling like a damn failure. I still have a few minutes until my meeting with officer Quintel, so I phone my dad. He's upset at the thought that Lara is going to get away with this; I can hear it in his voice. But since Dad knows little about criminal investigations, the most he can do is just listen. At the end he tells me, "Don't give up. You'll find something on him."

I force a light laugh, trying to lighten the conversation. "Oh yea," I say. "I forgot to tell you about an art exhibit I'm going to be part of. Some of my paintings will be on display at city hall, and I'd like you to come if you can."

"Wouldn't miss it." He hangs up without getting the date, but it doesn't matter. He's retired, and other than an occasional movie or a trip to the Indian casinos, his schedule is pretty much open.

When I call Marilyn Quintel into my office I can see that she's nervous. We don't really know each other very well anyway, and nobody likes getting summoned to talk with the captain.

Since I prefer that people be honest with me, that's how I proceed with Marilyn. I tell her flatly that she is failing the FTO program, and then I explain in detail the areas in which she is deficient. I don't put it off on anyone else—don't tell her the trainers won't pass her or that the chief wants her fired. I also don't front off the doctor, who was courteous enough to explain the situation to me—albeit straddling the gray area of medical privacy laws.

"What I propose, Marilyn, is that we remove you from the training program." I pause to give her a second to absorb it. "And assign you back to the jail as a community service officer." It's the non-sworn, unarmed position from which she came before going to the police academy. "I'd like to keep you in that position for a year, giving you more time to heal. During that time, I'd encourage you to keep a city map and a police radio with you in the jail, so you can listen and follow the activity on the street. You can also ride with patrol officers as much as you want, just to keep you up on things. Then, at the end of a year, we'll put you back into the police field-training program as an officer. Have you go though it again and see how you do."

Although Marilyn looks disappointed, I figure that saving her job, maintaining her income, providing a way to hone her skills, and giving her time to adequately recover, is a fair and equitable compromise. I know that it isn't what the chief wants, and it certainly isn't something we are obligated to do. But I feel that it's worth a try, and in the end, she agrees to it.

As Marilyn leaves my office, I notice Bobby Roselli and Gary Donahue pacing nervously in the hallway outside.

"The county sheriff is going to be one of the speakers at the council meeting tomorrow night," Gary says as they clamor in and close the door.

"The mayoral recall people are also going to be there in force," says Bobby, "including Danny Jenner!"

Bobby is using his clout as a former PBA president to talk it up among the association's board. A big turnout from the association members will send a message of solidarity. And having the former deputy chief speak, as well as the sheriff—one the most respected law enforcement officers in the state—ought to shake the hell out of Lara.

I stop at home after work on Tuesday, shedding my coat and tie and picking up Gale. Besides the fact that she wants to be there to support me, I figure that she, more than anyone else, has suffered the effects of this mess.

About a dozen of us meet at a restaurant near city hall, just before the meeting. We have some drinks and appetizers and then head over to the council chambers. I've had two martinis, just enough to give me a stupid smile.

The place is packed; not like the usual city council meetings where only a handful of *concerned citizens* show up to complain that their street needs repaving. Then the sizable group of cops files in, taking up two whole rows at the back of the theater-like room. The mayor and council eye us as they take their seats on a raised dais at the front.

The county sheriff walks in with a small gaggle of supporters, taking a seat, front and center, directly facing the mayor. Danny Jenner, our former deputy chief, shows up with Hank Barone, the guy who used to be an attorney for the city, and who now also works for the sheriff. Even Russ Emory, my furtive business owner friend and informant, shows up. I keep eyeing the door for my dad, but thankfully he's opted to sit this one out.

For over an hour, the mayor and council are criticized about their handling of the former police chief. Much of the heat is directed at Hector Lara, who sits there stone-faced, as if he's watching a documentary about the indigenous tribes of New Guinea.

The sheriff doesn't mince words though. He says that the mayor should be recalled and Lara should be fired. Adding, "If Hector Lara had any honor, he'd resign."

Many of the speakers implore the council to read what is now erroneously being referred to as the *Carl Bradford internal affairs report*. My buddy and former deputy chief says, "You have a duty and a responsibility to the truth, and to hold your appointee, Hector Lara, accountable."

I'm not expecting Russ Emory to speak, but I suspect he has been emboldened by the sheriff. "You're being fed a crock," he says to the council, warning them that this will cost them a public relations fiasco the likes of which the city has never dealt with.

I see the city beat reporter from the local paper, sitting in the front row scribbling notes as fast as she can. She's not the guy I've been cultivating, but I'm hoping she'll write a decent article.

Mayor Behrman sits red-faced, crossing her arms and turning away from the speakers like a scolded child. At one point she barks into the microphone, "There will be no more applause from the audience!"

I immediately start clapping loudly. She and Lara glare in my direction, but I don't care anymore. Maybe when the excitement of the night and the martinis wear off, I will care. But I leave the council chambers feeling supported and somewhat vindicated, for the first time in fourteen months.

I'm at work early the next morning, in my office reading the watch commander reports. Chief Vincent's secretary calls me to say that the chief would like to see me in his office, immediately.

I walk across the hall and there's Hector Lara sitting with the chief. Lara's got a look on his face like he ate some bad shrimp.

"Close the door," he says with a snarl.

Right away I don't like that he's ordering me around. Reminds me of that day at the animal shelter when he tried to bait me. Seems like he always pulls his tough guy act when he's either on the phone with me or he's got Vincent there to protect him. I close the door and take a seat facing him, looking right into his eyes. Vincent is sitting behind his desk watching the two of us with a look of dread.

"You needed to see me?" I turn to face the chief.

Lara barks, "I called you in here to discuss your conduct at the council meeting last night."

"Oh?" An insincere look of bewilderment is set on my face as I turn back toward the MA. "What conduct was that?"

"You are a captain," he says. "A representative of sorts of the police department."

"Yes, I am. And I'm also a resident of this city." My eyebrows dip. "Are you saying that because I'm a police captain I can't attend a public city meeting?"

"Well, no, I'm not suggesting that." He waves his hand like a wand from my head to my feet. "But you're attire. Your manner of dress was completely inappropriate."

I begin to defend myself, explain that I was still dressed in my work clothes—a collared shirt and slacks. But I stop myself, mid-sentence and shake my head. "No," I say. "No, I'm not doing this. You and I both know that if the sheriff hadn't called you corrupt and urged the council to fire you, we wouldn't even be talking right now."

Lara is struggling to come up with his next criticism, but can't find one.

"Was there anything else, Chief?" Now I've turned my back to the MA.

I feel Lara's eyes burning into me as I leave the chief's office. A momentary feeling of dread passes through me, like, what if he's now so pissed off that he *really* comes after me. Then I let out a little laugh. *As if, until now Lara hasn't already done everything he can to ruin me.*

He's the one who ought to be worried.

It's a Saturday afternoon; the kind of sunny day that reminds me there are better times ahead—a season when this will all be behind me. Today is also the city employee art exhibit at city hall. In addition to Gale and the girls, my brother's family is going, my mom, and my dad and stepmom.

I'm eager to see not only my artwork displayed, but also the works of other employees—many of whom I only know within the work setting. It's the first such event, and one I'm excited about. Beautiful artwork, hors d'oeuvres and wine . . . what could possibly go wrong on a day like this?

When I walk in and see Hector Lara working the crowd, I cringe. I'm not sure why he's here, other than he probably wants to show support for the city employees. And there's really nothing wrong with that, it's just that I wasn't expecting or wanting to see him. This was supposed to be a day when I could relax, forget about my troubles at work, and enjoy myself. Having him around is going to make that more difficult. So I make up my mind to leave the animosity at the door—something like a détente.

Unfortunately, my dad didn't leave anything at the door. He's still chaffing about the way Lara called me out after the council meeting, in addition to everything else that's gone on. I've got an eye on Dad and he seems okay though, just standing with my stepmom over by the cracker and cheese tray, checking out a macramé plant hanger crocheted by one of the librarians. In addition, Gale is right there beside them. My hope is that between the two women, they'll be able to keep my dad in check.

About this time I notice Hector Lara making his way along the display wall, gazing up at all the prints, paintings and tapestries as he passes. He's got a glass of wine in his hand and he seems to be particularly interested in a wood carving of a dolphin just a few feet from my dad. But Dad's got his back to Lara, and I'm hoping he hasn't noticed him.

The MA finishes admiring the dolphin and now he's sort of wedged between my family and the wall. He turns himself sideways and starts to squeeze behind my dad.

That's when it happens . . .

LESSON 22

"Beware the naked man who offers you a shirt."
~African saying

My brother walks over to me wearing just a trace of a smile.

"Please," I say to him. "Tell me Dad didn't just do that."

Tyler nods. "Oh yeah, he did it."

In a move that looked like a cross between a yawning stretch and a muscle spasm, my dad has just thrown an elbow into Hector Lara's neck, spilling the administrator's wine and momentarily pinning the guy against the wall.

"Oh, sorry about that," my dad says over his shoulder to the MA, who's now crumpled in a heap against a black and white photograph of Half Dome. A few gasps emit from the crowd. My dad turns to straighten the cockeyed picture, leaving Lara to help himself up.

I'm humiliated, Tyler is trying hard to keep from laughing, and Gale looks over at me with shrugged shoulders that say, *Sorry, but what could I do?*

* * *

Chief Vincent asks me to stay after our Monday staff meeting, and I'm half expecting to get walloped for disrespecting the MA the last time we were in his office, or if not that, for my dad's clothesline move at the art exhibit.

"I wanted to talk to you about a couple of things," says the chief, sliding a manila envelope across the table to me. "Congratulations, you're scheduled for the winter class at the FBI National Academy."

I'm speechless. This is a big deal for me; a very selective training program that I've waited a long time to attend. Worldwide, only a couple of hundred police executives are selected annually.

"It turns out that Bradford never submitted your applications," he says. "So when I explained the situation to the feds, they fast-tracked the process for us."

I'm having a difficult time believing that the MA would ever have approved it, but Vincent insists that it's going to happen. I realize, of course, that we've still got a few months before I head back to Quantico, and a lot can happen in that time. But as long as Vincent is chief, it seems I have a layer of protection from Lara. I start to thank him, but he holds a hand up to stop me.

"Hey, you've earned it" he says. "But that's just one thing I wanted to talk to you about. There's something else."

I watch him fidget in his seat, and I wonder if it's a good news-bad news thing.

"I'm going to be leaving."

Figures. Just when I can take a breath, the air gets sucked out again. "Leaving, as in you're not going to be the chief any longer?"

Vincent nods. "This was only intended to be an interim job, and my contract is up at the end of the year. Lara wants me to stay on for another six months, until he can find a replacement, but . . ."

His sentence hangs in the air, hinting that the reason the chief won't stay on is one he doesn't feel comfortable discussing. My guess is that it has something to do with working for Lara. His next words come as a surprise to me.

"I'm going to recommend you as my replacement," he says.

"Never happen," I say, shaking my head. "The MA wouldn't go for it in a million years. Hell, the council would never go for it. But thank you, I definitely appreciate the confidence."

He gives me a smile and a sort of nod that says, *tell me what you want, but I'm still going to recommend you.*

"Let me think about it," I say. "There is a lot more going on between me and the MA than you know."

About a week later a blistering article appears in the local paper. It's an uncomfortable read that unmistakably draws some battle lines that publicly advertise the main political event: Odell Graham vs. Hector Lara and his puppet council.

Graham, who is described as having broken ranks with the rest of the council, has actually filed a petition with the Superior Court. He's seeking an order compelling Lara (essentially his employee) to hand over the internal affairs report and other personnel documents relating to Carl Bradford. The story is written by my reporter friend and includes all of the details that I've passed on to him.

Teddy Rube, the newbie councilman who had stopped by my house to hear our side of the saga, shows a momentary flash of consciousness. He doesn't go as far as Graham, but Rube makes an on-the-record request to see the concealed documents.

But in a move so typical of Lara, he releases the report to the council later that same day—as if the MA had played chicken with Graham all this time, only to call his bluff at the eleventh hour. It was like Lara said okay, that report you have requested for several months, the one that I've refused to show you because it's a protected "personnel matter," well, I'll go ahead and give it to you now.

Not that any of them will actually see the true report. In the time that's passed, Lara, not unlike the Iranian government hiding evidence from nuclear inspectors, could show them a doctored version of the paperwork or something completely made up. And not knowing any different, the council will lap it up, *con gusto.*

Teddy Rube's entire spine falls out of his body and crumbles to dust as he immediately rescinds his request. Then he quickly follows up with a *Lara-inspired* press statement that says he no longer has a need to seek more information.

So in one swift move, Lara shut Rube up for good, made Graham look like a troublemaker, and rendered the superior court order irrelevant. But Hector Lara isn't done yet . . .

"Hello," I answer my off-the-grid desk phone.

"It's Russ," says a whispering voice. "Can you talk?"

"Sure." I stretch the cord over to the door, which I push closed. "Go ahead."

"Somebody shot at Odell," Emory says. "Tried to take him out."

"What?" I move back behind my desk and take out a notepad. "When? I didn't read anything about it in the log."

"He didn't report it," says Emory. "First someone tried to poison his dogs. Threw hamburger tainted with rat bait into his yard. Then someone fired at Odell's car when it was being serviced."

"Is he okay?"

"Yeah, he wasn't driving it at the time." Emory moves his mouth so close to the receiver that I can barely understand him. "The mechanic was driving it. The windows are blacked out and whoever did it must have thought it was Odell inside. Anyway, it shattered the windows of the car, but nobody was hit."

"You gotta be shit'n me."

"Odell thinks he knows who's behind it, but he doesn't want this to get out." Emory is now talking at a normal level. "He's pretty sure that this is retaliation for the petition he filed with the court."

"The councilman thinks Lara did it?"

Emory hesitates. "He doesn't think Lara actually poisoned his dogs or shot at his car, but he believes Lara is behind it."

"Like what?" I ask. "He hired someone to do it?"

"Yeah, like that." Emory pauses a beat. "Maybe Evan Casey."

My mind is trying to grasp a weasel like Casey attempting to kill the city councilman. Lara behind it? Sure, at this point I can believe that. But Casey actually having the balls to do it? Not so sure. The guy is a backroom manipulator and a snake in the dark. Maybe he'd poison the dogs, but I'm having trouble visualizing him pulling a trigger. This latest incident has me starting to wonder if Emory is pumping up these stories, possibly to benefit himself in some way.

Doesn't matter. Nothing would surprise me anymore—not Lara working with Casey, nor the two of them intimidating the lone dissenter on the council, even if it meant trying to kill the guy. I'm getting a better sense of what I'm dealing with now. This is no longer a game of strategy . . . it's a Goddamn battle. It's war.

So now that Hector Lara has released at least some version of the "Bradford internal investigation" to the council, he also tries to choreograph a citywide public relations blitz.

Shoring up what's left of her city council, the mayor comes out in the paper assuring the citizenry that there is nothing to the complaints against Bradford, stating that the misconduct allegations against him "in reality had no basis in fact." Mayor Behrman adds that she stands behind Administrator Lara 1,000 percent. And then in her condescending style says, "We extend an open invitation to everyone to join us in moving forward in a positive and collegial fashion." The subtext being that anyone who disagrees is neither positive nor collegial.

Our attorney uses the mayor's own "moving forward" pitch to make another run at the city to pay our mounting legal bills. This time it works. We don't hear it from Lara or the council, but Russ Emory calls to tell me that he got it straight from Councilman Odell Graham—"The council ordered Lara to cut you guys a check."

But after more than a week goes by without any word from Lara, I'm beginning to wonder if Emory heard wrong. Then, suddenly, Lara wants to meet with us, calls up as friendly as Captain Kangaroo and invites the remnants of our commander group to lunch.

236

I'm choking down my clam chowder as I listen to this guy tell us that we were all the victims of a big misunderstanding. He carefully avoids any mention of Bradford's misdeeds, or the whitewash investigation that supposedly cleared him. Nor does the MA mention the city council meeting that we all attended to support the sheriff's calls for his firing and the mayor's removal from office. He doesn't bring up our memo, how he's threatened us, how he forced Danny Jenner out, or how he's completely trashed each of our reputations. No, instead he smiles warmly.

My wait for the bomb to drop lasts until the coffees are ordered at the end of the meal. Then, with a most sincere expression, Lara says, " . . . and about the legal fees you've incurred." As if we've been talking about it all along. "I've decided to reimburse your expenses."

I've decided? The schmuck doesn't realize that I already know that the council ordered him to pay us weeks ago. Like we're now supposed to be grateful to him, as if it's coming out of his wallet.

He whips out a pen and a couple of pages clipped together, and slides them onto the table in front of me.

I glance through the document, a legal agreement of some kind. Clipped to the last page is a draft press release. It's from Lara's office to the local media, announcing that in an "effort to enable everyone to concentrate on the delivery of service, and to stop being distracted by extraneous matters," the city has agreed to reimburse all six members of the command staff for their legal costs.

"Just a couple of small caveats," he casually adds, motioning to the legal document. "You'll need to sign a hold harmless agreement with the city, and withdraw all your allegations of retaliation."

Oh, is that all? I feel the concussion of the explosion in the pit of my gut, rising through me until the mushroom cloud blooms over my head. The four of us, me, Claire, Bobby and Gary, exchange short glances, and I'm trying to read if they want to sign right now and move on in peace, or what.

"Sorry," I tell him, intentionally not speaking for the other commanders. "But I'll need to read this over in more detail."

Lara conceals his disappointment, or anger, whatever it is, and says nothing more about it. The hosted lunch comes to a quick conclusion and Lara takes off in his sports car. We mill around in the parking lot for a few minutes and then head back to the police department. There is a little bit of discussion, but it's without much substance. I get the feeling that after more than a year of fighting a battle in which we're no better off than when we began, my comrades are running out of steam.

I get to the coffee shop a few minutes before my dad—that's a first. It's cool and dark, and I sit parked under the streetlamp, thinking. Maybe it's time for me to do some self-reflection.

Deputy Chief Jenner has moved on, working for the sheriff now. Miguel Zavala is gone and Gary Donahue is retiring within the month. That leaves me, Claire and Bobby—hardly formidable against the omnipresent administrator and his legion of city attorneys. And Lara's milquetoast council is in lockstep with him. The only exception being poor Odell Graham—his dogs in the veterinarian hospital and his car windows shot out. Is this fight even worth it? What's left for me to care about?

I talk to my dad, tell him that the strategy of dragging this thing out for over a year has been intentional—a tactic straight out of Hector Lara's playbook. The MA knows that people change, people move on, people forget. And he's counting on the emotional potency of all this to wane—like a car that sits in a garage for a year; nobody deflates the tires, they just lose pressure and go flat over time. Lara knows that a year from now, nobody in this apathetic town will remember the former chief, much less care about why and how he left the job. But I'm not forgetting, and neither is my dad.

At least two people still care.

I wait a day or two, reading over the agreement that Lara wants me to sign. It's actually worse than I thought. By signing, I am giving up all rights to sue the city—not just for any injustices that have already been inflicted upon me, but for anything they may do to me in the future.

"Hello Mr. Lara." I have to keep reminding myself not to speak for the rest of the group. It actually might be in their best interest to accept the deal. Then again, if I don't sign, it's unlikely any of us will be reimbursed. "I've read over your proposed agreement and I'm not willing to release the city from liability. I have no plans to bring a suit, but I'd be stupid to waive my rights to anything that might happen in the future."

The MA seems unfazed. "I don't see why that's a problem."

"Oh, you don't?"

"No," he says. "I understand you're quite popular with the rank and file, especially given your powerful position as the patrol operations commander. If I were to take you on, mistreat you in some way, it would be tantamount to sticking my head into a buzz saw."

Interesting analogy. I'm not sure my popularity is as strong as he seems to feel it is, but after five years as patrol captain I do enjoy the influence of running the largest division in the entire city. Still, his argument does not compel me to reconsider, and I tell him so.

Chief Vincent calls me into his office less than a week later. "I'm thinking of rotating you out of patrol and into investigations."

I stare back at him without saying anything, searching for a hint of misgiving or guilt in his expression. Then I ask him, point blank: "Did this come from the municipal administrator?"

Vincent thinks. "He did mention that in the past the captains rotated assignments every few years. But he only suggested it."

"Lara wants to knock me out of the patrol division," I say. "He sees Patrol as the power seat in the department. This is just his way of retaliating, like not paying our out-of-pocket attorney fees."

"He has to pay you; the council already ordered him to."

"Yeah," I tell him, "but only if we sign away our rights."

The chief frowns, and I'm not sure how much he actually knows. "I think the reason he hasn't paid you guys yet is because he's afraid you'll use the money to help finance the mayoral recall."

I laugh. "Only a sleaze like him would think of something like that. I couldn't give a shit about the mayor. I need the money to pay for my daughter's college tuition."

"Anyway, Lara's not too happy with me either," says Vincent. "He was counting on a contract extension that would keep me here longer. I don't think he's been able to line things up yet."

By "line things up" I assume he means recruiting a chief that will get rid of me—something Patrick Vincent hasn't been willing to do. So, keeping Lara juggling problems and putting out fires has at least benefited me in that way. Less time for him to put his plan in place.

"What did he say when you recommended me for chief?"

Vincent laughs. "What choice does he have? You're the senior captain. When I leave, he's got no option but to put you in charge."

His non-answer tells me everything I already suspected. It's no wonder the MA is not happy with Vincent. If I know the guy at all, he'll start making Vincent's life miserable, now that he's leaving.

"And," he continues. "I didn't mention to Lara that you're going to Virginia in January. Less of a chance for him to derail it."

I thank the chief again for his efforts to get me into the FBI National Academy, and I also tell him that after mulling it over I've decided I'm not interested in the interim police chief's job when he leaves.

239

He shakes his head ruefully, but doesn't try to convince me otherwise. I think by now he knows enough of what I've been through with Lara. Realizing that the guy had also played him, Vincent decides not to move me out of patrol operations after all.

Later in the day the commanders hold a teleconference that includes the two who have already retired. We discuss the proposed settlement, and thankfully none of them like Lara's terms any more than I do. We agree to try another approach—one that might score us our reimbursement and embarrass the administrator and the council in the process. We draft a letter to the police union, laying out the reasons we hired an attorney in the first place, and of our failed attempts to get the city to pay us back.

By now the topic of us (the whistleblowers) having actually been told by Lara to hire an attorney, along with the fact that we have not been reimbursed by the city, has garnered a lot of press coverage— one of the main reasons that the council finally told Lara to pay us back. So when the PBA agrees to pay our out-of-pocket legal expenses, I seize the opportunity to strike another blow.

Next morning's headlines: POLICE UNION AGREES TO PAY FEES. So much for Lara's premature press release—the one he so badly wanted us to sign off on. I know that the council will be furious; it's been five weeks since they told him to pay us. Beating him to the punch, I've been able to word the article to look like the police commanders have taken the high road and are moving forward to bring about closure. And as an unexpected bonus—the PBA president states that the union has always stood "firmly behind the command staff and supported their actions."

A phone call from Russ Emory later in the day confirms it—the council is completely pissed off at Hector Lara for bungling their public relations opportunity. Instead of redeeming themselves in the community's eyes, they all came out looking like shit. The article's backlash only adds more fuel to the growing recall effort.

We're moving closer to the end of the year and I continue to gather evidence and document Lara's movements around town. I've also met with the department of justice in San Francisco, to go over what I've found thus far. By now I'm focusing my efforts on money laundering rather than actually trying to prove a case of soliciting a bribe. My thinking is that conducting a financial investigation will eliminate the need to deal with nervous developers and trying to persuade reluctant witnesses to come forward.

The agent I'm dealing with at DOJ tries to steer me towards the district attorney's office in my own county. Normally, it would be a logical move. But as I put together a list of former cops who now work as investigators there, it reads like a roster of Evan Casey cohorts. And with Casey so closely aligned with Bradford, and now suspected in Lara's dog poisoning and intimidation dirty work, the DA's office idea is quickly nixed.

Instead, I fill out a federal financial investigation application. It's a lengthy document containing all identifying information on a suspect, including known addresses, alias names, bank accounts, social security, passport, and drivers license numbers, etc. By the time I'm finished, the thing is several pages long. I use the report number from my original public corruption investigation, figuring that this is all part and parcel of the same case. Once filed, the application for information is distributed to all pertinent federal agencies, from IRS to INS. The results will take several weeks to research, so from this point on I'll need to be patient.

Not long after I send in the application I'm called into the chief's office again. And again, there's Hector Lara, sitting with a coffee mug in his hand and an expression of distain on his face. For a second or two I wonder if my investigation has somehow come to his attention. Not that I really care anymore, but it would definitely take an already uncomfortable situation and make it worse. Much worse. He turns slightly in his seat, as if the effort to talk to me is taxing.

"The chief tells me that you are not interested in the interim position when he leaves." Lara stares off, stone faced.

"That's right."

"I wanted to hear it directly from you," he says, finally looking at me. "Can I ask why?"

I pause long enough to slow my heartbeat and get my head straight. My dilemma is figuring out how truthful I should be. Right now, Hector Lara is like a naked man offering a shirt. It's an insincere gesture on so many levels—the most obvious being that he's really offering me nothing. He would sabotage my every move, poison the council against me even more, making absolutely certain that the permanent position never came my way. So, in reality, he has nothing to give and nothing that I want.

Realizing that I'm not telling him anything he doesn't already know, I decide to go ahead and speak frankly. "I'm pretty sure that you don't trust me," I tell Lara. "And I know for a fact that I don't trust you."

Chief Vincent nearly falls off his chair, but to Lara's credit he doesn't break stride. The MA takes a sip of coffee from his mug and nods thoughtfully. Almost as if he had convinced himself that I would jump at the job, but now that I've turned it down he's simply reassessing the situation and considering his Plan B.

I stay in the conference room with Vincent after Lara leaves. The chief asks me why I decided not to take the job, and I run down my list of reasons: how Lara has convinced the council that I led the charge against Bradford—made up false accusations just so I could get his position; that Lara sought a chief that would get rid of me; how Lara eliminated the deputy chief's position and then heaped an entire second division on me after Jenner left, then micromanaged everything I did, trying to find a flaw; that he criticized my decisions while Vincent was away, and how he promised Bradford that my career would never go anywhere.

Vincent listens without comment, thinking and nodding in agreement. After a few minutes of silence he says, "I think the MA was surprised that you turned down the position."

"I'm not stupid," I say. "It's a setup for failure, and I know that everything I would do, every decision I'd make, he'd be right there to berate me and then spin it to the council. I also know myself; I've managed to keep my anger in check thus far, but there is definitely a limit to my restraint."

The very next day Lara holds a departmental meeting at the police department. The assembly room is full and I'm sitting with the other commanders in the front row. I have an inkling that the MA wants to paint this thing between he and I a certain way to the troops—probably because of how "popular" he thinks I am.

Sure enough, after announcing that Chief Vincent will be leaving at the end of the year, he transitions to his search for an interim chief. Lara then motions to me with an open hand. "Phil and I have talked about him taking the position, but *he* feels that it would be best for the organization if somebody else were in the chief's office."

A low grumble rolls through the room like a wave, but what can I do? Stand up and tell everyone that those were his words, not mine? That Lara engineered this whole thing, trashed my reputation and ruined my career, and that he left me with no other choice? Lara's portrayal of our little talk made him look like the good guy, as if he had offered me the job, which he hadn't, and it made me look like a chump.

242

I walk out at the end of the assembly, pissed off and not talking to anyone. I close the door to my office and collapse myself onto my chair. I'm thinking about going to San Francisco and getting drunk again. I'm thinking about calling up the Indian woman—the one who loves me so damn much. I'm thinking about going back into the assembly room and kicking Hector Lara's ass.

Instead, I go home, pack up my little truck, and head up to my family's cabin in the mountains.

During the three-hour drive I listen to music and try my best to relax. I tell myself that it's only a job and it's not worth all this. I'm not doing myself any favors getting so upset, and this can't be good for my health.

I stop at the market in town to buy a New York steak, a potato, and some corn. I circle around the aisles, unfamiliar with the store's layout, searching for the damn steak sauce. I go back for some mushrooms—got to have sautéed mushrooms with the New York. This will be good, I tell myself. Alone up here in the woods I can get centered again. Wine, I'll need a bottle of red wine. I grab that, too.

I'm standing on the back deck, warming my hands over the glowing cask of the Weber. The smell of pine trees, the taste of wine, it all works together in my favor. Then, just when I think I've left my troubles behind, the phone rings.

Calls are so seldom at the cabin that I've almost forgotten there was a phone. I step inside and pick it up, wondering who even knows where to find me. It's Gale, calling to relay a message.

"A reporter from the paper called the house and wants to talk to you," she says. "I know you're trying to relax up there, but I think he wants to know why you turned down the police chief job."

I pour another glass of wine and contemplate my response before returning the reporter's call. For me to publicly say anything critical about the administrator, the city, or the council, could be a job-threatening mistake. But to word it in such a way as to get my point across, letting the readers draw their own conclusions . . . it's worth the risk.

The way I figure it, this is probably my last opportunity to make a public statement on this issue. And since Lara has already spun it his way to the department and undoubtedly to the city council, this is my only chance to even the score.

LESSON 23

*"The role of a writer is not to say what we all can
say, but what we are unable to say."*
~Anaïs Nin

My two-sentence quote in the next day's paper pretty much sums it
up: *"The municipal administrator and I don't place the same value
on integrity. For that reason, I don't care to work any closer to him
than I already do."*

Like it or not, I've finally said my piece. Sure, my career is over,
but then again it was over the minute I signed the memo accusing
Carl Bradford of malfeasance. At least now I've made it clear,
publicly, that I can't be bought. I'm not sure Lara was prepared for
that, and I'm pretty certain he feels that it weakens his hold on me.
In his eyes I'm more dangerous to him if he's got nothing to dangle
in front of me, such as the chief job.

I can only imagine that Hector Lara, white hot with rage after
reading my comments, ran straight into the city attorney's office to
see if he could fire me for what I said. But in reality, I said very little.
I'm guessing that the city attorney would have told him that
whatever *value* either of us places on integrity was never even
addressed—that was left for the reader to decide.

Anyway, mixed with the tang of venom in my mouth after
talking to the reporter, my New York steak doesn't turn out as tasty
as I had hoped it would. Probably serves me right.

Suffering through a few days alone at the cabin, jogging,
watching football and eating things that aren't good for me, I finally
head back home. It's been a nice couple of days to decompress, but I
return to the police department's theatrics feeling as if I had never
left—only to find out that Lara has announced his selection for the
new "interim" police chief.

Don't get me wrong; Thurmond Morris is a nice guy. There's not a mean bone in his body, but his strength is definitely not in decision-making. And although the troops like him, I'm not sure where he falls on the respect continuum. He's only a lieutenant, and for my money he's sort of out of his depth at that rank—probably hit his peak as a sergeant. He's the guy they call Morris Code, because of his big mouth. Thurmond doesn't live in the city and doesn't even come close to meeting the job's educational requirements.

This is the same guy who once reported to me that a ritualistic killer had disemboweled a prostitute. Same guy who accidentally fired a shotgun round over my head at the scene of a SWAT incident. And the same guy who once thought it would be funny to place a dildo on a lesbian officer's clipboard in the report writing room.

So I welcome my new boss, realizing that I turned down the job and now I have no room to talk about the guy who got it. I'll support him as best as I'm able, but I can already see why he was chosen. He's a jovial guy who gets along with the council, and he'll do whatever Hector Lara tells him to do—no questions asked. The MA will never have to worry about Morris making a decision without checking with him first.

"Hey," Morris says. "This feels a little awkward, seeing as how you've been my boss all these years . . . until today."

"Nothing to feel awkward about, Thurmond." I reach over and shake his hand. "You're the chief and I'm your patrol captain. It's as simple as that."

"Aw, well, you know, it'll always be me in this uniform—just the same ol' Thurmond."

Unfortunately, that's exactly what I'm worried about. My take on ol' Thurmond is pretty much confirmed right away when he tells me that I'm being transferred out of patrol operations.

"That didn't take long," I say.

"Well, yeah." Morris says, flashing a self-conscious grin. "The administrator thinks Desmond needs to get more experience, so he wants you guys to rotate."

I nod, forcing myself to appear agreeable. It's only a month or so before I leave for the East Coast, and I'm hoping I can just bear with it until then. The FBI has interviewed me, completed a background check and given me secret clearance. And I've already packed a box full of files, supplies and linens for my dorm room, to be shipped back to the FBI training facility. This three-month break from the headaches of the department could not have come at a better time.

"Oh yeah, another thing." Morris confers with his handwritten list of instructions. "The municipal administrator doesn't want you to attend the FBI training in Quantico."

My eyes settle on my new boss, but I can't even imagine what my face is saying. I'm fairly certain it isn't pleasant. I rub my chin and turn my gaze toward the window. There's the American flag, and next to it the California flag. The third flagpole holds the city flag—all three of them waving wildly in the wind outside the chief's office. They represent all the things I've stood for over the last thirty years, even longer. I'm so disappointed, on so many levels, that I can't even find the words. I just stare at the flags.

"But I told him . . ." Morris continues. "I told him that at this point, cancelling your training would appear retaliatory. It wouldn't go over well with the rank and file."

I turn back to Morris, still feeling like the energy has been drained out of me. His argument hadn't captured the true injustice of the administrator's subversive efforts, but I'm thankful that Morris actually said something in my defense. As it turns out, Hector Lara decides to back down—undoubtedly realizing that more alienation from the police wouldn't play well for him—i.e., his buzz saw analogy. Especially with the mayor's recall vote so close at hand.

Walking back to my office, I reconcile the bad with the good. I have to accept that I'm leaving the position I've thrived in for the last five years, but at least my FBI training is still on track. Barely.

Things don't stay quiet for long, and I begin to hear rumblings that some of the female officers are unhappy. I have no specifics, but the most common themes I'm hearing have to do with unfair treatment—either overt or subtle. I know I've been pretty wrapped up with patrol division issues, defending myself from Hector Lara, and with preparing for my three months away at the national academy. But having a wife and two daughters in the workforce, and also being a die-hard advocate of fair play, I roll up my sleeves and dive headfirst into it.

I call Nora Morales, a good friend and a respected homicide investigator, and I tell her what I've heard. Something of a wine aficionado, she invites me for drinks and appetizers one afternoon on her patio. We talk for two or three hours, at the end of which I think I have a pretty good handle on the issues. Some incidents can be chalked up to personalities or miscommunications; others are more troubling and have the smell of institutionalized favoritism. That bothers me.

The issues are wide ranging and it'll take a little time to put things in place. I'm fighting against the clock due to the upcoming training in Virginia.

When I bring it up in our staff meeting, the other commanders are just as committed as I am. We begin by putting together a department-wide training for every single supervisor—sworn or not. We also pay to bring in an attorney who specializes in gender discrimination and harassment lawsuits, and she speaks on the subject for two hours. Each of the commanders also addresses the group: me, Claire, Bobby and Desmond—the captain who is going to replace me in patrol. We give a clear vision of what we expect from leaders in our organization, focusing specifically on gender, fairness and favoritism issues.

The only commander who doesn't address the sixty supervisors and managers is Interim Chief Morris. It doesn't sit well with some of the people there, and they feel that it says something about the importance he places on it.

Between the rest of us, we're able to take care of a few of the other specific complaints—careless and insensitive comments, lack of recognition for good work, and some special assignment issues. I've also begun working with Scooter, now the personnel and training lieutenant, putting together a promotional training course to be offered to employees at all levels. That way those who may not have *friends in high places* will get the benefit of the same career and promotional advice as those seen as the *favorite sons*.

Tensions seem to be easing a little, but I know there is a lot more that can and should be done. In my mind it doesn't matter so much whether these issues of injustice are perception or reality, as I have come to know firsthand that to the offended person, they are one and the same. I'm hopeful that my FBI academy training might provide me with more ideas on how to address the subject.

A few weeks of a peaceful adjustment to the new chief turns out to be only a brief rest before the next punch. Morris calls me into his office, and once again, there's Hector Lara—a coffee mug in one hand and a fistful of papers in the other.

Doesn't the guy have an office of his own?

He's apparently come to share a series of letters with the chief, five documents in all, supposedly sent anonymously—each of them with accusations of harassment and discrimination.

"May I see them?" I ask. "The commanders and I have been working on some of these issues already."

"What issues?" Lara asks.

I feel my forehead wrinkle. "Complaints by some of the women employees?"

Lara hands me the letters. "These are complaints about you," he says.

Feeling like I'm about to hack up a hairball, I begin reading. The letters date back to just after Bradford left, coming in sporadically over the entire time that Patrick Vincent was here. They have nothing to do with the complaints raised by the women employees. Instead, these accuse me of running the police department with a racist and sexist agenda, disparaging blacks, gays and women. According to the anonymous author, I've been running roughshod over Chief Vincent, and now Chief Morris, showing favoritism to friends and SWAT team members and seeking retribution against anyone who was sympathetic to the former chief, Carl Bradford.

I shake my head in disgust. "The routing shows that these have all been sent to council members and to the NAACP."

Lara casually sips his coffee. "I wouldn't worry too much about it," he says. "Nobody puts a lot of credence into anonymous letters."

"Anonymous," I repeat, my eyes burning with rage. "Evan Casey might as well have signed his name on them."

"Yes, it occurred to me that Evan might have written these." Lara takes the letters back. "He was quite close to Chief Bradford."

"Look at the poor grammar and all the misspellings," I say. "They've got Casey written all over them."

Then it hits me. These could have been written by Lara himself, intentionally made to look like they came from some illiterate boob. Either way, I'm convinced that Lara is not going to defend me to the council or the local NAACP chapter.

"So, what happens now?" I ask.

Lara gives a slight shrug. "I'm not planning to take any action on these. I just thought it fair to let you and the chief know that they exist."

"Thanks." I'm unconvinced that after everything that's gone on between us, Lara's motives are so benign. Even if Casey sent the letters, the possibility remains that Lara masterminded and directed it. I ask to make copies of the letters, thinking that I'd like to keep them in my own file. I can just imagine that whoever sent them may send one to the FBI—trying to sabotage my appointment to the National Academy.

Luckily, none are received.

* * *

My flight to Washington, D.C. takes off at 6:05 a.m. on a dark, drizzly January morning.

I find myself surveying the other yawning passengers, wondering if any of them are part of the same program. Though I'm looking forward to meeting new people, students and instructors, I'm most excited about the respite from my turmoiled life at the police department, away from Hector Lara and corrupt city politics.

I'm thinking about the failed mayoral recall effort, and the fact that Lillian Behrman is still in office. Amazingly, 8,600 citizens signed the recall referendum, that's 1,400 more people than even voted for Behrman when she was elected to office in the first place. But the ensuing examination of signatures by the City Clerk—who, by coincidence, works for the municipal administrator—found discrepancies in enough of the signatures to prevent the referendum from making it onto the ballot. No real surprise there—score another one for Hector Lara.

I try to push all that crap out of my mind, soothing myself by envisioning the restorative break the next few months will bring. As eager as I am, the only source of reticence for me is the fact that I'll be rooming with someone I don't even know. According to the information they've sent, dorm rooms are laid out with two double rooms connected by a shared bathroom. Snoring, poor hygiene, personal quirks and language barriers . . . a variety of issues concern me. But still, I'm happy to be going.

The FBI training site is a highly secured facility—a mini-city set on 385 sprawling acres of Virginia countryside. It has six dormitory buildings, a dining hall, a classroom wing, a 1,000-seat auditorium, a multi-level library, a chapel, and a forensic science research and training center. The physical fitness facility is state-of-the-art, with a huge gymnasium, weight and cardio rooms and an outdoor track. The place even has its own bank, post office, and car rental desk. But beyond the comforts of a coffee shop and reading lounges, there are constant reminders that I'm on a government compound.

After winding through the security line, I finally step up to the welcome and orientation table. I'm given my I.D. and security badge, but as the woman checks my name off her list, I notice a slight wrinkle in her brow.

"Oh, I'm sorry." The woman takes the map from my information packet and draws a line through something, then circles another. "These dorm rooms have already been assigned, so unfortunately you and a handful of others in your class are going to have to be housed in The Jefferson."

"The Jefferson?" I'm thinking it sounds like a cheap hotel down the street. I should have known there would be a problem.

"Yes," she says, turning slightly in her chair. "The Jefferson is this building directly behind me. Your security badge will get you inside and up the elevator."

I shrug my thank you and head down the glass-enclosed hall. It feels something like a hamster Habitrail. Glancing at my security badge I see that I'll be housed on the sixth floor. When I get off of the elevator and find my room, I hesitate a second to prepare myself. It's been years since I've shared a room with anyone besides Gale . . . probably not since the police academy. I've found that at my age I'm much more sensitive to things like bad breath, body odor and other hygiene problems. As a result I've come to place a very high value on personal space and my own privacy.

Anticipating the worst, I slowly push the door open. The last thing that I expect is exactly what I find: a single room with its own bathroom, a solitary bed, a small desk and a chair. I'm on the top floor, and the room has a window that overlooks a thicket of white oak and chestnut, stretching eastward toward the Potomac River as far as I can see. Quiet, peaceful, and best of all, private.

It's been a couple of weeks, and I come out of class one day to find a light snow falling on the clear roof of the Habitrail. We're going on a long run tomorrow morning and the outside temperature is hovering around seventeen degrees. This is great!

A message tacked onto the class information board says that I have a package at the post office. I stop by and find a bulging legal-size envelope from my secretary, Carmen. I had asked her to keep an eye out for my financial investigation report, and to forward it to me here, without a word to anyone. Now that I finally have it, I spend the evening in my room pouring over its contents.

I'm not a money guy, and numbers just make my head spin. Looking over these documents makes me wish Bobby was here to help me; now that guy gets numbers. So does Gale. No offense to Bobby, but between the two, I'd rather Gale were here. Anyway, I need to befriend an FBI agent who can help me understand this stuff.

As big as this place is, and even with the number of agents and instructors here, it's not as easy as it might seem to find just the right person to help me out. I'm not sure how I'd even ask an agent in the first place. I guess I'd have to lay out the whole story. They'd probably think I was nuts.

Turns out that I love running in the snow. What a blast, seeing my steamy breath puffing out in front of me as I navigate the ice-covered running trails. I even go back out alone on the weekends, early, while most of my classmates are still sleeping. I've lost nearly fifteen pounds and I've never felt better. The best part is stepping into the heat of the sauna at the end of the run—the smell of the hot wood, the creak of the redwood planks.

I'm sitting in the dark sauna, naked and alone, stretched back against the warm wall, meditating. This has to be the most relaxing place on earth. The door opens with a sudden swoosh, as a gust of cold air replaces the warmth. I'm staring at a young man dressed like a spy—black suit, white shirt and thin black tie. I can't see his eyes because he's wearing reflective sunglasses—yes, in the sauna.

"Uh, hi." I self-consciously slide a hand over my groin.

The man looks at me for a second then says, "I'm sorry, but you can't be here."

"Oh, I didn't know." I gather the towel out from under me. "I thought the gym was open on Sunday. Sorry."

"No, it's not that. The gym is open on Sunday." He glances back over his shoulder, around the locker room, still holding the sauna door open. "It's just that the President is going to be here."

"The President? Of what?"

He tilts his head like he's speaking to a foreigner. Then, with exaggerated articulation, he says, "Of the United States."

It takes a second or two to sink in. "Here?" My voice comes out a little high and squeaky. "The President is going to be here? In this sauna?"

The secret service agent sighs. "No, he's not going to be in the sauna. He's going to be outside, riding his bike. And we have to clear this whole area, so you're going to get dressed and go. Now."

As I hastily make my way out of the locker room, unshowered and half-dressed, another man with sunglasses passes me with a German shepherd on a leash. He guides the dog along the rows of lockers, motioning at each one and snapping German-sounding commands.

I loiter around the outer hallway for a while, trying to appear as if I'm waiting for a friend. Another agent stationed in the corridor glances suspiciously at me.

"Hey," I say, as if we're on the same team. "A few years ago I worked a protection detail for the President's father, George Bush Senior, when he came to the Bay Area."

The agent looks on without changing his expression. I might as well have told him that my grandmother had a hip replacement.

He nods. "On behalf of a grateful nation, we thank you."

It would have been better if he had said nothing. Anyway, a half-hour passes and a parade of vehicles arrives. I think I see the President getting onto his bicycle, but there is another guy dressed exactly the same—yellow and black riding suit and helmet. Must be a decoy, I think to myself, probably a routine precaution.

As the cluster of over a dozen agents on bikes takes off, followed by a black command van and an ambulance, I am amazed at all the precautions they've taken. And this, a Sunday morning bike ride on a highly secured government facility that houses only FBI agents in training and 150 police executives. Amazing.

I'm suddenly struck with the fantasy of finding myself alone with the President, one-on-one. And I tell him the whole story of what I've been going through: about Hector Lara and the corrupt politicians who are running my city. I'm sure he would help me.

I'm taking a police ethics course as one of my electives. It's actually taught by a pair of FBI instructors, and just about every student in the class is a city police chief, county sheriff, or at least a high-ranking commander in their respective agency. It's a great class and every presentation has me pinned to my seat. Our course project is a research paper, describing a situation where the student's ethical integrity was in question and how we handled it.

Perfect, I think to myself. This one is right up my alley. So I spend every free minute putting together a chronology of the whole Chief Bradford story and the ensuing retaliatory actions by Hector Lara and his council. I turn in the paper, second-guessing myself as to whether it's even what the instructors wanted. I mean, there are a lot of good, moral, ethical examples out there, and my story doesn't really even have an ending. In fact, it's less about anything I've done and more of a report about people who lack moral integrity.

A day or so after the instructors receive it, they approach me at the end of class. "Would you mind making an oral presentation of your paper to the rest of the students?"

I agree to present my paper in front of the class, and I spend the entire next meeting giving my fellow students a condensed account of the past two years of my life. Afterwards I'm peppered with questions. The other police executives, with an array of shocked expressions, are absorbed in the drama and want details about it.

How did the rank and file feel about the former chief? How old was he? What kind of street cop had he been? Other questions revolved around the shenanigans coming out of city hall. *Why were they all protecting the chief? Were they hiding criminal behavior that they were also involved in? Could you bring in the feds to investigate all of them?*

I answer their questions as honestly as possible, still other students want to talk more in the hallway after class. One of them, a wiry guy from somewhere in the Midwest, pulls me aside to tell me that he was faced with a similar situation in his organization.

"We had a police chief that was involved in all kinds of mischief," he says. "Never showed up at work, took the city car for his personal use, and did the same thing as your guy; falsified his time sheets."

"Were you involved in bringing it to light?" I ask.

"Sure was. Me and the corporal, we went to the mayor and let him know what was what."

His situation doesn't sound exactly like mine, but there are enough similarities to capture my interest. "So how did it turn out?" I ask.

The guy smiles as if he's been waiting for me to ask. "Well sir, the chief got fired and now I'm the chief."

I shake my head. "And nobody was pissed off at you for blowing the whistle on your former boss?"

My classmate wrinkles his nose. "Well, only the guy who got fired. Everybody else was thankful that we didn't let the sumbitch get away with it."

I think I need to go work for the city of Milford.

Only two dozen of us are being housed in the Jefferson dorms, having been selected, apparently, at random. Because we are all on the top floor of a newer building with single rooms, we've jokingly become known throughout the national academy as "The J Boys."

I make a lot of good friends from all over the country, as well as from around the world. One of them, a guy who rooms across the hall is from a large department on the East Coast. His organization cycles so many people through the training that they actually keep a car at the campus for their use. But since my neighbor has brought his own car, he's given me the keys to his department car, told me I could use it whenever I need. Not wanting to take advantage of what has become an added perk, I use his car sparingly—only to get out and see a movie, or buy a pizza when I tire of the cafeteria food. It's also great to be able to drive to some of the historic sites in the area.

I've spent the day off visiting the Holocaust Museum in D.C., and return to the dorms with barely enough time to wash up and get down to the cafeteria. As surprised as I was at the invitation to present my ethics paper to the rest of the class, I'm even more shocked when I sit down at my table to eat dinner that evening.

Both of my instructors seek me out, joining me at my table with their trays of food. We talk lightly for a few minutes, and I'm thinking that they are just being friendly.

Then one of them says, "We've been talking among the staff about your paper. The story is exactly the type of situation we want the other executives to think about in the context of leadership. We feel that your paper would be an excellent training tool."

I'm unsure where he's heading with this, but I put down my forkful of meatloaf and thank him for the compliment.

"We'd like your permission to publish your paper," he says. "We'd keep it in the FBI library, and use it for some of our courses."

The vindication I feel is indescribable. For the first time in more than two years, someone other than my family and the five other signatories of the now infamous memo are telling me that what I did was important and worthwhile.

"And there's a guy I think you ought to talk to," says the other instructor. "He's got an office in the administrative wing, and he used to be in charge of a political corruption unit in one of our field offices. I know he'd love to meet you."

The next day I find the agent's office at the end of a labyrinth, on the forth floor of a building I've never seen before. The agent smiles comfortably, stands to shake my hand, like a tax preparer or a banker who I've been working with for years. He's actually eager to talk, heard about me from my course instructors.

I start out slow, explaining my background with Bradford and the memo that started the wheels turning on this whole thing. I explain about Z, the informant who told me about Lara's solicitation for a payoff from the San Francisco company. And then about my efforts to focus on what Lara did with his money rather than how he got it.

The agent nods, occasionally glancing sideways at my bulging file, as if he's trying to see into it.

"These guys usually follow a pattern," he says. "They like to fly under the radar. The last thing they want is to draw attention to their money. Anything you've noticed in that regard?"

I think a minute. "Yeah, sort of. Our city is in the top third of the state, size wise. Yet the administrator's salary is among the lowest."

The agent nods, writes something down on his pad.

"And he lives in an average home. Nice, but modest." Then it occurs to me, a rumor about Lara moving into a newer home. "He's been working hard on behalf of another developer, trying to push through a huge residential and commercial project in the hills. It may be a coincidence, but no sooner did they finish building the place and I hear a rumor that the municipal administrator has a new house in the same development. What he paid for the property, if anything, I have no idea."

He flashes a smile, and I immediately feel stupid for mentioning an unsupported rumor. Maybe I'm shooting too high here. Better to just stick to the facts.

"So I conducted this search of his financial records," I tell the agent. "And there are a few things of interest, things that piqued my curiosity."

He picks up his pen again and leans forward.

"The municipal administrator is involved in a lot of trust deeds," I say. "Like a dozen or so properties, spread out in different states. Most seem to be around $10,000. I don't know anything about them, but it seems to me--"

"What else you got?"

I flip open the file and pull out a single sheet. "His name was flagged by INS, something about a boarder entry. I believe he was coming into the U.S. from Canada, up around Detroit, I think it says."

The agent takes a few notes and then looks up at me.

"Then there's this," I say, sliding another couple of clipped pages toward him. "He's registered under NAICS as the principal in a religious organization—a church. The corporation supposedly employs a staff of two, and reports an annual income of $120,000."

"What is he, a pastor or something?"

I shake my head. "He's only the city's municipal administrator, as far as I know. I don't see him as too much of a holy man."

"Is it a legitimate church?" he asks.

"I doubt it." I point to the listed address. "The organization is registered to a condominium he owns."

The agent finally eases back in his chair. "Okay, good. So this is how it works," he says. "Money gained by illegal means—like under-the-table bribes, political payoffs, money from contractors to influence development projects, etc.—is referred to as dirty money. Typically, the process of making the money appear clean takes three steps: placement, layering and integration.

255

The first stage involves introducing the dirty money into a legitimate financial system. Then the money is transferred around, sometimes through different accounts, in order to create confusion. Lastly, the money is integrated into the financial system through additional transactions until the money can't be traced back to its original source."

Now I'm the one nodding and taking notes. Like I said, I'm neither a money guy nor a numbers guy. But he's explained the process pretty simply for me.

"So when you look at these systems your municipal administrator has set up, think in those terms." He picks up the list of trust deeds. "Could these involve large amounts of cash to either purchase the property or secure the loans? Could that money be later transferred into multiple accounts to appear as repayment of a loan or the sale of property? And finally, could the funds be put into a legitimate bank account, savings, property purchase, or an investment that would make the funds appear completely legal?"

I now actually understand a little bit about how this works. But I also understand enough to know that this is way over my head.

"Same with this one," he says, picking up the other clipped papers. "Religious organizations presumably take in a lot of cash. Cash is difficult to trace, especially in smaller amounts. The question you'd want to ask yourself is whether illegally obtained cash can be integrated into the financial system under the guise of religious donations?"

At the conclusion of our meeting, the agent makes it clear that because of his assignment at the training facility, he's no longer in a position to either investigate or help on this case.

"Here's the number of a friend of mine," he says, handing me the business card of another FBI agent. "She heads up the political corruption unit out of the Oakland office. That's close to you, right?"

I nod.

"When you get back, bring her what you've shown me here," he says. "I'm sure her unit will be able to help you. In the meantime, relax and enjoy your time at Quantico. This case will still be there when you get home."

That's exactly what I'm afraid of. This case has been a cancer inside me. It's a burden that's taken up more than two years of my life already. As much as I want to bury the MA in his own shit, I'd also like to finally get this investigation off my plate.

Six weeks into the Quantico program I come out of class to find a phone message from Interim Chief Morris. I duck into the library where it's quiet, and listen to the message.

"Hey Phil, it's Thurmond. Well, I just wanted to tell you that . . . well, the municipal administrator has just promoted me to the permanent chief job. He hasn't announced it publicly yet, but it's pretty much official. I just figured you'd want to know."

LESSON 24

"Occasions do not make a man either strong or weak, but they show what he is."
~*Thomas à Kempis*

I return to the department refreshed and ready to begin my new assignment. For me, the position of investigations captain feels like a big step down from what I've been doing, in terms of number of personnel under my command, division budget, and overall pace of the work and activity level. But maybe I'm ready for that.

The criminal investigators are for the most part a competent and talented group. They have their downtime, but when the big stuff happens they're usually on top of their game. The only downside for me is that a handful of them are still followers of Evan Casey, who ran this division before he retired. And I suspect a few of them still see Casey for coffee from time to time.

Since Casey is still actively involved in undermining the current administration, and me in particular, the situation leaves me a little worried. Add to that the retaliatory attacks against Odell Graham's dogs and his car, I wouldn't be surprised if Hector Lara is working with Casey—most likely pulling the levers from behind the curtain. For that reason, I'm concerned that Evan Casey's little disciples in my division may also try to undermine me.

One of the first things I do upon my return is buy a wireless RF signal detector and use it to sweep my office for bugging devices. I then commandeer a pinhole camera from property and evidence—which is now under my command—and mount it on a bookcase behind my desk. In the event anyone enters my office when I'm not here, I'll have a video record of it. In my entire career I never would have considered such things, but if I've learned anything during the past couple of years is that trust may be a nice goal, but in my position it's an unrealistic one.

So I've been back now for a few weeks, still getting comfortable with my new role. Not much more has been done with regard to the women's issues, and I don't want to let their concerns just drop off the radar. While I was in Quantico, I met a female deputy chief who works in Dallas, Texas. We spent a lot of time discussing the issues brought to my attention before I left, regarding perceived inequities towards women in the department. She turned out to be a great resource, partly because she had suffered through some of the same issues and partly because the large agency she manages has instituted some progressive programs to address similar problems.

I'm eager to put one of her ideas into action as soon as I return. Assembling a small representative group of women employees, we begin meeting regularly so that they can pass on any issues of concern. Some of the women have apparently expressed anxiety about being labeled troublemakers, so I've promised to keep their identities to myself.

I present weekly updates during our command staff meetings and we brainstorm how to deal with the particular issues raised, with an emphasis on sending the right message throughout the department. I've provided no names and have avoided specific details, so that there is no chance that staff can identify those involved.

Chief Morris, who seems only lukewarm on the whole thing, laughingly refers to the group as *Phil's girls*. Thus far, however, he has approved, with a dismissive wave of his hand, each of my proposed corrective actions against male offenders. Apparently he's much more comfortable having me take the lead on this.

I finish giving my report at the end of one of our meetings and we all get up to leave.

"Not so fast," says Claire. "We've got a problem with one of our watch commanders."

My head tilts back and I sigh. Then I suddenly remember that I no longer oversee Patrol, and a smile spreads across my face. The watch commanders are now Desmond MacLeod's responsibility. Mac's expression turns painful as Claire continues to fill us in.

"I was going through the phone tapes, trying to track down a call to dispatch, and I stumbled onto something. It sounds like the watch commander was having some kind of phone sex, right on the taped line in his office."

Mac puts a hand to his forehead, and then pulls out a pen and notepad. "Please, tell me it wasn't with one of the dispatchers."

Claire shakes her head. "It was an outside line."

The chief is clearly distressed. I'm not sure if it's because he's uncomfortable talking about sex, or because the watch commander in question is one of his good buddies. Whatever the reason, Chief Morris dismisses the rest of us from the room and keeps Claire and Desmond behind.

I later learn that because of the watch commander's rank, the chief wants Mac to investigate the lieutenant himself, instead of assigning the internal affairs sergeant to do it.

Now I'm actually glad that I was transferred.

* * *

I've got a phone message waiting for me when I get into work. It's from a sergeant in the patrol division—a young woman who as far as I know is doing fine. I guess the word is out that I'm a soft touch for the gender issues in the organization, because the fact that she wants me to meet her somewhere outside the city hints at a new problem I'm about to inherit. I call her back and arrange to rendezvous at a Starbucks in the valley.

I find her sitting by the window wearing dark glasses to hide her tear-filled eyes, an eerie reminder of my Indian friend. I had helped the sergeant's partner with an issue several months back, coached her on how to prepare for a special assignment that she had applied for. I'm hoping that this meeting is something as simple as that, but unfortunately it's not.

"My partner doesn't like me," she blurts out as soon as I set my coffee on the table. "Doesn't even acknowledge me. Treats me like shit."

"Your partner?" I'm still thinking her lesbian girlfriend.

She frowns. "John Flores, my patrol partner, the other sergeant on my shift. The guy doesn't like me."

I don't know if I've oversold myself as someone who can help, but I want to tell her that I can't *make* someone like you, if they don't like you. In fact, I sort of want to tell her to stop whining and just do her damn job. *How many people don't like me?*

But of course, I don't say any of that.

I ask if they have any history, anything that would motivate him to dislike her so much. I know John pretty well; in fact he's one of the guys who's helped with the Hector Lara surveillances. He's also worked for me a number of times and I've never known him to have a problem with people. Then again, I've never known her to have problems with people, either.

She doesn't want to make a formal complaint, doesn't want to talk to her own lieutenant, and doesn't feel "comfortable" confiding in her own captain. I offer to mediate an exchange between her and John, but she doesn't want that. And she doesn't want to transfer to another shift. Kind of feels like my hands are tied, but I agree to get back to her after I've had a chance to look into it.

Back at work I learn that her shift partner, John Flores, was just selected to head up a gang enforcement unit and he's being transferred off of her shift at the end of the week. Fantastic—problem solved. He's outta there and she gets everything she wants. I still have no idea what their friction was all about, but it no longer seems to matter. I call the sergeant back and let her know what I learned. She thanks me, and that's that.

* * *

I'm on my way to work one morning. Got my windows open and my brown bag with a sandwich and an apple sitting on the passenger seat next to me. I'm motoring down the hill in my little Toyota truck; past the high school I used to attend. A school bus stops on the opposite side of the street and the little red stop paddle flips out to stop traffic in both directions. So I stop.

A black Lincoln Town Car behind me pulls right up to my bumper and I hear the horn honking. I can't see anyone in my rearview mirror, just dark windows. Apparently the driver isn't familiar with the vehicle code section requiring traffic in both directions to stop for an on-loading or off-loading school bus.

The bus finally leaves and I start driving again. A block later, a group of school kids are crossing at a crosswalk, so I stop again. The black Town Car, still right behind me, pulls right up and starts with the horn again.

Half a block later, traffic starts backing up where the parochial school, the middle school and the high school traffic all converge in one miserable intersection. Out of the corner of my eye, I'm aware that the black car has pulled into the right-turn lane next to me. Good riddance. But then the car stops.

The first I see of the guy is when his driver's door is flung open next to me, smacking into the side of my car. Then, all six-foot-three inches of his 270 pound body dives in through my open passenger window. He's swinging wildly, punching my face and head, and I haven't even had time to remove my seatbelt or take the truck out of gear.

It crosses my mind to drive off with the son-of-a bitch hanging from the window, just like in the movies, but traffic is still stopped in front and behind me. My gun is somewhere nearby, either in the glove box or in a holster under the seat, I can't remember at the moment. But it wouldn't be a justified shooting anyway, though the threat of a gun in his face might get him to back off. Instead, I swivel in my seat and rear back with my legs. I do a sort of mule kick, catching the guy square in the face. I know I got him good because his nose immediately starts to bleed.

The guy backs out through the window and straightens up. "I'm going to kill you," he says.

My throbbing eye socket tells me that he already tried. I don't know if the guy's on drugs or just having some sort of meltdown because he's late for work. In any case, the car door that he threw open is now wedged into my bumper and the meathead can't pull it loose. As he drives away, part of his door trim comes with it.

I use my cell phone to call dispatch and ask for some assistance. I give the description of the car and the guy—a *very large* male, Pacific Islander, with a bad temper.

As I take inventory of myself I realize that one of my contact lenses has been punched out of my eye, and is somewhere on the floor mat. My watchband is broken and my dress shirt is torn. I also find that the nice sandwich that Gale made me is now as flat as a breakfast crêpe.

Within a half hour the responding cops figure out where the guy lives, find the Town Car in his driveway, and arrest him for battery. Turns out he is the bodyguard of the wealthy sports team owner, and he's out on parole for a prior felony weapons conviction.

I go back home to change clothes, and by now the area around my right eye has turned into a puffy red and blue crater. Returning to work, I find that I am now the one wearing dark glass inside.

Definitely not one of my better days, but it's about to get worse. For whatever reason, Chief *Morris Code* has decided to call the administrator and fill him in on the morning's ass kicking. But rather than inquire about my injuries, Lara wants to know how many cops are working the case and whether or not he can trust them to be objective—seeing as how their captain is the victim.

The investigators have contacted the suspect's parole officer for permission to search the residence—a legal condition of his being on parole. But Lara orders Morris to have them immediately halt the investigation.

By this time the cops have already interviewed the suspect's kids, who were apparently in the car during the incident and saw the whole thing. They've already given statements that their dad was mad because "the guy in the truck" made them late for school by stopping for everyone. They told the cops that their dad got out of the car and attacked the other driver—me. The statements against their own father pretty much negates the suspect's story that I ran into him and tried to drive away, and that he only got out to ask nicely for my license.

For me, a couple of messages are received loud and clear: my time away has changed nothing between me and Lara, and Morris is never going to think for himself or stand up to his boss. All this does is make me more committed to my cause—ensuring that the municipal administrator gets what he's got coming.

It doesn't take long before all of us know the details of Captain MacLeod's sex-talking watch commander investigation. I find that part of the case amusing, but it disappoints me to learn that several additional violations have come to light. This apparently was not a one-time thing; in fact there were other such calls. In one instance the watch commander was involved in an explicit sexual conversation, during which a critical incident was unfolding on the street. But rather than take command of the crime scene, the lieutenant stayed on the phone, with his office door closed.

According to Mac, some of the watch commander's phone transcripts suggest that the guy may have also left the city to meet a girlfriend on the other side of the bay while he was on duty. These kinds of things are game changers in terms of disciplinary options. When someone in a leadership position doesn't perform their duties, they're usually facing termination.

It's also the type of thing that never would have happened prior to Bradford's poor example, so visibly lowering the bar. I feel as if some of the weaker people in the organization have fallen victim to the lack of discipline, using the chief's immorality and the department's disarray as an excuse for their own misconduct. We've sadly come to accept the abnormal as normal around here.

The one person in our command group who is least amused with the situation is poor MacLeod, who's had to listen to hours of X-rated phone conversations. None of us are sure how much Mac is telling Chief Morris, and how much Morris is telling city hall. My guess is that neither Morris nor Hector Lara knows the specifics yet. But I get the feeling that all that is about to change.

One particular phone number shows up often on the naughty lieutenant's desk phone, and it happens to be the other participant in several of the tape-recorded sex calls. One conversation even suggests a rendezvous had occurred in the hot tub at the woman's house while the lieutenant was working his shift.

It's late in the afternoon when Mac visits me in my office. He closes the door and takes a seat without a word. I ask if he's alright, but he only shakes his head. My eyes keep drifting down to the folder in his hand, and I'm guessing that whatever is inside has something to do with his morose state.

"What is it, Mac?" I ask.

"This case," he says. "It's a mess. The leads I'm following just keep expanding. I finally got the subscriber information for the number our boy keeps calling." Mac lifts the file. "Comes back to a fancy home up in the hills."

"Here in the city?"

MacLeod nods. "Some chick by the name of Joy Talbot."

A wonderful image flashes through my head, of the municipal administrator tucked away at the end of the bar with a little blond businesswoman. "Joy Talbot? Are you sure?"

MacLeod double-checks the phone records. "Yeah, why?"

I feel the grin stretch across my face, pulling my jaws from ear to ear. "Mac . . . Joy Talbot is the MA's main squeeze. He's been seen all over town with her."

MacLeod rolls his eyes and the folder drops onto the floor. "You gotta be fuck'n kidd'n me."

We call Claire and Bobby into the office and tell them. Bobby looks stunned, but Claire just laughs. "Men are such pigs." It's a sentence she repeats several times until I finally remind her that not all men are. I don't think she believes me.

The way I figure it, either the horny lieutenant doesn't mind playing second fiddle to the municipal administrator, or he doesn't know who else has been nibbling on his little peach pie. My guess is that neither of them knows . . . yet.

"Have you told Morris?" I ask MacLeod.

"Not yet."

I let out a hardy laugh as I imagine the look on Morris' face. "Once the chief catches wind of this, he'll shit his pants. Morris will hit speed-dial to Lara's office so fast that his cell phone might actually combust. This thing is about to get really interesting really fast."

"Maybe I should interview this Talbot woman first, before I tell Morris," says MacLeod. "I mean, maybe there's some sort of mix-up, or possibly it's a case of mistaken . . ." Mac's voice drops off as he's unable to convince anyone, even himself, that there has been a misunderstanding.

"Yeah, right," Bobby says. "By the way, Joy Talbot belongs to the chamber of commerce and owns a business downtown."

"She also has a husband," Claire adds. "I'm guessing you're going to have to interview her."

"Of course I am," says Mac. "I have to. She's a key witness in my case. I need a statement from her about all the phone calls and visits from numbnuts."

* * *

I love to cook. That and my artwork are my favorite ways to take my mind off of work. I'm in my kitchen one Saturday afternoon, putting the finishing touches on a red sauce that I plan to use on my Chicken Parmesan dinner tonight. On other days like this, when I feel most separated from my job, something always happens to draw me back in. Today it comes in the form of a knock on the front door.

Gale answers it, and I listen from the other side of the kitchen threshold. I think it's someone stumping for a political seat, no, running for re-election of some kind, a woman it sounds like, Dorothy Easter, a fairly new city councilwoman, but I can't hear too much of what she's saying. Just enough to make my blood boil.

Then I hear Gale's response, loud and unmistakably clear. "You have some nerve. Coming to my house, to my door, after what you and the rest of your spineless city council did to my husband!"

Now I sense the woman back pedaling. She's making excuses, apologizing, blaming it on the more seasoned councilmembers.

"Don't you dare come to my door ever again, Mrs. Easter," Gale barks. "And tell the rest of your cohorts down at city hall to stay away from here. Now go on, scat, get off my front porch!"

It is one of the most belittling putdowns I've ever heard. No cursing or threatening, just a complete disregard for the woman, as if she had no more value in the world than a cigarette butt.

The grin is still on my face when Gale returns to the kitchen.

"You're not mad at me?" she asks.

"Hell no." I grab Gale in a tight embrace and hold her there. "That was beautiful." I pause a second to replay the scene. "Scat? Like what is she, a cat pissing on our lawn?"

Then we both start laughing.

Meanwhile, back at work, the women's issues that I thought had died down, have not. My friend, Nora Morales, tells me that some of the women have been talking about getting an attorney and filing suit against the city.

"For what?" I ask.

"Discrimination?" She sighs. "I don't know, whatever. They don't see things changing around here. The chief isn't taking our issues seriously enough."

"He is," I tell her. "The entire command staff reviews each and every complaint during our weekly staff meetings, and we've tried to address all of them."

Nora shrugs. "Don't know what to tell you."

After talking with Nora, I go downstairs and try to catch up with another friend. She works as the district attorney liaison officer, and I find her finishing up at her desk when I step into her cubicle. I give her a quick rundown of what has happened since the end of last year—the complaints that were brought to me and about the steps I've taken to address them; educating the managers, gaining compliance, working to change perceptions, and so on. She nods and smiles as she listens, her expression indicating at points that she's already heard some of what I'm telling her.

"Yeah," she finally says. "They approached me, too. Wanted me to sign on to their cause."

"And?"

"I don't want to be any part of it," she says. "Not interested. Not that I disagree with some of their issues, but I don't think their way is the way to accomplish what they want."

"What *do* they want?" I ask.

She tosses out a laugh, but she's shaking her head. "I don't think *they* even know what they want. That's part of the reason I'm steering clear of them."

As it turns out, the complaining women account for only about half of the female officers in the department. And there appears to be no common profile—with an even racial, ethnic and gay-straight mix on both sides of the coin. In any case, I continue working on the issues that the ever-shrinking representative group of women brings to me, and I continue making those issues part of the weekly command staff agenda. And like I promised them at the beginning, I continue to keep all of their identities confidential—even to the chief and the other commanders.

266

At our next meeting I bring up the subject again. "I'm hearing that some of the women employees are still unhappy. They're dissatisfied with what's going on, and they see our efforts to address their issues as insincere."

The chief groans and shifts on the big pillow that's sandwiched beneath him. "Now what?"

I tell Morris that even after several group discussions and one-on-one meetings, I'm still not really sure what they're after.

"Does this have to do with the SWAT team?" he asks. "The big saying around here is . . . 'SWAT or nothing.'"

Bobby speaks up. "It's actually, 'SWAT or not', Chief."

Morris waves his hand in front of his face like he's shooing a fly. "Whatever."

"Yeah, anyway," I continue. "No, nothing has come up about the SWAT team. But their frustration is getting to the point that some of them are talking to attorneys about filing some sort of lawsuit. Not sure if it's discrimination or harassment, or whatever. But you should know that this issue is not going away. In fact, things seem to be getting worse instead of better."

Morris shrugs. "Well, if the girls want to file a lawsuit, let them file a lawsuit. Nothing we can do about it."

Claire, Bobby and I look at each other with a lot of apprehension in our eyes. Poor Desmond MacLeod is only half-listening, staring down at a bulging file folder full of the tapes and transcripts of his night shift lieutenant's antics.

"You guys can go," says Chief Morris, with a swipe of the hand across our side of the conference table. The three of us gather our things and walk out, closing the door with MacLeod and the chief alone in the room.

An hour passes and Mac hasn't come out yet. Bobby and Claire are sitting in my office, discussing strategies to mitigate the growing nightmare involving some of the women employees. Meanwhile, we wait to find out what's going on with Mac's case. It seems as if we're the only ones who can sense the pressure building under the department's tectonic plates. And we all feel that the big earthquake is definitely coming.

Finally, after nearly ninety minutes behind closed doors, Desmond MacLeod emerges from the chief's conference room. He looks haggard and his eyes are bloodshot; not from crying apparently, but from anger. He tosses his case file onto the empty seat in my office and toes my door closed. Then he flips off the wall, in the general direction of the chief's office.

"What?" says Bobby.

Claire is shaking her head, not sure what's coming, but knowing it's going to be bad.

I get up and walk around my desk. "Go ahead, Mac. What is it?"

He takes in a breath and holds it. He finally lets it out, into his balled fist. "Morris," he says. "He called the administrator, blabbed everything to him. Told him all about my investigation."

LESSON 25

"How people treat you is their karma;
how you react is yours."
~Dr. Wayne W. Dyer

"The chief ordered me to terminate the investigation."

"What?" Bobby jumps out of his seat. "What the hell are you talking about? You're not even finished . . . haven't even interviewed any of the witnesses yet."

"That's just the point," says MacLeod. "I've been prohibited from talking to any witnesses, specifically Joy Talbot."

Claire smirks. "Gee, I wonder where that came from."

MacLeod looks like he wants to punch something, or someone. "Oh, the chief told me exactly where it came from. He said flat out, this comes directly from the municipal administrator—'You will not interview any more witnesses.' Morris said the city is not going to go for termination either; they're cutting a deal so this thing is done. Finished."

"That came from Lara, too," I say. "He doesn't want Joy Talbot interviewed because she might mention him, might say something about *their* relationship. And Lara must know that this thing will end up in court if we go for a termination, with lawyers and witness depositions. Once it gets to that point, it's out of his hands—they'll subpoena Joy Talbot, and Lara won't be able to control what she says. And it'll be too far down the road for him to cover it up. The only way the administrator can keep a lid on this thing is by halting the investigation right where it is, and cutting a deal with dumbass."

"What kind of deal?" Bobby asks MacLeod. "Did the chief say?

"Nope." Mac gathers his file from the chair. "Morris took it out of my hands, completely. He said he's going to deal with the PBA lawyer himself. I'm done, completely off of the case."

Speculation turns to confirmation on this point a week or so later. We're in the middle of our weekly staff meeting, discussing the budget, when Morris suddenly changes direction and spills the whole thing. He tells us that Lieutenant *Happy Pants*, who had abdicated responsibility to his night shift squads in lieu of his own libido, will be allowed to keep his job.

"I know you guys don't agree with this," says Morris, flustered and red-faced but trying to appear in control. "You think he should have been fired . . . but *it is what it is,* and it's out of my hands. They're going to demote him a rank, and that's it. And we're done with it."

The chief's use of *"they're* going to . . ." makes my skin crawl. Who in the hell are *they?* This is his department, and it should have been his decision to make. But Morris seems more than content to let everyone else pull his strings.

* * *

The lieutenant who works for me in investigations is at the end of his three-year assignment and is scheduled to rotate out soon. It was great having him here to help me transition into the division, but it's also good that he's moving on. He's a little too comfortable and a little too egocentric for my taste. An old school type that I'm not sure I can trust to promote the all-inclusive agenda I'm trying to bring into the mainstream.

His is an important position though, because the person I select will stand in for me during my absences. That lieutenant also has the department's press information officer responsibility and needs to carefully navigate the interpersonal minefield of the sedentary investigators. And since I've inherited everyone else in here, it will be nice to handpick the outgoing guy's replacement.

But as I look at the list of lieutenants around the department, many of the good ones are already in special assignments. Others are either too new or happy in their current role as patrol watch commander. Except for one.

Cory Unger is lesbian and an informal leader among the woman employees. From all that I've heard lately, she is also spearheading the move to bring a suit against the city. On the other hand, Cory is known for her strong people skills. She's a competent program manager and a flawless public speaker. If it weren't for the lawsuit thing, this would be a much simpler decision for me. But now it's one that I spend several days mulling over in my head.

Had this just been a discussion about taking the position, she and I would have had it in my office. But I want this to be more honest and personal, and off the record. In order to do that, I've asked her if she'd mind meeting off-site.

We get together on a Thursday night, at a quiet restaurant just outside the city. I guess I have a thing for food and wine and talk—seems to make things go easier, more cordial, especially when it's a conversation that is likely to be a little awkward anyway.

Cory seems a little nervous when she first arrives. "I have to say, I'm a little surprised that you're even considering me for the job. More than a little surprised," she says.

"To be honest, I had to do some serious thinking." I order a glass of wine and Cory does the same. "And in the end, I had to consider the big picture and do what's best for everybody. I actually believe that you are the right person for the position, and it would also be good for you and your career. Having your skills in the bureau would also be a big help to me."

"I'm really glad to hear you say that," she says. "But you do know the entire situation . . . I mean, are you aware that we've retained an attorney?"

I nod.

She runs her finger around the rim of her glass, staring down at it. "It isn't the way I wanted this thing to unfold," she says. "And I know you've been working to help us--"

I shake my head and she stops talking. "I'd rather us not get into that conversation right now. We're both doing the best we can, so let's just leave it at that."

"Right." Cory lets out a sigh. "I've got to be honest, some people warned me about taking this job, said it could be a setup—leaving myself open for you and the administration to make me look bad."

"Yeah." I'm gazing out the window now, thinking of how many times I've had those same worries about my own situation. "Well, it's my decision and I'm telling you that you're the one I want to work with. I think we could both find reasons to be suspicious. You're not the only one who might benefit from being guarded, but that won't make for a good working relationship. If this is going to work, it'll take a little trust on both our parts."

Cory agrees, and by the time our meal comes we're settled. The rest of the talk is lighter and more comfortable, discussing the job and sharing ideas for improving the bureau. By the end of the dinner I'm convinced that I made the right decision. She gives me a hug and thanks me again.

Chief Morris thinks I'm nuts when I tell him who I've selected. And I get the feeling the rest of the command staff has their doubts as well. Maybe they're right, but I have to go with my own instincts. Sure, I would probably never sue the city, but then again, I don't know what she and the other women have gone through. And if I allow myself to become paranoid and distrustful, then what does that make me? I wouldn't be living up to the sense of fair play that I've been expecting others to live up to. I'd be no different than them. So, I have to do what I believe is right.

On another front, the discipline against the former lieutenant, now a sergeant, is a done deal. The personnel action of a one-rank demotion has been ratified and signed off on by all of the appropriate parties. It's too much deception and manipulation of fact for me to take in, and I'm beyond disappointed. I'm sickened.

Just like former chief Bradford, the watch commander should also have been fired—not protected and taken care of. In both instances, the standard of acceptable conduct was manipulated to fit the situation. And both of those situations were solely to benefit and protect the administrator. I can accept that Hector Lara dislikes me, even hates me. And I can even accept that he would get rid of me in a heartbeat if he could find a way to do it. But what I can't accept is all the hypocrisy.

The final straw comes a few weeks later at an award ceremony at city hall. I'm sampling the snacks laid out on a table in the rotunda. The cheese tray has the horseradish cheddar I like, fantastic. And those little poppy seed crackers, excellent. I'm staying out of the way, minding my business and trying to be as inconspicuous as possible. But as much as I hate being here, I'm still cordial, making an effort to be the respectable police captain.

The city's department heads trickle in, followed shortly after by the council—Dorothy Easter, Teddy Rube, and the guy with the bad breath. They move around the room, phony smiles pasted on their faces, congratulating a handful of longtime employees who are there to receive longevity awards. The council members avoid me like death, which is fine with me. Then there's the high-pitched squelch of the microphone, and Mayor Behrman moves to the podium with the municipal administrator gently guiding her by the elbow. Always the consummate gentleman in public.

The mayor begins her speech with her usual sallow script—same one she uses for everything from retirements and promotions, to DARE graduations.

I roll my eyes as she dons her bifocals and begins her address to the employees. "Our city thrives," she says, "under the skilled and competent leadership of our municipal administrator, Hector Lara."

Lara smiles bashfully. And then just out of microphone range, I hear him say, "Thank you, Madam Mayor."

"Service to the public," she continues. "It is why we are here. But this cooperative relationship could not be accomplished without you, the employees we hold responsible for carrying out that important mission. All one has to do is look at our city seal, the four corners of our foundation: honor, integrity, accountability and honesty—these are the values we hold sacred. Fair and ethical treatment of others are not just words, they are more than what we just say, they are the ideals that we live by."

About this time I can feel the burn of the horseradish inching up my throat. *Honor? Integrity? Accountability? Honesty?*

Hector Lara smiles, nods, and does a little clap of his hands behind her. Members of the city council have all taken seats in the front row. They're clapping, too, glancing around the rotunda as well. All one big happy and honorable group, full of all the values we hold so fucking sacred.

I leave city hall, feeling sick to my stomach. I drive back to the station, open my office safe and take out the entire Hector Lara case file. Without even taking time to edit or organize its contents, I drive to the Oakland FBI office and walk in. I'm unannounced and without an appointment, and all I have to go on is a name scribbled on the business card. Some agent, assigned to the training division on the opposite end of the country.

The head of the political corruption unit is a black woman who looks to be a little younger than me. She steps into the room, accompanied by a younger Hispanic guy. They listen to my spiel, a rambling and unrehearsed composite of my last three years on the job. I'm emotionally spent by the time I finish talking, and to this point neither of them has uttered a single word.

"I'm done," I finally say. "Not only am I done explaining this screwed up situation, but I'm done fighting. I'm not going to take this case any further than right here. It's eaten up enough of my life. This thing has taken enough of a toll on me and on my family."

The woman has a skeptical expression on her face, as if I'm too emotionally caught up in the investigation to be objective. And maybe she's right. I have no idea if these case notes and documents even mean anything, or if anyone besides me gives a shit.

The Hispanic agent, on the other hand, looks worried. "Are you going to be available to speak with us if we have questions?"

I nod. "Sure, yeah, whatever."

"This sounds like a good case," he says. "I'd like to look into it."

His supervisor isn't showing the same enthusiasm, but I don't care anymore.

"I am going to retire in six months," I say. "You are my last stop with this thing. I'm going to leave after thirty-one years of service and I'm going to move out of that Goddamn city. I'll probably move out of the Goddamn state, and I'm never going to look back. So you guys do whatever you want with this crooked son-of-a bitch. Or you can toss the entire case file in the shitter. It doesn't matter to me. Like I say, I'm done."

They're kind of quiet after that. I get up, thank them and shake their hands. Then I leave them with my paunchy case file sitting in the middle of their laminate conference table.

My little truck feels lighter without the huge folder sitting in the passenger seat. And I feel lighter, too, as I head home without the mammoth weight of the city's problems on my shoulders. I'm counting down toward the end of my career now, and I can't wait. It finally seems within reach.

I'll hold my head up and work through the next few months with honor and integrity. I've kind of poured myself into these harassment and discrimination complaints, helping the women as best I can. It's almost like I'm accomplishing something on their behalf, that I've been unable to accomplish for myself. That's probably one of the reasons I've been so passionate about their issues.

* * *

I answer my desk phone one day and it's one of our former police chiefs who left several years ago for a prestigious position in the federal government. In fact, he was the chief who preceded Bradford and who recommended him as a replacement.

"I just wanted to say that I admire and respect what you and the other commanders did," he says. "It took guts and a lot of moral courage, and I'm proud of you."

Surprised wouldn't describe my feelings. More like shocked.

The former chief goes on to tell me that in retrospect, he now realizes that Bradford wasn't ready for the job. He admits that it was a mistake on his part to ever recommend him.

274

The ex-chief asks me how Hector Lara has treated us in the aftermath, and I tell him honestly. Disheartened but not surprised, he confides that his distrust of Lara was a motivator for his leaving. He also offers his help, but at this point it's futile. The damage is already done—to the department and to me, personally.

There is only one real upside to the conversation: the modicum of comfort I feel that this is now the third former police chief to corroborate the character flaws in Hector Lara that I've experienced since the commanders came forward.

I've nominated one of my most trusted friends, Paul Longmeyer, for an award. He was known as an outstanding undercover narcotics investigator, was selected to the county task force, and has served as a board member on the state narcotics officers' forum.

The phone call telling me that Longmeyer won the award comes at the end of a long, tiring week. The forum's president tells me that Paul will be honored during a presentation at this year's conference in Reno, Nevada.

I'm sitting in my office, thrilled at the news.

"And since you nominated him," the president continues, "You are invited to attend the ceremony, on us. The forum will pay for your food and lodging, so all you have to do is show up at the hotel."

Sounds even better.

I've decided to take the scenic route to Reno, stopping at the family cabin for the night and then continuing up Highway 4 over Ebbetts Pass. The pass is closed during the winter months, but it's a beautiful and tranquil drive in the spring. I even pull off along the way, stopping to sit by Mosquito Lake, where I feel like everything in my life is finally coming back into balance.

On the other side of the curvy mountain road is the small town of Markleeville. It feels like Nevada, but it's actually the last little corner of California. I could make it to the host hotel tonight easily enough, but decide to stay at a cozy motel just off the highway. I've just hit the parking lot, and apparently the first area of cell phone service, when a buzzing noise erases the calm of the Sierras.

The message from Chief Morris is in the form of a text, left on my phone sometime during the drive over the pass. "The girls filed the law suit," he writes, most likely with a mix of shock and annoyance. "And you're named in it." He included a link at the end of the text, directing me to an online version of the entire affidavit—posted by the local news media.

I register at the motel desk, and then take my passkey and my laptop down the hallway into my room. I spend barely a few seconds taking in the tenor of the knotty pine timbers and the smoky scent of the fireplace, but the inevitability of more disappointment awaits me like a fatal prognosis. I open my laptop and bring up the link.

My heart drops and tears well in my eyes as I read what some of the women wrote about me; the women who I tried to help, and who I fought for as if I was fighting for my own wife and daughters.

I want to call and ask them why they would say these things. I can't understand why Marilyn Quintel would turn on me after I sat half the night in the hospital, comforting her family while she was in surgery. And after I fought for her job when she was failing the training program and the chief wanted her terminated.

And the sergeant whose work partner didn't like her . . . what in the world would make her lash out at me? Accuse me of siding with John Flores, and rewarding him with a promotion to gang unit supervisor. That's not what happened at all, and she knew it.

Others state how I've done nothing to help them, that I've used our meetings to vet out the troublemakers, and then violated their confidentiality by identifying them to the police chief and the other commanders. But none of that ever happened.

They wrote that I was part of the problem, actually naming me as a member of the regime of privileged white males at the top who have held them down. I can't believe what I'm reading. It's all been twisted to appear differently than it was. It's nothing but lies.

The suit asks for millions of dollars from the city, and all I can figure is that these women have sold their souls for blood money. Could it really be so important to them?

As I go through and read it again, I'm struck by the fact that my road here was no picnic. I worked for supervisors who disliked me, who mistreated me, and who failed to acknowledge my work. I've been passed over, ignored and treated unfairly more times than I can count. The victim of cliques and alliances, a hundred times I've been left feeling like an outsider looking in. I spent nearly three miserable years under Bill Preston, completely buried with *his* ridiculous projects, only to have him embarrass me and take the credit for the work I did. I served under a chief who never came to work and never did his job. I've been bullied by a municipal administrator who turned friends, co-workers, department heads and council members against me, singlehandedly destroying my reputation.

276

Maybe a result of my gender, or my color, or because of the position I've attained in the police department—but whatever blinders people had on when looking in my direction, I feel as if I've spent my entire career without any protection from mistreatment and harassment and retribution.

I attend the awards ceremony in Reno, numb and only halfway engaged in it. Longmeyer and his family are there, and it clears my head to be around them—good people who have real integrity. I get to spend some time with a couple of the old narcs that I worked with back in my day. If I could end my career right now, I'd walk away. But I have to go back when it's over.

After dinner I'm talking with a couple of guys who know Evan Casey. They don't seem to care for him any more than I do, and they're telling me about Casey's new job.

"He was hired at a police department across the bay, as a captain in charge of special investigations," they say. "What a sweet gig. The little slime ball always seems to land on his feet."

That figures. It just tears the wound open a little further.

I return to the department to learn that Chief Morris is retiring. Whether it was the lawsuit or Morris's mounting health problems that did him in, I don't know—nor do I care. He'll have to live with himself and his decisions, just as I'll have to live with mine.

This whole thing with the women, biting and slashing me along with everyone else in their lawsuit, squeezes the last drop of resolve out of my soul. I have no cause left in which to focus my energy. I do my job, but little more. Most of my time is spent alone in my office, planning for the day when I won't have to come here.

The mayor is finally gone, voted out, I guess, or maybe finally realized she had backed the wrong horse. And a new mayor is in her place—a guy I've known for years, and who is no stranger to the local political scene. A new assistant administrator has also been hired, a woman who brings experience, through not from this city. Between her and the new mayor, I'm hopeful that Hector Lara will be under greater scrutiny. But he's their problem now, not mine.

A few months pass and we've also got a new chief—a nice guy who they pulled out of retirement from another comparable sized police department. I'm guessing that he's been told a load of shit about me, but I'll not be any problem for him, or for anyone else. They could have brought Carl Bradford back for all I care, because there's no fight left in me. *They* won.

I pick up the paper one morning and the headlines reach out and slap me: MUNICIPAL ADMINISTRATOR LEAVING HIS POST.

The accompanying article is more of a full-page tribute to the guy, most of it clearly choreographed by Lara himself. It includes a list of his accomplishments and a host of glowing comments from his flunkies on the council. All of that is probably to be expected. What is unexpected is the fact that Hector Lara is leaving in the first place, especially now. Buried deep within the adulation and flattery, is one tiny fact—easily overlooked by one unfamiliar with the public employee retirement system. It's that the 53-year-old Lara has decided to quit, very suddenly I might add, less than two years shy of his retirement age. Not for health reasons or to take a better position with more pay, but to do what? Try his hand at consulting?

My mind goes back to how hard he worked to keep Bradford on the payroll until his retirement age. Seems like Lara would work at least as diligently on his own behalf. All that money, those medical benefits, the power? All that access to lucrative city development projects? Would the municipal administrator simply walk away from all those things of his own free will?

I don't think so.

There is only one way a guy like Lara leaves on his own, and that's if it benefits him. And since quitting before retirement age will cost him so dearly, I'm convinced that regardless of the public spin he's managed to put on his departure, the guy was forced out.

During morning coffee with my dad, I let him know that I have decided to leave as well. Even though it was never my goal to outlast Hector Lara, it gives me a tiny feeling of triumph that I will.

I sense a look of relief on Dad's face. Probably how I would feel if one of my daughters had gone through what I have. I've always felt that the worst pain a man can have, is to feel the pain of his child. And that's what I think my dad has been feeling for these last couple of years.

"We have an extra desk at the office," he says. "You know that you're always welcome to come by and use it. You can relax and write your books, or bring in your paints and do some artwork." And then he adds, "You could even start up a private investigations business."

We both laugh at that one. I'm done with investigations, and he knows it better than anyone.

* * *

I decide to invite three of my nephews to the police department on my last day. The boys are my brother's kids, and I've always been extremely close to them. To those guys I'm just crazy Uncle Phil, the one who does and says anything to get a laugh. And although they've always known I was a cop, until today I don't think they could actually picture it.

Gale and my oldest daughter are also with me, and if anyone has endured as much as me during the past three decades, it's my wife and my daughters. I couldn't end my career without Gale, because I could never have survived my career without her.

We hug friends and say goodbye to those I've seen day in and day out for nearly all of my adult life. Good, hardworking people who have held their heads up through their times of adversity, and who have supported me through mine. People I've cared about in a way few outside our work could understand—a mutual trust and respect that only comes from years of putting our lives in one another's hands.

I remove the lock from my locker, now empty after decades of use, and I walk down the familiar hallway for the last time. As I drive out of the back lot with Gale, Cari and my nephews in the car, an entire brigade of police motorcycles joins us. They surround the car with lights flashing, acting as escort on my final drive home. I pull slowly around the front of the police building and see that people have lined both sides of the drive—dozens and dozens, maybe hundreds. Most of them are in uniform, but others are in plain clothes—dispatchers, jailers, analysts and clerks. Some have even come in on their days off. They stand at attention as I drive past, and then they salute me.

The emotion of it all squeezes the breath from my lungs, and I'm unable to talk. My family stares out the windows in amazement. I'm looking at my entire division, along with most of the police department. Even the former deputy chief, Danny Jenner, is here— having shown up from his job as a sheriff's deputy. He's standing at the front of the group, saluting in his county sheriff's uniform. His eyes lock onto mine and I know that he's one of only a handful who realizes the price I paid to make it to this day.

To my surprise, several of the women who were involved in the lawsuit have also come out, standing at attention and saluting me. Another of them has pulled her police car over to the side of the road. Her lights are flashing and she's outside the car, standing at attention and saluting me as we drive by.

I'm not sure that I'm able to understand any of it, but I hold no grudge against her or any of the rest of them. We've all made our choices and now we all have to live with them. And just like the former chiefs, they'll have to look at themselves in the mirror every day of their lives.

When I turn onto my street, the contingent of motor cops breaks off. They hit their sirens in one final whelp, and then disappear in my rearview mirror.

I sit parked in my driveway as Gale, Cari and the boys get out and go into the house. I'm left with a hollow feeling inside, an emptiness that is neither good nor bad, right nor wrong. It's the remnants of a career left fluttering like a tattered flag over a bloody battlefield. What remains for me is the mournful sensation of a true potential only partially realized.

But even in these waning moments of nostalgic remorse, my emotions are trumped by a wonderful feeling of relief.

They can't get to me anymore. *I'm finally done.*

EPILOGUE

"We must be willing to let go of the life we have planned,
so as to have the life that is waiting for us."
~Joseph Campbell

What can a man receive in exchange for his soul? Certainly not his dignity. We must all reshape ourselves to some degree, and conform in one way or another in order to be successful in our chosen fields. But there is a limit, a horizon line, beyond which compromise becomes dishonor. We should all be so lucky as to recognize where that line is.

I can honestly say that during my entire career I never considered selling out or compromising my values—not for a promotion or to become a police chief, not for the lure of money, or for a lawsuit, or for a disability retirement that I did not deserve. The cost of personal disgrace was one I was never willing to pay, even if nobody else knew the truth but me.

My family and my upbringing can be credited for the values that sustained me through all of this, but none as important as those given to me by my dad. I'm also thankful to have had strong and ethical mentors throughout my career—men who knew what was right and refused to stray from those ideals. All of them helped prepare me for many of the challenges that lay ahead. Challenges I could never have even imagined when I began my career as a nineteen-year-old kid.

The job and the life of a police officer turned out to be more difficult than I anticipated. They were full of hurt, pain, challenge and disappointment. What I thought at the beginning of my career would be the most difficult—the bad people on the street who do bad things to others—was actually the easier part. I expected their hostility and aggression. What I never even anticipated was the measure of evil inside the people that I worked with and worked for.

Those were the people I trusted, and when they turned on me I was devastated. It was in this final season of my career that I came to realize that power and greed, the root of most evil things, runs rampant in municipal government and throughout the public safety ranks. Sadly, I found that unfortunate truth to be the true pain of being a policeman.

The awareness of this created inside me an anger that exists to this day—anger that I must continually work to overcome. I've had to ask myself: What is the final destination of hatred? If love and forgiveness is the goal, then I'm not there yet. Not by a long shot. But I am nowhere near where I once was—wearing my bitterness and anger in retirement like another uniform.

Finally, having had time to create distance and gain perspective, I am able to view my history with more clarity. Also, perhaps, with more compassion. After all, we are only products of how we were raised and the sum of our life experiences. Those who lash out at others are often most angry about something within themselves. Usually it is a trauma so deep or so ugly that they may not even have the capacity to face it.

The distance between my present and my past life in the police department has enabled me to see beyond what I was able to see while embroiled in its toxins. Through this growth, I have found that the cast of characters who once had such powerful impacts on my career and on my life, no longer play a role in my happiness. I believe that each of us has taken away our own lessons, applied them to our lives, and now live with the outcomes of our decisions:

Carl Bradford: The former police chief never made a public statement after our memorandum was submitted. He severed all ties and friendships within the department and never again worked in law enforcement. He continues to collect his full pension at police chief's pay, and has since remarried and moved out of state.

Hector Lara: The former municipal administrator struggled to get his local consulting firm off the ground, without much success. Making a few failed runs for public office, he finally wangled an appointment to the local school board. An illicit sex scandal derailed Lara's marriage and his reign on the board, and he has since moved out of the area with his new girlfriend. Though his resignation from the city was spun to appear as Lara's decision, it remains unknown what impact, if any, my corruption investigation played in his abrupt departure.

Evan Casey: The former police captain worked for a short time for a South Bay police department, until it was discovered that he had lied on his employment application. Unable to produce the college diploma that he claimed to have, Casey was fired from the job. He has also severed most ties within the department, though still meets for coffee regularly with his small group of loyal disciples.

Odell Graham: The only elected official to publicly back the police commanders, retained his spot on the city council for another eight years. With a newly elected mayor and council, Graham was able to be effective despite his poor relationship with Hector Lara. He is now retired from city politics.

Teddy Rube: The rookie councilman who showed a brief flash of support for the police commanders, only to be slapped back into line by the administrator, continued to serve on the council. He later ran successfully for the state assembly, where he now chairs the state's public safety committee.

Dorothy Easter: The flighty woman who had the misfortune to show up at our front door, continued to serve on the city council for several years. She successfully ran for mayor of the city, and now holds that position.

The Women: After the attorneys collected their tidy sum, the fourteen females involved in the lawsuit split the remains of a five million dollar out of court settlement. Most of them never progressed in their careers, even after the city brought in a female police chief to "change the culture." Within a few years most of the plaintiffs had left the department for various reasons; six retired with disability claims, four were fired, one was demoted, one left for another department, and to date only two remain working there—one having been promoted and the other still a patrol officer.

Patrick Vincent: The transitional chief who followed in the wake of the Carl Bradford incident, retired after a year on the job. He suffered a mild stroke shortly after he left, leaving him with a slight limp. He now freely admits that he was miserable working under Hector Lara—the man his wife credits with causing her husband's health problems.

Thurmond Morris: The municipal administrator's handpicked chief of police retired less than three years after being appointed—a retirement that coincided with the women employees announcing the filing of their lawsuit. Morris continued to suffer from a debilitating illness after he left, and took his own life seven years into his retirement.

Danny Jenner: The former deputy chief left the department under subtle and not-so-subtle threats and intimidation by the former administrator, Hector Lara. Jenner was hired by the county sheriff's office and worked his way up to the rank of commander. He is now a popular and successful police chief of a contract city.

Miguel Zavala: A newly appointed captain at the time he joined the commanders in submitting the Bradford memo, Zavala finished his career overseeing the investigation division and then retired with his wife to a home on a golf course out of state.

Gary Donahue: A lieutenant in charge of personnel and training at the time he signed the Bradford memo, Donahue also left the department within two years. Gary spends his retirement playing golf and getting together with other retirees.

Bobby Roselli: The internal affairs lieutenant when he signed on as one of the six authors of the Bradford memo, Bobby was the only participating commander to promote in the memo's aftermath. Bobby ultimately attained the rank of captain, and then retired after serving ten more years on the job.

Claire Melville: The only non-sworn signatory of the infamous Bradford memo, Melville worked ten more years in her position before retiring. During her career Claire served under eight different police chiefs, successfully navigating the dicey law enforcement environment as both a woman and a civilian.

Greg Diaz: The gallant firefighter who climbed over the hood of a homicide victim's car to hold up his baggie of drugs for everyone to see, continued in the fire service. Even though that was only one of many career screw-ups, Hector Lara still saw fit to promote Greg to be the city's fire chief.

* * *

There are a number of ways one can move on from the kind of disappointment that comes with the job I did for thirty-one years. I briefly considered continuing my career in another department, possibly as a police chief, or by applying my anti-terrorism training as an analyst for a state or federal agency. But unlike many of my contemporaries who took their policing skills to another organization, I finally decided what was best for me was to leave law enforcement behind altogether—the rigid structure, the dominating, power-hungry higher ranks and the perpetual sniveling of the lower ranks. Mostly though, I chose to leave behind my city's political apparatus and its intrinsic, almost fashionable, acceptance of misconduct, abuse of power and dereliction of duty.

In what has been the best decision I could have made, mostly at my wife's urging, I've turned toward my long-held love of the arts. The paintings that have always been an escape, I now have time to work on whenever I want. I've tried my hand at acting, having appeared in a few TV shows, and then as a writer—this being my fourth book.

My family has also taken on a more meaningful role in my life now, one that I have a greater appreciation for every day—my wife, my daughters, my son-in-law, and my two grandsons, especially. And though I lost my dad to cancer a short time after my retirement, he was able to see me finish my career with honor and dignity. I think he knew how much he inspired me, and how much his teachings guided me. He was the one who set the bar for me.

It's a nice feeling to wake up every morning, look in the mirror and have no regrets about what I did. Well, almost none. I only wish that I had picked up the sword to fight sooner. But then again, I can look at that as another lesson learned—one I sincerely hope I will never again have to put into practice.

And like the five other police department administrators who sacrificed their reputations to do what was right, I am grateful for recognizing the line beyond which I would not cross—just one more experience that I had to live through in order to appreciate its value.

This final lesson has also allowed me to understand that the key to serenity is to stop the struggle to live the life I had planned, and accept the life that awaits me.

The end of a career full of life lessons . . .

Made in United States
Orlando, FL
10 October 2023

37750353R00163